and Postmo

Modernity and Postmodernity

Knowledge, Power and the Self

Gerard Delanty

SAGE Publications
London • Thousand Oaks • New Delhi

First published 2000

 SAGE Publications Ltd
6 Bonhill Street
London EC2A 4PU

SAGE Publications Inc
2455 Teller Road
Thousand Oaks, California 91320

SAGE Publications India Pvt Ltd
32, M-Block Market
Greater Kailash – I
New Delhi 110 048

British Library Cataloguing in Publication data

A catalogue record for this book is
available from the British Library.

ISBN 0 7619 5903 3
ISBN 0 7619 5904 1 (pbk)

Library of Congress catalog card record available

Typeset by Photoprint, Torquay
Printed and bound in Great Britain by Athenaeum Press,
Gateshead

Our age is, in especial degree, the age of criticism, and to criticism everything must submit. Religion through its sanctity, and law-giving through its majesty, may seek to exempt themselves from it. But they then awaken just suspicion, and cannot claim the sincere respect which reason accords only to that which has been able to sustain the test of free and open examination.

Immanuel Kant, Preface to the *Critique of Pure Reason* (1929 [1781], p. 9)

Besides it is not difficult to see that our time is a birth-time and a period of transition to a new era. Spirit has broken with the world it has hitherto inhabited and imagined, and is of a mind to submerge it in the past, and in the labour of its own transformation. Spirit is indeed never at rest but always engaged in moving forward. But just as the first breath drawn by a child after its long, quiet nourishment breaks the gradualness of merely quantitative growth – there is a qualitative leap and the child is born – so likewise with the Spirit in its formation matures slowly and quietly into its new shape, dissolving bit by bit the structure of its previous world, whose tottering state is only hinted at by isolated symptoms. The frivolity and boredom which unsettle the established order, the vague foreboding of something unknown, these are the heralds of approaching change. The gradual crumbling that left unaltered the face of the whole is cut by a sunburst which, in one flash, illuminates the features of the new world.

G.W.F. Hegel, Preface to the *Phenomenology of Mind* (1977 [1807], pp. 6–7)

Science today is a 'vocation' organized in special disciplines in the service of self-clarification and knowledge of related facts. It is not the gift of seers and prophets dispensing sacred values and revelations, not does it partake of the contemplation of sages and philosophers about the meaning of the universe. This, to be sure, is the inescapable condition of our historical situation.

Max Weber, 'Science as a Vocation' (1948a [1917], pp. 152–3)

The contemporary philosopher meets Freud on the same ground as Nietzsche and Marx. All three rise before him as protagonists of suspicion who rip away masks and pose the novel problem of the lie of consciousness and unconsciouness.

Paul Ricoeur, *The Conflict of Interpretations* (1974 [1969], p. 99)

No one has ever been modern. Modernity has never begun. There has never been a modern world. The use of the present perfect tense is important here, for it is a matter of a retrospective sentiment, of a reading of our history. I am not saying we are entering a new era; on the contrary we no longer have to continue the headlong flight of the post-post-modernists; we are no longer obliged to cling to the avant-garde of the avant-garde; we no longer seek to be cleverer, even more critical, even deeper into the era 'era of suspicion'. No, instead we discover that we have never begun to enter the modern era. Hence the hint of the ludicrous that always accompanies postmodern thinkers, they claim to come after a time that has not even started!

Bruno Latour, *We Have Never Been Modern* (1993 [1991], p. 47)

On double truth and the right distance. How to avoid seeming complicitous with the object analyzed (notably in the eyes of those who are foreign to it) or, conversely, reductive and hostile (especially to those who are caught up in the object and who are inclined to refuse the very principle of objectivation)? How to reconcile the objectivation of belief (religious, literary, artistic, scientific, etc.) and of its social conditions of production, and the sensible and faithful evocation of the experience of belief that is inherent to being inserted and involved in a social game? Only at the cost of a very long and very difficult work – and one that is the more invisible the more successful it is – to put oneself at a distance from the object and then to surmount this very distance, a work that bears inseparably on the object and on the relationship to the object, thus on the subject of the scientific work.

Pierre Bourdieu, 'Scattered Remarks' (1999, p. 334)

CONTENTS

PREFACE AND ACKNOWLEDGEMENTS

This book can be read as a response to two kinds of transition in modern society. The first concerns cultural changes in the worldview of society, that is, changes on the level of the prevailing model of knowledge and, more broadly, changes in the cultural self-image of the age, the models by which a society interprets itself. The second kind of transition concerns changes in the social, economic and political structures of modern society. The issues that these questions raise directly relate to the debate on modernity and postmodernity, which has been one of the central controversies in social and political theory for almost two decades. It is a striking feature of social and political thought over the last two decades that these two dimensions of transition coincide in certain respects. On the one side, the older and Marxist-influenced debate on the transition from feudalism, and somewhat later from mercantilism, to capitalism from the sixteenth century onward has now been seen to be part of the more general transition from tradition to modernity, whereby the transition could also be theorized in terms of a conflict between capitalism and democracy, or, as more recent formulations would put it, as a struggle between an instrumental rationality of domination and a cultural critique animated by a communicative rationality deriving from civil society. In this debate, the idea of modernity suggests more than merely capitalism – or, in other formulations, industrialism – and therefore the direction in which the transition may be leading is at best an open agenda, since the struggle between power and culture, capitalism and democracy, cannot be so easily concluded. Indeed, the normative critique of capitalism can no longer be conducted from the vantage point of democracy. It is not surprising, then, that one of the conclusions to this debate has been a recognition, at some level, that the idea of a cultural and societal transition must be theorized as an opening within modernity itself of alternative logics of development, ranging from hidden histories, civil society, social movements, to Soviet statism. Thus with the shift to modernity as a frame of reference the idea of a further transition from capitalism to socialism becomes just one developmental logic. Whether it was because this debate congealed in the seemingly permanent structures of the Cold War or because no movement emerged dominant or because of an institutional compromise between capitalism and democracy, a credible, though contested, conclusion that could be drawn from this was Habermas's notion of the incomplete project of modernity – incomplete because modernity's work could not be concluded for a variety of factors which were best summed up in his later announcement of the 'new obscurity' into which the late modern age had entered. The implicit theme now is that time might have run out for a project inaugurated at the beginning of the modern age.

The second debate concerns the question that it is modernity itself that may be defeated, not by a victorious capitalism – though some are decidedly ambiguously about this – but by the transition to a new age, the postmodern era, which has allegedly arrived, at least according to some of the more programmatic formulations of this way of thinking. If this is so, then one of the first casualties of the fall of modernity is the tension between democracy and capitalism, and all the developmental logics that this tension opened up. This, of course, does not mean that capitalism has disappeared, but it does mean that the tension between capitalism and democracy has weakened, and in this there can be no doubt as to who is the winner. More importantly, however, when put in the context of the fall of communism and the ending of the Cold War from the early 1990s, we are faced with an entirely new kind of a transition, and one that was considerably aided by the survival, even under the conditions of totalitarianism, of democracy, albeit a democracy confined to the margins of civil society. I am referring to the transition from communism to capitalism. The uniqueness of this transition was that several developmental logics unfolded more or less simultaneously: capitalism, democracy, nationalism. What is particularly notable in this is that this second transition – which could be seen as delayed moderniza- tion – has been accompanied by a wider mood of a transition from modernity to postmodernity, culturally, politically and socially, for the fall of communism occurred at a time when postmodernization was par- ticularly pronounced in the West (for instance, the questions of globaliza- tion in cultural production, communications and finance, the rise of the information society, European integration, transnational communities, new discourses of human rights, ecology and the politics of nature). Many theorists, such as Alain Touraine, who are critical of postmodern arguments have argued that the older struggle of democracy and capital- ism may be overtaken today by a new conflict between the forces of rationality and an authoritarian neo-communitarian politics of identity. As a result of the apparent supersession of the social question with the challenge of culture, which is no longer contained within the relatively stable paramenters of the national state, one of the greatest and most urgent tasks facing democracy, and for which it is ill equipped, is to deal with conflicts relating to cultural identity, not to mention issues relating to ecology and nature (which is part of the new cultural self-image). This framework suggests that modernity – which was dominated by the political question concerning democracy and the social question relating to capitalism – may now be refracted through the prism of culture and in this reconfiguration of the modern worldview there has been a turn to issues of identity and community, a movement that could be seen as the extension of the aesthetic into everyday life.

Clearly there are two ways of looking at this situation. Either one could say the transiticn from communism to capitalism in the former Soviet Bloc has been the last phase of a modernity organized along the lines of instrumental reason, differing only from the West in that the forces of domination have been concentrated more in the state than in the mode of production – the position I more or less take – or one could argue that this event has been part of a more wider transition to the postmodern era, a transition that is related to the current debate on globalization. In my view, postmodernism had its roots in the late modern West – having emerged in Europe, it became an American cultural product in the 1970s – but has reached its fullest expression in cultural forces far beyond the West, for it is in parts of the non-western world, Japan and much of the Islamic world, for instance, that post-modernization in the domain of culture has been able to give expression to the creative integration of tradition and modernity that would be impossible in the West, but even more impossible in the former Soviet Bloc, whose modernity was constructed on the basis of the destruction of tradition in the name of an ostensibly victorious modernity framed not just in the image of the Enlightenment but by totalitarianism. Thus one logic of modernity – the struggle between capitalism and democracy in the West – led to a movement from organized modernity to a post-modernity that was still within the confines of modernity, and another, carried forward by the state, which had suppressed both democracy and capitalism, led to totalitarianism, which must be seen as the other face of modernity. In the former, cultural modernity preseved some pre-bourgeois and Christian traditions; in the latter the destruction of all tradition, premodern as well as modern, was near complete. Only in parts of the non-western world, particularly those parts such as Japan, which were untouched by westernization, or where colonialism was incomplete, as in much of the Islamic world, did tradition adapt itself to varieties of modernity, thus easing the transition to postmodernity. Here a different logic of development has prevailed; rather than one of a struggle of democracy and capitalism or one led by statism, it was one animated by community.

Whatever position one takes, it is clear that the alternatives to capital-ism do not lie in modernity's other face, state socialism. This leaves three available options, of which two have been widely discussed and are the subject of this book: either a position is sought within modernity – the promise of a democracy to come – or one abandons European modernity altogether in favour of postmodernity. The latter position has been complicated, even confused, because the postmodern position, which originally arose in certain developments in poststructuralist thinking in France in the 1960s and early 1970s, became tied to quite independent developments in the arts and architecture in North America in the 1970s to become a powerful intellectual movement in the 1980s, when it privileged cultural issues precisely at a time when neo-liberalism was in the ascendancy in politics and economics, a time when the left's main intellectual response was rational choice theory. By this time postmodernism had used up its original political ambitions, either because it had achieved some of its goals or because it had become absorbed into the relativism of an age that has rendered materialism culturally soft. The debate on postmodernity became further complicated by a deepening in the sense of a global transition. Globalization, which is only another word for accelerated change, gave credence to much of the postmodern stance, whereby 'positions' which had already become 'postures' could now be reproduced in timeless space and in non-verbal modes of communication. Clearly this was an expression of an intellectual milieu which had witnessed the disappearance of alternatives and could only find a virtue in mobility. Beyond the West, however, postmodernity and globalization became linked to a growing consciousness of a postcolonial world emerging.

I mentioned a third option that the final collapse of modernization has opened up. For those who want to turn neither to modernity nor to postmodernity, the cosmopolitan idea offers a way of linking the idea of modernity, divested of the Enlightenment, with postmodernity, divested of globalization and relativism. For this position is reducible neither to modernity nor to postmodernity and it may be the only means of linking the idea of universalistic morality with cultural pluralism. Epistemologically, in this book I have linked this perspective to new debates on constructivism.

This book is a study of the background to these issues. It is written with a view to making some of the main classical debates on modernity and postmodernity available to the general reader and the advanced student in social science. It is also intended to provide the scholar with an argument to address. My own position on these debates is expressed in the Introduction and in the final chapter, though the main strands of it run throughout the chapters of the book. The essence of this position is the thesis that instead of seeing modernity and postmodernity as opposed positions, or as stages in modern society, that they be seen as more continuous. In short this is a book which offers a thesis of continuity between modernity and postmodernity, though one conceived of in terms of the idea of a developmental logic. This developmental logic is one of a movement from a concern with scepticism (in the domain of knowledge) in the premodern era, to one of discursivity (in the domain of power) in the modern period, to a preoccupation with reflexivity (in the domain of the self) in the postmodern era. Thus postmodernity can be seen as an augmented consciousness of a problematic that preceded the advent of modernity. By reducing the identification of modernity with the Enlightenment, effectively projecting it backwards into history, I hope to have also underpinned the postmodernist alleged rupture with modernity. The thesis of the book can be summed by saying, with Bruno Latour: we are not postmodern because we have never been modern.

I wrote most of this book in Toronto when I was a Visiting Professor in Sociology at York University in 1998. I am grateful to Professors Jos Lennards and John O'Neill of York University for their generosity during this time. Thanks are also due to Professors Gordon Darroch and Des Ellis. Acknowledgements are due to the graduate students who attended my course and to many members of the Department of Sociology and The Programme in Social and Political Thought. I am grateful to Piet Strydom, Tony King and Patrick O'Mahony for reading and commenting on an earlier draft. Finally, I would like to thank Chris Rojek and the anonymous referees for Sage as well as the copy editor, Justin Dyer.

Toronto and Liverpool, 2000

INTRODUCTION
Knowledge, Power and the Self

The central thesis of this book is that the divide between modernity and postmodernity obscures the radicality of the modern itself. My argument is that the postmodern impulse has been with us from the advent of modernity itself and that the discourses of modernity began earlier than the conventional watershed of the Enlightenment, which was less a rupture than a culmination of a process that had begun much earlier. Modernity, for me, entails the very experience of scepticism that is normally attributed to postmodernity, which is not, consequently, the radical and ruptural break that it is often held to be. Modernity is itself founded on a scepticism concerning some of the central dimensions of human experience, in particular relating to knowledge and power, but also the very idea of the self. But since scepticism derives from a premodern epistemology, we can say, not only have we never been fully modern, as Bruno Latour (1993) has famously put it, but we have also never been postmodern. However, the argument advanced in this book departs from Latour's position in its assessment of modernity, which I see as characterized not just by scepticism in the realm of knowledge but also by the discursive contestation of power, which can be seen as communicative scepticism.[1] The postmodern, then, is the extension of this logic of development into the domain of the self and is best characterized by a deepening of scepticism and discursivity into a wider and more culturally pervasive reflexivity.

Taking the domains of knowledge, power and the self, I believe the radicality of the modern project can be found in the experience of limits which is central to these domains and which justifies the claim that a profound scepticism is deeply embedded in modernity, a scepticism whose augmented forms are discursivity and reflexivity. Scepticism entails the experience of limits; that the possibilities of knowledge are defined precisely by an awareness of limits. The modern alternatives to scepticism are rationalism (the belief in the limitless nature of knowledge, the centrality of the cognizing ego) and relativism (the rejection of absolute certainty, the historicization of subjectivity, a turn to culture).

Scepticism, in my view, best captures the modern spirit for it steers a mid-course between the illusions of certainty and the dangers of relativism. Kant, not Hume, is the true modernist sceptic. In recognizing the limits of knowledge, experience and action, scepticism offers a radical alternative: our experience of the world may be mediated by the cognitive structures of the mind and cultural models of interpretation, but a reflexive relation to the awareness of limits can allow us to transcend those very limits by transforming them. Thus, the radical impulse to overcome limits is central to scepticism, marking it off from rationalism and relativism. Part of this striving to overcome limits is the negation of foundations. Modernity can be seen to give expression to the desire to overcome an origin.

The conventional view of modernity as substituting ecclesiastical legitimation for one of scientific certainty – whereby one origin, one founding act, is replaced by another – needs to be revised for the epistemic culture that modernity brought about was one of a deepening of uncertainty which came with the conviction that human cognitive powers can wield merely cognition of possible worlds, for knowledge is always constrained to be mediated experience. Postmodernity, I suggest, is nothing but the self-consciousness of this experience that there are limits to what can be said and done. The writings of some of the central figures in modern social and political thought demonstrate precisely this awareness of limits and, I shall argue, the scepticism that this entails is also evident in a certain tradition in theology, namely negative theology, wherein a radical reflexivity has been held to be a core feature of the human condition, which is one of anxiety, doubt and uncertainty. My most far-reaching argument is that modernity entailed the deepening of a discourse of uncertainty that began within premodern theological debates, and the discourses of postmodernity can be seen, likewise, as a deepening of the modern quest to solve a problem that was originally posed within the domain of religious experience: the conflict between belief (the realm of possibilities) and knowledge (the realm of limits), a conflict that laid the basis of modern scepticism, as is revealed in the writings of Pascal (Bourdieu, 2000). The modern solution to this problem was to locate transcendence in a self-limiting subjectivity. But the price of this epistemic shift in western cognitive culture was a radicalized scepticism which imposed limits on all aspirations to transcendence. Under the conditions of modernity, transcendence is simply the awareness of limits and is expressed in the belief in the finitude of knowledge and the unattainablity of perfection. The critical power of knowledge derives from this recognition that all forms of human experience are mediated. To uncover these structures of mediation is one of the central tasks of the theory of modernity that is being proposed here.

This is also true of the domains of the self and of power. The quintessentially modern discourse of the self is also one that is based on the recognition of both limits and possibilities. This has received expression in the quest for identity and community in modern culture. The foundation of modern culture is the doctrine of the autonomy of the self and its project of self-determination, a doctrine that has presupposed particular spatial and temporal structures, such as those associated with the nation-state, the industrial and urban life-world, and the sites of massified education and consumption which have all provided the foundations of a unified self. Central to this is the relation of the Self to the Other, a relationship which is never transparent but, like all experiences, is a mediated one. The modern quest for identity and community can be seen as the medium by which the Self and Other are actualized. The self received its affirmation of identity only by reference to an unknowable other, be it God, exotic and primitive peoples, nature, a myth of primordial origins, adversaries of war, the mad, the poor, criminals. For modernity, this was a project of mastery, for self-determination was also a project of the determination of the Other. Self-legislation and violence were closely bound up with each other. Modernity reached its limits with the recognition that its most cherished discourses were founded on an act of violence against the Other (de Vries and Weber, 1997). Postmodernity, I would suggest, involves a deepening of this problematic, and in its most recent forms, it marks a shift in the priority of the Self over the Other. Much of postmodern literature today is an expression of the return not just of the banished subject, but of the Other. If the Holocaust marked the culmination of the modern quest for mastery and the determination of the Other by the Self, postmodernity as a post-colonial and post-Holocaust discourse forces us to see the Self through the eyes of the Other. In this reversal in the priority of Self and Other, subjectivity is reconstituted around a new responsibility for history and nature. Underlying these shifts in the constitution of subjectivity is a certain scepticism in the durability of any narrative of the identity of the Self for the question of non-identity must always be posed. In the context of value pluralism and multiculturalism and the collapse of the self-confidence of the Eurocentric worldview, the prospect of any universal discourse of identity is very much in question. The reinvent of the Self under the conditions of difference is one of the central tasks in the new 'social' postmodernism, a project which in fact can be seen as a return to the modern discourse of the Self, but under the conditions of a more radicalized reflexivity whereby a relational conception of the Self emerges.

The sceptical impulse is also evident in the modern discourse of power. What is sceptical about modern discourses of power is the view that power must be limited and is ultimately legitimated by the social contract of rulers and the ruled. The conversion of power into legitimate authority is one of the central tenets of modernity. The solution that modernity found to this problem was one that committed the modern to a certain contingency and indeterminacy: power can never be once and for all justified as authority and therefore the moment of closure can never be instituted. The mediatory domain that is required to bring this about shifts from the ancient authorities to public discourse, the chief characteristic of which is its radical indeterminacy. In so far as public discourse is constituted in communication, the moment of closure can never be totally instituted. The centrality of communication to modern societies has been one of the most important expressions of the modern impulse (see Styrdom, 2000). This has been one of the main lessons of Habermas's social theory and is also the inspiration of Unger's theory of 'society as artifact' (Unger, 1987). Lying at the heart of modern forms of communication is the experience of an emptiness. According to Claude Lefort (1988, p. 17), this is evident in the modern sense of democracy as an empty space, a space that is never inhabited by power. The negation of democracy, and its particular model of modernity, is totalitarianism for this has attempted to bring about a total fusion of state and society in order to obliterate any empty spaces that might be inhabited by public discourse. I see modernity as the extension of a radicalized discourse of publicity to all spheres of society, and what we call postmodernity is only the completion of this project, which received its greatest impetus from the invention of printing and the rise of a reading public.

The central argument in this book is that postmodernity is deeply rooted in the culture of modernity, just as modernity itself was rooted in the premodern worldview. I have stressed a particular set of problems relating to knowledge, politics and the self, for instance the discourses of scepticism, discursivity and reflexivity. I see the movement from pre-modernity to modernity to postmodernity as a gradual distanciation of subject from object, first in the transformation of knowledge, then in the transformation of politics/power, and finally in the transformation of the self. In the spaces that are opened up in these cultural shifts – from scepticism in knowledge to discursivity in the political regulation of power to reflexivity in the identity of the self – new cultural logics emerge.

First, in premodernity, subjectivity rebels against objectivity, establishing itself as autonomous, though it is not until the postmodern age that there is a loss of autonomy as the distancing, decentring and relativizing logic reaches completion in what now becomes reflexivity. I have argued that postmodernism can be traced to premodern, or 'protomodern', scepticism, which transformed knowledge and prepared the ground for the second step in the distanciation of subjectivity and objectivity: the modern turn to discursivity. This was essentially an achievement of modernity, which prioritized communication. By means of the power of discourse, the revolution, begun in the domain of knowledge, enters the caesura of modernity, bringing scepticism into the sphere of power in the unleashing of a discursively constituted politics. Finally, in post-modernity the decentring and relativizing logic of scepticism and dis-cursivity extends from the domains of knowledge and politics to the realm of the self, bringing to completion the work of modernity. The postmodern, then, is merely the bringing to completion of what had already taken place in the spheres of knowledge and politics, for its greatest impact has been on the self and the possibility of identity.

I would like to take this one step further. The contemporary period cannot be reduced to either modernity or postmodernity, for there are in fact two logics of reflexivity unfolding, one of deconstructionism and one of constructivism. Deconstructionism – the dissolution of the self – represents the first stage in postmodernity, with constructivism coming into its own today, as new selves are constructed. To appreciate this we need to go beyond the discourse of postmodernity, but we must also resist the temptation to return to an incomplete project of modernity, as Habermas would wish. To go beyond modernity and postmodernity is also to move beyond the limits of the European/western project of the Enlightenment to new constructions of human experience in a world which is neither modern nor postmodern (Dallymar, 1996; Varela et al., 1991). These constructions can only be grasped from the perspective of the new cognitive-constructivist approach that is emerging in social science today.

Three conclusions follow from this. The first is that modernity involves not so much an overcoming of religion as a continuation of it in a higher order of reflexivity. In order to appreciate this deepening of the reflexive impulse we must distinguish between religion as a belief system and theology as metadiscourse on the limits of belief, for it is in the latter that we can see how some of the central concerns of both modernity and postmodernity have been posed. Modernity, while being on the one level 'posttraditional', on another was a discourse that took up in a more reflexive key the central question of theology, namely the possibility of transcendence.

The second conclusion is that postmodernity is also a continuation of the modern project, which must be seen as one of radical scepticism, the penetration of scepticism into the identity of the self. What is coming to an end today is postmodernity in so far as this has construed itself as the successor to modernity. Postmodernity can no longer claim the mantle of scepticism for itself, for, as I have argued, this is part of the modern itself, and goes back as far as the Pyrrhonnist movement in the third century BCE.[2] Postmodernity is better understood as a deepening of the reflexive and sceptical moment of the modern itself. If modernity was a critique of objectivity in the name of a self-legislating subjectivity who becomes the order of all things, postmodernity can be seen as a dissolution of this very subjectivity.

The third conclusion is that the deconstructive project of postmodernity is now complete. The discourses of scepticism, discursivity and reflexivity as they unfolded in the domains of knowledge, power and self in the movement from premodernity to modernity to postmodernity are now released from this framework.

****

Chapter 1 offers the argument that resonances of postmodernism can be found in many modernist thinkers. I begin by looking at the rise of the discourse of modernity in the early modern period, with particular reference to Kant and the idea of enlightenment. The chapter explores the theme of the crisis of modernity in the writings of Hegel and Marx, and the emergence of high modernism, as is exemplified in Baudelaire and Joyce. I then focus on two principal traditions in *fin-de-siècle* European thought, the critique of the Enlightenment (Nietzsche, Freud, Heidegger) and the sociological interpretation of modernity (Durkheim, Weber, Simmel).

In Chapter 2 I discuss the debate on the relationship of modernity to premodernity and religion. The focus here is on Hans Blumenberg's critique of the secularization thesis of Karl Löwith, who argued that modernity is a copy of Judeo-Christian eschatology and is therefore unable to legitimate itself by its own categories because these categories are not 'authentic'. This controversy will provide the background for more recent debates on religion and tradition with respect to modernity and postmodernity, since postmodern theory is increasingly seeking to address the question of theology. Conceptions of negative theology challenge the conventional distinction of modernity as posttraditionalism. My central argument is that the terms of the older debate on secularization must be revised since the principal challenge to the identity of modernity is no longer the thesis of historical illegitimacy, the target of Blumenberg's work, but the postmodern challenge, which has rehabilitated theology as a metadiscourse of negativity and alterity.

The theme of the dark side of modernity is explored in Chapter 3 by the idea of modernity as a pathogenesis. The main positions will be Horkheimer and Adorno's *Dialectic of Enlightenment*, Reinhart Koselleck's *Critique and Crisis*, Stephen Toulmin's *Cosmopolis: The Hidden Agenda of Modernity* and Eric Voeglin's *New Science of Politics*. The chapter also includes a discussion of Hannah Arendt's vision of modernity as a conflict between the political and the social.

In Chapter 4 I look at a number of *posthistoire* positions on the impossibility of modernity. Modern culture, theorists such as Arnold Gehlen and Leo Strauss argue, has entered the stage of crystallization, which results in the loss of coherence and certainty. Under these circumstances the problem of contingency has become more acute, since there is no clear cultural solution to the dilemma of choice. The chapter begins with Arnold Gehlen's notion of cultural crystallization and 'posthistory' and goes on to discuss Francis Fukuyma's somewhat different version of the end of history thesis. I then discuss Leo Strauss's theory of modernity, as outlined in his essay 'The Three Waves of Modernity' and, finally, I look at Niklas Luhmann's theory of modernity, with particular reference to his *Observations on Modernity*.

Moving beyond theories which are broadly anti-modern or deeply pessimistic of the possibility of modernity to provide a foundation for politics and society, I discuss in Chapter 5 theories which share a concern with the recovery of modernity as a project needing completion. The chapter deals with the theory of modernity in the work of Habermas, Lefebvre, Heller, Castoriadis and Touraine. A reading of their work suggests a conception of the social defined in terms of communication. Modern societies, I argue, are essentially communication societies for communication is the principal medium of integration today.

In Chapter 6 I take the theme of community to attempt to bridge the divorce of modernity and postmodernity. Whereas modernity was allegedly constructed on the destruction of community and postmodernity on the eclipse of the social which had characterized the age of modernity, we can see how community has in fact become a key concern of postmodernist approaches. Tying community to a notion of citizenship, I examine community in a variety of debates cutting across the modern and the postmodern. I draw from Michel Maffesoli's concept of 'emotional communities', Jean-Luc Nancy's theory of the 'inoperative community', Maurice Blanchot and William Corlett's conception of community beyond unity and identity, and Bill Readings's notion of the 'community of dissensus'. These approaches provide us with a means of seeing how community can be understood in terms of an 'imagined community' which is always incomplete and constested.

In Chapter 7 I discuss the main debates on postmodernity by taking four main movements which constitute postmodern culture. First, the question of the aesthetic, looking at the relation of postmodernism to the avant-garde and modernism. Second, I examine the theoretical turn to poststructuralism and the method of deconstructionism, with reference to Foucault, Derrida, Vattimo. Third, I deal with the sociological and cultural analysis of postmodernity in terms of postmodernization, that is, as a social condition. In this context the work of Lyotard, Jameson and Harvey will be discussed. Fourth, I look at postmodernism as a particular kind of political practice. Finally, by way of conclusion, I will look at the possibility that postmodernization may be detaching itself from the framework of European/western modernity and suggest that the genuinely postmodern world is now in areas beyond the West.

In the conclusion, Chapter 8, the postmodern emphasis on the symbolic is contrasted to the theme of reflexivity and it is argued that this should be recognized as the key category today. This is briefly discussed with reference to the work of Pierre Bourdieu and developments in cognitive and constructivist theory.

1

THE DISCOURSES OF MODERNITY
Enlightenment, Modernism and
Fin-de-Siècle Sociology

In this chapter my aim is to outline some of the classical discourses of modernity in order to provide a foundation for the subsequent chapters, where the focus is more on the debates of the second half of the twentieth century when 'organized modernity' – the Enlightenment construction of modernity – entered into its final phase of crisis.[1] Taking the central themes identified in the Introduction – knowledge, power and the self – I begin by looking at the rise of the discourse of modernity in the early modern period, with particular reference to Kant and the idea of enlightenment. Second, I look at the theme of the crisis of modernity in the writings of Hegel and Marx, and the emergence of high modernism, as is exemplified in Baudelaire and Joyce. I argue that the crisis of modernity in high modernism resulted in the fragmentation of the discourse of modernity into two principal traditions in *fin-de-siècle* European thought: the radical critique of the Enlightenment (Nietzsche, Freud, Heidegger) and the sociology of modernity (Durkheim, Weber, Simmel). To trace the contours of these movements is the subject of the final section of the chapter. The central argument is that resonances of postmodernism can be found in all of these *fin-de-siècle* thinkers, whose work reflects a gradual turn to a vision of culture that embraces reflexivity and scepticism. In other words it might be said that the critique of modernity was always built into the very idea of the modern, which can only be seen as a contest term. The theme of this chapter is suggested by a remark of Paul Ricoeur in his book *The Conflict of Interpretations* (1974, p. 99): 'The contemporary philosopher meets Freud on the same ground as Nietzsche and Marx. All three rise before him as protagonists of suspicion who rip away masks and pose the novel problem of the lie of consciousness and unconsciousness.'

The Emergence of Modernity

The idea of modernity found one of its first expressions in the seventeenth- and eighteenth-century debate between the 'ancients and the moderns', or the 'battle of the books', concerning literary style and the status of the classics, as represented in, for example, William Temple's *Essay on Ancient and Modern Learning*, published in 1690, and William Wotton's *Reflections upon Ancient and Modern Learning*, published in 1696.[2] The moderns were those who had rejected classic style, such as the idea of timeless beauty or the reverence for the Augustan Age, in favour of the contemporary, which was characterized by a strong belief in science and progress. In England modernity was more closely associated with the rise of modern science, and is best exemplified in Francis Bacon's opposition to the wisdom of antiquity. By this time, modernity – and the modern – had already come to designate a particular kind of time consciousness. The modern was defined by an orientation to the past and postulated an origin from which the present was both a derivation and a distanciation. For the Christian thinkers of the early medieval age, the modern referred to the contemporary period of the early Church. Modernity was thus defined in opposition to the pagan period, which had been overcome. To be modern was to be contemporary, to witness the present moment. The idea of 'the moment' is central to the time consciousness of modernity and expresses a tension between present and past (see Friese, 2001). The seventeenth-century debate can be seen as a heightened consciousness of the uniqueness of the present moment. The moment of modernity exists in the space between present and past for the modern is not only an epoch that lives for the future, but is one that is formed out of a particular conception of history. The critical appropriation of the past provides the modern spirit with its central driving thrust. The overcoming of an origin is part of this way of thinking, which ties the moment of the present to an act of historical appropriation.

One of early uses of the term modern, which goes back to the fifth century, refers to the retrieval of ancient culture: the moderns were the 'new ancients' (Schabert, 1986, p. 9). According to Jacques le Goff in the twelfth century the word 'modernitas' was used, in what was one of the first quarrels between ancients and moderns, to mean the critical assessment of an evolution which had already lasted for centuries (cited in le Rider, 1993, p. 27. See also Lichtblau, 1999 pp. 15–16). The idea of modernity is thus a projection backwards as much as forwards, and it is for this reason that many of its formulations embodied nostalgia as much as utopianism. Modernity could also be a political project, and the early Christian thinkers of the late Roman period were able to define their age as modern in opposition to the pagan world of antiquity, a term that was associated with the opposition of civilization to the pagan culture of the barbarians, while drawing its force from an even more primordial origin. In this binary construction, an opposition between Self and Other enters the discourse of modernity. This will not be pursued here, beyond remarking that one dimension to the formation of European modernity has been a polarity of Christians versus the internal enemies (Jews) and the external enemies (Muslims) (Delanty, 1995a, 1996a). In other words the temporal dimension to modernity has been closely associated with a logic of exclusion and inclusion.

Returning to the idea of time consciousness, we can say modernity is also an awareness that 'the moment' is an 'epoch', stretching forward as well as backwards in time. The future is seen as emanating not from the present as such, but from an event which preceded the present and from which the present also derives its strength. In the age of the Enlightenment, the epoch of modernity is thus seen as the period stretching from the sixteenth century to the eighteenth century, when, as a result of the scientific revolution, the Renaissance, the Reformation and the age of discoveries, the old certainties of the Middle Ages were shattered. The Enlightenment gains its legitimation from a rupture which had already occurred in recent history, that is, with the beginning of modern times. As Jürgen Habermas (1987, p. 5) has put it, 'the secular concept of modernity expresses the conviction that the future has already begun: It is the epoch that lives for the future. In this way, the caesura defined by the new beginning has shifted into the past, precisely to the start of modern times.' The idea that the present has already begun is one of the hallmarks of the modern consciousness of time, distinguishing it from the postmodern conception. One possible place to look for this caesura might be in the culture of the baroque. In this period, which covers most of the seventeenth century, a break had already occurred without which the Enlightenment project would not have been possible. The baroque can be seen as occupying a position between traditional society and modernity, and its social basis was the beginnings of mass society. Its most notable feature was the growing consciousness of the present as a period of crisis (Maravall, 1986).[3]

The notion that the future has already begun is central to the time consciousness of the modern, which derives its legitimation from its own self-projection back on history. The early modern idea of revolution, for instance, not only signified a radical break from the past and an embracing of the future, but signalled a cyclical conception of history by which the future was a returning and appropriation of the past. The later idea of revolution, while abandoning the cyclical conception of history, always retained a relation to the idea of redemption, that is, the return and overcoming of an origin. The problem of modernity – and, indeed, the problem of scepticism – was always the problem of justifying itself by means of criteria that could be derived neither from what had been rejected nor from its own self-legitimation.

It may be suggested, then, that the idea of modernity expresses an ambivalence on modernity as an epoch – a period in historical time – and as a time consciousness – a consciousness *of* time. Clearly it is both, and many of the great visions of modernity were attempts to reconcile these two ways of conceptualizing the present moment: modernity can be seen both as an idea – a cultural impulse, a time consciousness – and as a historical event, a social condition, an epoch in historical time. Modernity has primarily been understood to be an idea, but it is one that has a pronounced temporal resonance.

A particularly striking example of modernity as an idea is Kant's essay 'An Answer to the Question: What is Enlightenment?' In this famous essay, published in 1784 and the subject of much of the subsequent discourse of modernity from Hegel to Foucault and Habermas, Kant answers the question 'Do we live in an *enlightened* age?' by saying 'No, but we do live in an age of *enlightenment*' (Kant, 1996, p. 62). By this he meant that the age itself was not coeval with the culture of enlightenment. In other words, there was a disparity between culture and society, between norm and reality: the forces of enlightenment had not fully penetrated the age. 'As matters now stand,' Kant argues in the same passage, 'much is still lacking for men to be completely able – or even to be placed in a situation where they would be able – to use their reason confidently and properly in religious matters without the guidance of another.' Kant clearly equated enlightenment with a particular way of thinking and one which exemplifies the spirit of modernity. 'Enlightenment is mankind's exit from its self-incurred immaturity,' he argues. In his words, 'immaturity' is the inability to make use of one's own understanding without the guidance of another and it is 'self-incurred' when there is a lack of resolution and courage to use it without the guidance of another. Thus '*Sapere aude!* Have the courage to use your own understanding! is the motto of the Enlightenment' (Kant, 1996, p. 58). This is a very clear statement of enlightenment as an idea, as well as capturing the central ideas of Kant's philosophy, which can be summarized as revolving around the themes of autonomy, critique, publicity. Enlightenment as a condition may have emerged out of the historical age of modernity, but is defined as much by opposition to the present as it is to the past. The condition of enlightenment is one of autonomy, critique and the 'public use of reason'.

Kant's whole ethical philosophy was a defence of the autonomy of morality, which for him cannot be derived from anything other than the moral law, in other words from itself. Morality is autonomous of all worldviews that postulate conceptions of a unified worldview, for under the conditions of modernity the principle of differentiation and decentring is irreversible: the cognitive, the aesthetic and the moral are differentiated from each other and from religion. Religion no longer provides a principle of cultural unity because the modern age has witnessed the separation of the cultural spheres of knowledge, art and morality from each other. Modernity thus presupposes autonomous logics of development. The project of autonomy and the principle of cultural differentiation constitute the foundations of the Kantian idea of modernity. Though Kant rejects the principle of unity in favour of autonomous logics of development with respect to the principal cultural spheres, he retains a firm belief in the unity of the subject. The Kantian Self is a centred ego who inhabits a culturally decentred world.

The second main plank in Kant's philosophy and conception of modernity is the idea of critique. Earlier, in 1781, in the preface to the *Critique of Pure Reason*, Kant (1929, p. 9) argued for the need 'to institute a tribunal' – 'This tribunal is no other than the critique of pure reason,' that is, a critique not of all knowledge but only of knowledge that cannot be related to experience:

> Our age is, in especial degree, the age of criticism, and to criticism everything must submit. Religion through its sanctity, and law-giving through its majesty, may seek to exempt themselves from it. But they then awaken just suspicion, and cannot claim the sincere respect which reason accords only to that which has been able to sustain the test of free and open examination.

In this work Kant gave one of the most sophisticated epistemological defences of critique as a form of cultural suspicion. He was the first major thinker to formulate the idea of critique, which for him was the recognition of the limits of knowledge, and not a celebration of the open horizon of knowledge. The Kantian transcendental critique is a procedure that is negatively defined, for Kant believed the greater danger lay in making false claims for reason, which happens when reason strays into the realms of the rationally unknowable. Thus, the critique of reason was a critique of the false claims of reason, which in its 'pure' form must be severely delimited to particular domains of knowledge. Kant called his method transcendental critique, by which he meant the search for the conditions of the possibility of knowledge, or, as he called it, 'self-knowledge'. All knowledge is mediated knowledge for knowledge is conditioned by the cognitive structures of the mind, and therefore, he argued, reason cannot always be used in its pure form. In postulating the existence of the mediating structures of the mind – such as the *a priori* concepts of space and time – Kant rejected the claims of rationalism, in particular in its Cartesian form, namely that pure, objective knowledge is possible. However, Kant was not announcing a retreat into subjectivism, such as the empiricist variety associated with Hume or the idealism of Berkeley. The Kantian solution was to find a mid-way between these two approaches. The answer that Kant found was a qualified scepticism with regard to objective knowledge but a retention of the world of objects, albeit at the cost of their ultimate unknowability. It was a scepticism that found its expression in the form of critique. By confining the search for knowledge to the uncovering of the transcendental conditions of possible knowledge, Kant was able to wed critique to the sceptical tradition. As I argue in the next chapter, the significance of critical philosophy is not appreciated unless it is seen in the context of an attempt to make room for religious faith: by restricting the scope of reason, Kant believed religious faith, within the bounds of secularism, could be possible – so long as it surrenders all claims to rational justification.

In his disparate political writings, Kant revealed a profound under-standing of the nascent culture of critique which had arisen with modernity. This was manifest in the emergence of the public domain. He argues enlightenment is possible only when a certain kind of freedom exists. The essence of this freedom is the 'freedom to make a public use of one's own reason in all matters' (Kant, 1996, p. 58). Kant argues the public use of reason must at all times be free, for it alone can bring about enlightenment. The public use of reason is to be contrasted to the 'private use of reason'. Of what does the distinction consist? Public reason, for Kant, is essentially reflective, intellectual discourse, whereas private reason is primarily institutional, specific to particular non-public contexts. The discourse of the scholar and the horizons of scholarly discourse are ultimately those of cosmopolitan society:

> I understand, however, under the public use of his own reason, that use which anyone makes of it as a scholar before the entire public of the reading world. The private use I designate as that use which one makes of his reason in a certain civil post or office which is entrusted to him. (Kant, 1996, p. 60)

It is clear that the public use of reason pertains to academic discourse, of which the chief characteristic is argumentation. Private reason, in contrast, does not require argumentation, since Kant feels this would be disruptive for the smooth functioning of society and he, in no way, was defending popular radicalness. Indeed, public reason, institutionalized in a republican order, could be used to justify authority. Thus Kant's vision of modernity was one both of political conservatism and of intellectual radicalness, of ever-expanding horizons of cognitive experience. The target of critical argument for Kant was religious and ecclesiastical dogma, since he believed this was the only remaining obstacle to enlightenment, for the arts and science had emancipated themselves from the prince's consciousness. Kant, like many of the moderns, did not reject Christianity but believed that its cognitive and institutional jurisdiction must be restricted. Thus the idea of the critique of tradition enters the discourse of modernity, whose self-consciousness is one of argumentative renewal and the rejection of foundational acts, other than that of the 'tribunal of reason'. In another work, published in 1798, *The Conflict of the Faculties*, the appeal to academic discourse becomes even more apparent. Kant's aim in this highly influential essay was to defend the autonomy of philosophy as the foundational faculty in what was to become the neo-humanist University of Berlin, for philosophy, unlike law, medicine and theology – which express the private use of reason – is based on the vocation of free thinking and does not serve any institutional function. It is ultimately the trustee of public reason and the neo-humanist university is the institutional guarantee of the freedom of critical inquiry.

In sum, modernity in Kant is associated with the spirit of enlightenment, which on the whole is an idea, or a cultural impulse, the rule of secular reason. There is little indication that modernity is an epoch in time, rather it represents the consciousness of new horizons in epistemic structures and moral awareness. With Kant, scepticism in the domain of knowledge reaches a new level of intensity with the idea of critique and is extended into a wider commitment to discursivity in matters pertaining to the legitimation of power.

Towards Modernism

With Hegel the idea of modernity becomes wedded to a philosophy of history.[4] Modernity is both a time consciousness and a theory of history, an epochal concept. In his *Lectures on the Philosophy of History*, modernity designates the emergence of the new, but not just in terms of chronological time. Modernity entails a reflective consciousness of history, which sees the future as already having begun in the recent past. In fact, for Hegel, modernity is conceived in a way that expresses the unity of past and present, with Greek civilization, Christianity, the French Revolution and the modern state forming a totality. In the Preface to the *Phenomenology of Mind*, he wrote:

> Besides it is not difficult to see that our time is a birth-time and a period of transition to a new era. Spirit has broken with the world it has hitherto inhabited and imagined, and is of a mind to submerge it in the past, and in the labour of its own transformation. Spirit is indeed never at rest but always engaged in moving forward. But just as the first breath drawn by a child after its long, quiet nourishment breaks the gradualness of merely quantitative growth – there is a qualitative leap and the child is born – so likewise with the Spirit in its formation matures slowly and quietly into its new shape, dissolving bit by bit the structure of its previous world, whose tottering state is only hinted at by isolated symptoms. The frivolity and boredom which unsettle the established order, the vague foreboding of something unknown, these are the heralds of approaching change. The gradual crumbling that left unaltered the face of the whole is cut by a sunburst which, in one flash, illuminates the features of the new world. (Hegel, 1977, pp. 6–7)

Here, the consciousness of the present moment is stronger than in Kant, for whom modernity was essentially the experience of enlightenment within a cultural modernity that had not yet found a political form. For Hegel, modernity is more than enlightenment but is also a relationship to history. Hegel's philosophy can be seen as a historicization of Kant's critique, for morality is deemed to be created in society and is articulated in human history. With Hegel, epistemology thus becomes social theory rather than just a theory of knowledge. It is a question of how knowledge is constituted in history. For Hegel, reality is constituted by knowledge, which is always critique. By critique, Hegel means a form of knowledge that transforms its object as opposed to being merely self-limiting, as in Kant. In this way, knowledge and reality are dialectically shaped. Critical knowledge, then, for Hegel is a form of consciousness raising, and the highest form of knowledge is consciousness as self-consciousness. Critique thus ultimately becomes for Hegel a kind of constructivist activity, or world constitution. We can thus say that critique means more than criticism. Criticism does not question the critic, only one's opponent; critique questions both oneself and one's opponent. Kant's critique remained bound to a model of criticism, for the self remained untouched by the critical philosophy, which almost entirely referred to the model of knowledge. In Hegel, on the contrary, critique as reflective consciousness refers to the transformation of Self, Other and world, reaching into the domains of knowledge, power and the self. With respect to the themes of scepticism, discursivity and reflexivity, we can say that while Kant gave expression to the necessity for a degree of scepticism in knowledge and discursivity in the legitimation of power, Hegel marked the inauguration of reflexivity – to be sure, within the limits of the philosophy of history.

Hegel's social theory was of course highly idealistic: the evolution of forms of knowledge corresponds to phases in the development of society and the 'universal' and the 'particular' are united in the formation of ever-higher forms of knowledge (which eventually transcend society). This is essentially a process of displacement, or 'overcoming', and constitutes what he called the 'phenomenology' of mind, the evolution of forms of knowledge. For Hegel, like Kant, knowledge was always self-limiting, but he differed from Kant in his view that knowledge – as the self-consciousness of the spirit of the age – always comes too late, unable to be realized in political practice, for social actors cannot conceive of their age in pure thought. Historical self-consciousness can ultimately, by dint of the 'cunning of reason', be available only to the philosopher, who transcends the age by being its principal expression. In this way, Hegel – whose thought was a combination of radical liberalism and conservatism – was able to justify the French Revolution while rejecting the idea of revolution and, in particular, revolutionaries.

The result of Hegel's endeavours was a conception of modernity that stressed its internal ambivalences and struggles: self, knowledge and power are severely delimiting, both realizing and making impossible their autonomy. For instance, in the *Philosophy of Right*, published in 1821, Hegel outlined a theory of civil society which gave expression to a vision of modernity as a process of negation. Ethical life (*Sittlichkeit* or ethical community) is constituted in the private realm, the public realm (or civil society) and the state (the political realm). Civil society creates and destroys ethical life because the 'system of needs' is realized under the conditions of capitalism: 'ethical life is split into its extremes and lost' (Hegel, 1952, p. 123). For Hegel, the state is a higher expression of community than civil society, and the function of the state is to compensate for the shortcomings of civil society (it is both interventionist and welfarist). In sum, the theme of Hegel's social theory is that of the fragmentation/alienation of consciousness in civil society and the search for a political solution for the realization of community. Modernity is the motif which gives expression to this struggle.

This pessimistically tinged sense of modernity – the note of sadness and of desire – that is evident in Hegel is also to be found in the writings of the German Enlightenment figures, many of whom – for instance Schlegel and Schiller – combined republicanism with romanticism (unlike Kant, who combined republicanism with reason). In the Sixth Letter of his *On the Aesthetic Education of Man*, Friedrich Schiller contrasted the 'moderns' with the Greeks, who alone have humanity and imagination:

> How different with us Moderns! With us too the image of the human species is projected in magnified form into separate individuals – but as fragments, not in different combinations, with the result that one has to go the rounds from one individual to another in order to be able to piece together a complete image of the species. (Schiller, 1998, p. 86)

Modernity produces fragmentation, a contrast to the wholeness of the Greeks. Schiller was no reactionary conservative – unlike, for instance, his contemporary Novalis in *Christianity or Europe*, published in 1799 – and did not think this lost unity could be recovered under the conditions of modernity. It is for this reason that Schiller argued 'only the aesthetic mode of communication unites society', for all other forms divide society (Schiller, 1998, p. 93). The idea of an 'aesthetic education' always remained very fundamental to the romantic spirit of modernity, linking the desire for freedom with reason and sentiment. Its legacy was an ambivalent attitude to modernity: on the one side, a great faith in the promise of reason to bring about freedom, and, on the other, a nostalgia and sadness for the passing of an unretrievable organic unity. These two attitudes shaped much of the subsequent understanding of modernity, with one tradition drawing its inspiration from the promise of reason (revolutionary romanticism, nationalism, fascism, Marxism and liberalism) and another (much of the modernist tradition, Nietzsche, Heidegger, Freud, Wittgenstein, Benjamim) reconciling the promise of freedom with a melancholic pessimism about modernity.

The realization that modernity is inherently contradictory became more pronounced with Marx. Modernity is seen at odds with its own project, which becomes a revolutionary process. Instead of historical constitution, we now have self-constitution as the essential driving force of modernity. The self is a collective social actor who must be historically constituted. This view of the subject differs from the Kantian one in that autonomy is no longer the starting point but an aspiration. The focus of critique shifts from epistemological issues, as in Kant, or the philosophy of history, as in Hegel, to the social relations of capitalism and its system of domination. Still, the act of historical overcoming is strongly present in Marx, though the orientation is more to the future than the past, which loses its hold over the present. It may be suggested that with Marx modernity is neither exclusively an idea – as with Kant – nor an epoch in history in which an idea is realized – as with Hegel – but a radical project of action. The crucial factor now is the increasing recognition that cultural idea and social reality are contradictory. As a result, modernity as a project is expressed less in the overcoming of an origin than in the struggle to overcome alienation and exploitation.

It makes sense to characterize this development as an anticipation of modernism. The term 'modernism' can be used to designate the radical turn in the culture of modernity. Modernism, strictly speaking, refers to developments in aesthetic modernity, and is not normally applied to the other dimensions of cultural modernity such as cognitive rationality and morality. But some of the core features of *fin-de-siècle* modernism are expressed in the writings of Marx and Engels, such as the vision of modernity as a dynamic force by which subjectivity and objectivity are forced asunder, the fusion of consciousness with historical experience, the transformative power of consciousness, the confluence of politics and aesthetics in the expressive potential of creativity and violence (see also Crook, 1991; Lunn, 1982).

The early discourses of modernity, epitomized in the writings of Kant, took the central characteristic of modernity to be the differentiation of cognitive spheres from each other in the wake of the fragmentation of the unified worldview of medieval Christendom and the doctrine of the divine right of kingship. By the end of the nineteenth century, this all changes. The aesthetic dimension undergoes an increasing formalization of style, which can be seen as an immanent development of the autonomous institution of art as a professional activity by which art ceases to be the representation of orders (social or religious) other than those of art itself (Bourdieu, 1996b; Bürger, 1984; Cascardi, 1992). Occurring at the same time, but becoming increasingly intensified in the early twentieth century, the aesthetic imagination – which had purged itself of all unmediated social content – reestablishes its connection to morality and politics. In this politicization of art and literature, which is always indirect and highly mediated, the separation of cognitive spheres is rendered more diffuse. In its most radical form, the avant-garde, art enters the life-world as social critique, and, on a different front, many of the leading expressionists believed their art bordered on a new spiritualism, a transcendental principle of unity, though one that could offer no political possibilities. The more artists, such as Franz Marc, Paul Klee, Vassily Kandinsky, explored the abstract possibilities of the formal structure of art, the more they became aware that the aesthetic imagination could give expression to a spiritual reality beyond the reach of all other forms of experience. This spiritualization of the aesthetic was explored by Kandinsky in his extremely influential book *Concerning the Spiritual in Art*, published in 1911. Aside from the example of the avant-garde, in most of its guises, in particular in painting, the tensions of modern society are represented in an anti-representational form, and in many cases border on an extreme reflexivity and preoccupation with abstractness. But it would be a mistake to reduce all of modernism either to the politicized avant-garde or the de-politicized formalism of early expressionism and its quest

for a spiritual order. Too much of the debate on modernity and modernism
has resolved around the example of the avant-garde to the neglect of the
historical time consciousness of modernism.

The spirit of modernism was one of creative expression, be it in art or
in politics. From the vantage point of the autonomous institution of art
and the aesthetic form, modernism, for the greater part, was able to
express social content in new creative ways. Even Kant in one of his later
works, the *Critique of Judgement* (published in 1790), argued that the
aesthetic imagination could be a means of giving expression to a new
kind of community, a view that was made more explicit by Schiller.
Modernism as exemplified in Baudelaire, Flaubert, Joyce, Yeats, Woolf, did
not purge the aesthetic of all social content. In radicalizing the nature of
narrative, these authors were able to portray the tensions within society
and provide consciousness and experience with new forms of expression.
For Flaubert, the novel was akin to sociological critique (Bourdieu, 1996b).
Joyce's *Ulysses* explored the consciousness of the city. The city thus
becomes a social text in which history and consciousness are blended. In
Joyce's work the city becomes the dominating motif, as it is in the sociology of Georg Simmel and the early Chicago School. The experience of
modernity in Joyce is also bound up with a reading of the western canon,
such as Homer and Dante, for history is something inescapable.

This latter point – the intertwining of modernity and history – draws
attention to the experience of ambiguity which is central to modernity.
Modernism can be a repudiation of history as much as a nostalgia for
it. Modernism can reflect a desire to escape from modernity as much
as it can be a celebration of the modern world. In 1893 Hugo von
Hofmannsthal remarked that to be modern could mean reflection on the
age or it could mean escape from it into a fantasy world: 'Today, two
things seem to be modern: the analysis of life and the flight from life. . . .
One practises anatomy on the inner life of one's mind, or one dreams.
Reflection or fantasy, mirror image or dream image' (quoted in McFarlane, 1991, p. 71). The desire to escape from modernity can be either a
romantic antimodern animus, for instance a longing for a lost object,
nostalgic and melancholic in tone; or it can take the form of a search for
an alternative modernity, the enchantment of the Orient or some kind of
exotic primitivism, or even the image of America. It is in this spirit that
Alexis de Tocqueville's *Democracy in America* can be read. Published in
1840, this work saw the coming age of democracy to be in America, not
in Europe, which was entering into decline. Tocqueville gave expression
to what was to become a widespread view, namely that the American
Revolution had been a success while the French Revolution and all
European revolutions – 1789, 1848, 1917, 1968 – were failures, resulting in
terror, restoration, despotism or compliance with power.

One of the chief characteristics of modernity which invites this kind of
an ambivalent reaction is the sense of contingency. Modern society, in
particular urban life, is never based on the direct experience of reality,

except only in those fleeting moments which for Charles Baudelaire epitomized modernity: 'By Modernity I mean the transient, the fleeting, the contingent; the half of art whose other half is the eternal and the immutable' (Baudelaire, 1964, p. 13). The modern is the condition of perpetual motion. In his writings on Baudelaire and other works, Walter Benjamin (1973a) speaks of the 'prehistory of modernity', by which he meant the actual experience of modernity. The kind of experience that modernity creates is a highly mediated one, for society is never experienced in its totality; nor is it experienced directly. We experience society through a whole variety of forms, ranging from art itself, commodities, conventions, fashion, technology, the medium of print and public communications – and today TV and the internet. This sense of the moment is stronger in Simmel, for whom modernity is best expressed in diverse 'momentary images' (*Momentbilder*), or 'snapshots' (Frisby, 1986, p. 6). Modernism juxtaposes the worlds of autonomy and fragmentation. Modern society is both based on autonomy – the autonomy of the self – and the fragmentation of experience. With authors such as Marx, Baudelaire and Joyce, the theme of fragmentation grows in importance. Modern society shifts the quest for autonomy inwards towards subjectivity, which is capable of reconstructing out of the fragments of experience a new principle of unity. For Baudelaire, modernity signified the aesthetic portrayal of the fragments of beauty in everyday life. To be modern is to seek everywhere after 'the fugitive, fleeting beauty of present-day life, the distinguishing character of that quality which, with the reader's kind permission, we have called "modernity" ' (Baudelaire, 1964, p. 40).

It is, then, in the context of the move towards modernism that Marx, as a theorist of modernity, must be located. As Marshall Berman (1982) has argued, Marx's writings, in particular the dominant motif of the *Communist Manifesto* – 'all that is solids melts into air' – reflects the spirit of modernism.[5] Marx's vision of modernity was one that celebrated the dynamism of modernity, a social formation that had built change into its very structures. His analysis of the capitalist mode of production sought to reveal the process by which objects become fetishized, separated from subjectivity. Capitalist society is a society which reduces all social relations to commodities, which are not just mere objects but 'fetishisms' in that they are made up of distorted relations between subjectivity and objects. His concept of the 'fetishism of commodities' demonstrated how structure and cultural reproduction are intertwined and that therefore culture cannot be seen as something that transcends social reality but is produced within it in structured forms of relations. Marx's theory of commodification thus anticipates postmodern theories of cultural production and consumption.

There are essentially three concepts of culture in Marx: culture as ideology, as class consciousness and as fetishization. In the earlier writings, such as the *German Ideology*, where the focus was a critique of idealist philosophy, which overstated the role of cultural processes, culture is seen as part of the superstructure, an epiphenomenon. Existing alongside this conception of culture is a notion of class consciousness, which is the opposite to ideology in that it is the authentic expression of reality that is to be transformed by action. The idea of class consciousness is to be contrasted to false consciousness. In *Capital* Volume 1, in the section 'The Fetishism of the Commodity and its Secret', there is the suggestion of a more relational concept of culture as containing a secret for which the power of reflection is called: 'Reflection on the forms of human life, hence also scientific analysis of those forms, takes a course directly opposite to their real development. Reflection begins *post festum*, and therefore with the results of the development ready to hand' (Marx, 1976, p. 168). As we shall see in the course of this book, this third notion of culture as entailing a secret which must be revealed by reflective consciousness has proven to be more important than the other two conceptions.

The key idea in Marx's writings is the notion that capitalism is a reality-creating force that has built the means of its own destruction into itself. Capitalism creates reality by generating the social conditions of forms of consciousness and the social relations which generate consciousness. However, capitalism is essentially contradictory, since it is based on a structural relationship of inequality by which the conditions of the existence of one class are determined by the labour of another. The relentless pursuit of profit, which is not reducible to agency for capital has its own dynamics, transforms all social relations. This transformative dynamic is also built into the actual experience of social reality, and it is in this intertwining of structure and culture that class consciousness is raised. The Marxist self is, like the subjectivity of aesthetic modernism, a decentred one; it is an essentially relational definition of subjectivity, as well as one that points to its creative potential. In this respect there is a pronounced postmodern theme in Marx's writing (Carver, 1998). The creative dimension to Marx's thought is not always stressed, and as Hans Joas (1996) argues, it can be seen alongside the idea of the creativity of action in authors as diverse as Schopenhauer, Dewey, Simmel – the philosophy of life and pragmatism.

The theme of the crisis of modernity can be traced back to Hegel's pessimistic account of civil society and his notion of the 'cunning of reason'. Marx's writings displayed an even stronger conviction of the promise of modernity than Hegel, who ultimately retreated into speculative thought and redemption through philosophical reflection. After Marx, the theme of the crisis-prone nature of modernity becomes ever more pronounced, with modernity becoming inseparable from critique. We can in fact say the discourse of modernity – the developmental logics of scepticism, discursivity and reflexivity – undergo a crisis, collapsing into several, quite different discourses, many of which are hostile to modernity. It is possible to trace two main strands in the *fin-de-siècle* critique of modernity: the radical rejection of the Enlightenment conception of modernity (Nietzsche, Heidegger and Freud) and the social theory of modernity in the works of Durkheim, Weber and Simmel.[6] These will be discussed in the next section.

The *Fin-de-Siècle* Critiques of Modernity

Towards the end of the nineteenth century the dark side of modernity becomes more apparent. The first intimations of this were in post-revolutionary romanticism, the resonances of which can be found in the thought of Hegel. In the period after the French Revolution, modern society is portrayed as destructive and alienating, a turn that was possibly related to the failure of the revolutionary dream (Heilbron, 1995). While the forces of liberalism and socialism grew in strength from mid-century onwards, the romantic quest for subjective autonomy and a retreat to culture and away from civilization and the social remained a powerful force in European thought, one which was to dominate the twentieth century as the other side of reason (Hughes, 1958, 1966; Poole, 1991; le Rider, 1993).

A significant figure was Matthew Arnold, whose *Culture and Anarchy*, originally published in 1869, presented an influential defence of culture as a force of stability in modern society. For Arnold, modernity is perpetually prone to anarchy and the only antidote is culture, by which he meant the arts. Such figures as Schopenhauer, Kierkegaard and Nietzsche also began to have a major influence on late nineteenth-century thinking. The impact of their ideas lay in a new emphasis on a creative spiritual rediscovery of the self. Schopenahuer, for instance, had written a short essay on suicide in 1851, which Durkheim would have read, undoubtedly inspiring him to write his own famous work on the subject (Schopenhauer, 1970; see Morrison, 1998). Schopenhauer in general exerted a pessimistic influence on European *fin-de-siècle* thought. Indeed, Durkheim's concept of 'collective representations' is directly related to Schopenhauer's *The World as Will and Representation*, written in 1818. Weber was heavily influenced by Nietzsche, and to a lesser extent by Kierkegaard, and in 1907 Simmel published what he regarded as his major work, *Schopenhauer and Nietzsche*. Kierkegaard also had a major impact on late nineteenth-century conceptions of modernity. While history and modernity were not important to him, he did have a notion of the modern self that was significant in shaping the reflexive turn. As Arpád Szakolczai argues, Kierkegaard added a crucial dimension to reflexive sociology by developing the idea of a relational self. According to Kierkegaard, the

> self is a relation that relates itself to itself or in the relation's relating itself to itself in the relation; the self is not the relation but is the relation's relating itself to itself. . . . The human self is such a derived, established relation, a relation that relates itself to itself and in relating itself to itself relates itself to another. (Kierkegaard, 1980, pp. 13–14, quoted in Szakolczai: 1998, p. 214)

Nietzsche rejected the historicist tendency in nineteenth-century thought, the view that meaning is revealed in history, as he did the Enlightenment belief in the emancipatory power of reason and science. The philosophy he proposed – nihilism – rejected the search for emancipation in either science or history. This radical critique of the Enlightenment ultimately entailed a rejection of politics in favour of an ethics of autonomy, the rediscovery of subjectivity. Though Nietzsche has been appropriated by poststructuralism and by neo-Heideggerianism, he can in fact be seen as more of a proponent of radical modernism than is suggested by these traditions.[7] Far from rejecting the centrality of the self in favour of a presuppositionless discourse or the collapse of self and world into the notion of Being, by means of the concept of power Nietzsche sought to emancipate the self from the illusions of both Platonic philosophy and historicism. History is not the unfolding of an Idea, but the creative appropriation of tradition by the self. The idea of the 'eternal reoccurrence' can be seen as the rejection of the Enlighten-ment notion of time as historical and linear in favour of a conception of time as a series of positions which can be occupied by the self in the affirmation of a certain type of life that we would willingly return eternally to. One might say Nietzsche was a modernist – in so far as this was a doctrine of the autonomy of the self, power and knowledge. What he rejected was the Enlightenment's vision of history and reason.

Heidegger devoted himself to a radical critique of modernity, seeking a new normativity outside the parameters of modernity (Ferry and Renaut, 1990; Zimmerman, 1990). Rejecting all previous humanisms, be they those of communism, Sartrian existentialism or Christianity, Heidegger, in the 'Letter on Humanism' (1978), looked to a new humanism beyond modernity, which is merely the expression of technology and rational-ism. He warned of the descent into 'homelessness', and the need to recover a primordial rather than a modern conception of the world.

> The danger into which Europe as it has hitherto existed is ever more clearly forced consists presumably in the fact above all that its thinking – once its glory – is falling behind in the essential course of a dawning world destiny which nevertheless in the basic traits of its essential provenance remains European by definition. No metaphysics, whether idealistic, materialistic, or Christian, can in accord with its essence, and surely not in its own attempts to explicate itself, 'get a hold on' this destiny yet, and that means thought-fully to reach and gather together what in the fullest sense of Being now is. (Heidegger, 1977, p. 221)

It is particularly significant that the 'Letter', which was the expression of Heidegger's mature thinking, was written in 1946 when a world-wide consensus was emerging about the need for a new culture of inter-nationalism to solve the problems engendered by fascism. Heidegger rejects both 'nationalism and internationalism as being out of touch with the "truth of Being": Nationalism is not overcome through mere internationalism; it is rather expanded and elevated thereby into a system. Nationalism is as little brought and raised to *humanitas* by international- ism as individualism is by an ahistorical collectivism' (Heidegger, 1978, p. 221). The political ideologies of modernity – individualism and collectivism, liberalism and collectivism – are equated with the rise of technological forms of mastery. In the *Introduction to Metaphysics*, in 1935, Heidegger wrote:

> This Europe, which in its ruinous blindness is forever on the point of cutting its own throat, lies today in a great pincers, squeezed between Russia on one side and America on the other. From a metaphysical point of view, Russia and America are the same: the same dreary technological frenzy, the same unrestricted organization of the average man. (Heidegger, 1959, p. 37)

Heidegger's critique of modernity was a total one. He rejects the political culture of modernity for a spiritual dimension prior to the modern which he accuses of having brought about the 'spiritual decline of the earth'. His philosophy as outlined in *Being and Time* called for a return to early Greek thinking as well as an interest in the works of Nietzsche and a critique of technology, the result of which was a rejection of the Enlightenment heritage: language, not reason, was the foundation or ontology of human society. Modernity, for Heidegger, is not a process of emancipation but one of 'forgetting'; it is a forgetting, an 'oblivion', of the meaning of human existence, the question of 'being'. Modernity is the separation of subject and object. Heidegger's call for a return to the pre-Socratic Greek notion of Being saw in ancient thought an inalienable unity of subjectivity and objectivity, which was destroyed from Plato onwards. In 'The Age of the World Picture' Heidegger sees modernity as an attempt to construct (to 'represent') the world as a picture, which he sees as an act of objectification: in the act of 're-presenting', the world is converted into an object that can simply be represented as an object for a subject. What defines modernity is precisely the emergence of a view of the world as picture: 'the fundamental event of the modern age is the conquest of the world as picture' (Heidegger, 1977, p. 134). This is essentially a cognitive development, and one which is constructed on the basis of the violent separation of subject and object: 'The world picture does not change from an earlier medieval one into a modern one, but rather the fact that the world becomes picture at all is what distinguishes the essence of the modern age' (Heidegger, 1977, p. 130). The other side of the world picture is a subject who observes a world outside itself. 'That the world becomes picture is one and the same event of man's becoming *subiectum* in the midst of that which is' (Heidegger, 1977, p. 132).

Heiddeger rejects this Enlightenment tradition, which has degenerated into 'Americanism' and has corrupted the original European essence that is to be found in early Greek thought. He praises the 'West's last thinker', Nietzsche, who wrote 'when he was "most distant from cloudy, damp, melancholy Europe" ': 'The wasteland grows: woe to him who hides wastelands within' (Heidegger, 1968, p. 51). Nietzsche, Heidegger (1968, p. 55) argues, 'sees clearly that in the history of Western man something is coming to an end'. But it is an ending that is also a beginning, an 'unspoken gathering of the whole of western fate, the gathering from which alone the Occident can go forth to meet the coming decisions – to become, perhaps and in a wholly other mode, a land of dawn, an Orient' (Heidegger, 1968, pp. 69–70). The name 'Europe' means for Heidegger the 'late-comers': 'Europeans are living in the twilight of a world on which sunset is about to fall and the new age that is to dawn will be a post-historical age but one in which the original Greek insight into the most fundamental questions of human existence will be revealed' (Heidegger, 1957, pp. 300–1). As has frequently been pointed out, his primordialist critique of modernity has been tainted by its close association with the Nazi ideology, which he willfully supported and sought to legitimate. From the early 1930s Heidegger began to explore the political implications of his ontology of Being.

Freud, too, was responsible for a major onslaught on the idea of modernity, though not one that can be compared to the Heideggerian primordialism. For all his critique of civilization, Freud retained a great belief in the need for a social order of restraint against the destructive forces of primordialism. In demonstrating that beneath the rational consciousness and the unity and coherence of personality are the deep irrational forces of the unconsciousness where the prehistorical conflicts of civilization are played out, he effectively undermined one of the major premises of the Enlightenment, namely the coherence and unity of the self, which is seen as a struggle between the ego and id. Rather than the promise of freedom through reason, modernity is based on a lost object and the desire for its recovery places civilization ever under the strain of a pathology. In his later works, written after the First World War as Europe began its descent into antisemitism, Freud speculated that the love of the aggressor may be a greater force than the oedipal complex in shaping modern consciousness. From Freud onwards, modernity and violence cannot be so easily separated. Freud believed the political mission of psychoanalysis was to reduce the hold of the id – from where the powerful and destructive forces of the unconsciousness derive – by strengthening the ego, the social apparatus of control: 'Where id was there ego shall be' (Freud, 1946 p. 106).

This strand in the discourses of modernity was on the whole one that tended to reject the Enlightenment model of modernity. It was reflected in a great variety of sociological and philosophical positions, as varied as Tönnies's *Community and Society* (1963, originally 1887), Husserl's famous essay on the spiritual decadence of European modernity, 'Philosophy and the Crisis of European Man' (1965, originally 1936), Ortega y Gasset's *The Modern Theme* (1961, originally 1923), Max Scheler's *Ressentiment* (1972, originally 1915) and Georges Sorel's *Reflections on Violence* (1950, originally 1908). Tönnies was a curious figure, who, like Borkenau (1981), was very sympathetic to radical socialism while being very hostile to modernity, which for him was epitomized by 'society', or associational forms of relations. Drawing from the still potent forces of revolutionary romanticism, he looked to the idea of community for a spiritual alternative to modernity. For Husserl, modernity was characterized by the forgetting of the fundamental condition of intentionality in human self-constitution. But modernity, too, is based on a struggle of recovery, which for Husserl is the recovery of something that has been lost as a result of the rise of modern positivism or naturalism. This is held to be the unity of spiritual life and creative activity, as well as a recovery of a sense of objectivity, eclipsed by the rise of subjectivity. The Spanish social philosopher Ortega y Gasset also saw history as leading to stagnation and decadence, for which he blamed 'mass society', in which there was a decline in spiritual leadership. In his terms, 'reason' and 'life' were totally split apart.[8] For Max Scheler, in a famous work, modernity is a descent into the cultural condition of 'ressentiment', a concept that derives from Nietzsche. For Scheler, who wanted to reconcile Christian morality with modernity, human values are essentially objective and embody an independent meaning, but in modernity there is a descent into ressentiment against those values. The morally weak fear those who are able to accept that they are to be judged by ultimate values.[9] Finally, for Georges Sorel, an anarchist syndicalist, wrote of modernity in terms of a struggle between a myth of violence and reason. Violence was necessary in order to overcome capitalist rationalization, he believed. But violence – the movement of the masses against the institutions of modernity – needs recourse to a myth in order to awaken the spirit of socialist revolution. This way of thinking, with its resonances of an aesthetic politics and primordialism, reflected the romanticist revolutionary strand in modernity.

The second strand I mentioned is the more restrained sociological discourse of modernity in the works of Durkheim, Weber and Simmel. These were all major theorists and critics of modernity, liberals by political conviction and conservatives by cultural inclination. Of the three, Durkheim was the one who tended to be the most reconciled to modernity. The mark of modernity for Durkheim was a form of social integration that did not rest on a mechanical relationship between culture and society, by which individuals unthinkingly reproduce cultural norms, but was one of differentiated systems of communication. He believed the society of his time had reached a point of transition in which mechanical forms of integration had broken down and genuinely modern 'organic' forms had not yet emerged. This possibly explains his interest in studying 'anomie', the breakdown in social cohesion in the manifestation of pathologies of normlessness such as suicide. His famous treatise Suicide, published in 1897, can be read in this light as a comment on the ills of modernity, or rather the incomplete realization of modernity. Recent interpretations of Durkheim as a postmodern thinker

(Meštrović, 1991) emphasize the impact of idealism in his work, in particular the impact of Schopenhauer and cultural pessimism. This, however, is much disputed, since Durkheim, methodologically a positivist, was ultimately more of a realist than an idealist (Morrison, 1998). It might make more sense to emphasize the enduring impact of Kantian ideas in Durkheim, as in Weber and Simmel, who, all in their different ways, converted Kantian cognitive epistemology into a cultural theory, though in the case of the latter two, Weber and Simmel, their reading of Kant was mediated by Nietzsche. For Durkheim, culture is a medium through which the world is experienced. Though his notion of collective representations may have been derived from Schopenhauer, his vision of modernity was a much more optimistic one than that of many thinkers of his generation. Yet, a note of pessimism can be found in his writings. In the conclusion of *The Elementary Forms of the Religious Life*, Durkheim wrote of a cultural void in modern society:

> we are going through a stage of transition and moral mediocrity. The great things of the past which filled our fathers with enthusiasm do not excite the same ardour in us, either because they have come into common usage to such an extent that we are unconscious of them, or else because they no longer answer to our actual aspirations; but as yet there is nothing to replace them. . . . In a word, the old gods are growing old or already dead, and others are not yet born. (Durkheim, 1915, p. 427)

It was Durkheim's firm belief that all societies need some kind of 'collective effervescence' to affirm their unity and identity. In this work on the sociology of cultural forms of knowledge, he outlined the cognitive structures of religion as a cultural model for society, but held that there is no essential difference between religious feasts and ceremonies and those of the modern national state. The decline of the old gods refers not just to the demise of religion but also to the waning appeal of the greatest myth of modernity, the French Revolution, which produced a series of national holidays to perpetuate its founding act: 'A day will come', Durkheim speculated,

> when our societies will know again those hours of creative effervescence, in the course of which new ideas arise and new formulae are found which serve for a while as a guide to humanity; and when these hours shall have passed through once, men will spontaneously feel the need of reliving them from time to time in thought, that is to say, of keeping alive their memory by means of celebrations which regularly reproduce their fruits. (Durkheim, 1915, pp. 427–8)

It would appear what animated Durkheim was the possibility that modernity might be able to recover something like the revolutionary effervescence and give a new meaning to modern society.

Unlike Durkheim, Max Weber did not tend to see modernity as an incomplete project. In fact, the problem of modernity for Weber was precisely that it had been completed and exhausted the possibilities of cultural renewal, leaving in its wake an inner-directed self, asceticism without a cultural mission. He was heavily influenced by Nietzsche, who led him to see that modernity had exhausted cultural meaning. In an intellectualized and rationalized world, meaning consequently would have to be found anew, in an inner-worldly attitude and, what intrigued him, the rediscovery of charisma. There is undoubtedly some parallel here between Weber's fascination with charisma and Nietzsche's 'supreme being' (*Übermensch*), for both ideas suggest an emphasis on a creative individualism which can re-create enchantment in a disenchanted world. Thus, it may be suggested that Weber read Kant through the eyes of Nietzsche, whereas Durkheim's Kant remained oblivious to Nietzsche.[10] Both, however, can be seen as reflexive sociologists. Szakolczai (1998, pp. 210–13) argues that while their earlier works formed the basis of the sociological canon, their later works, which were never fully integrated into the mainstream tradition, reveal a common concern with reflexivity, and one which only in recent times is being appreciated.

One of the central themes in Weber's sociology is the exhaustion of culture as a resource of meaning, which consequently must become inner-directed. For Weber, culture provides individuals with the resources for meaning and an orientation for their interests, but, like all of society, it undergoes a process of rationalization. Culture, for Weber, and unlike Durkheim, is underpinned by the subjectivity of actors, making meaningful action possible. For Durkheim, in contrast, culture has a greater force of objectivity. What is specific to western rationalism is the confluence of the economic and the cultural, the famous thesis of Weber's *Protestant Ethic and the Spirit of Capitalism* originally published in 1904–5. This leads to the 'paradox of rationalism': the western quest for meaning generates a rationalized order which then destroys the very possibility of meaning. As Weber expressed it in the essay 'Religious Rejections of the World and Their Directions': 'The paradox of all rational asceticism, which in an identical manner has made all ages stumble, is that rational asceticism itself has created the very wealth it rejected. Temples and monasteries have everywhere become the very loci of rational economies' (Weber, 1948c, p. 334). This argument – which can be stated more broadly to be that the spirit absorbs the ethic – leads Weber, ultimately, to a thesis of the cultural exhaustion of modernity, which becomes an 'iron cage'. However, it is crucial to appreciate for Weber there is not a total absorption of subjectivity into the iron cage, for religious asceticism has escaped the cage it helped to build:

Since asceticism undertook to remodel the world and to work out its ideals in the world, material goods have gained an increasing and finally an inexorable power over the lives of men as at no previous period in history. Today the spirit of religious asceticism – whether finally, who knows? – has escaped from the cage. But victorious capitalism, since it rests on mechanical foundations,

needs its support no longer. The rosy blush of its laughing heir, the Enlightenment, seems also to be irretrievably fading, and the idea of duty in one's
calling prowls about in our lives like the ghost of dead religious beliefs.
(Weber, 1978, pp. 181–2)

The problem is not subjectivity – and its most elevated form, religious
asceticism – but the neutralization of culture to inspire and provide
leadership for society.

Weber sees modernity caught up in a double struggle. On the one
level, there is the Kantian conflict of the separation of the cultural
spheres of science, art and morality from each other and from religion,
which no longer provides a cultural foundation for modern society. But
for Weber, Kant is to be interpreted through the eyes of Nietzsche: the
differentiation of cultural spheres is now seen as the 'ethical irrationality'
of modernity and the principal expression of its 'disenchantment'. Meaning becomes more and more subjective and the cultural spheres of
science, art and morality can never be reconciled under the conditions of
modernity. As a result, the quest for meaning must shed the possibility
of enchantment. The second level concerns the conflict between culture
and rationalism in other domains of society, in particular the economic.
On this level the conflict is greater since what is under threat is the very
possibility of culture itself, and even the possibility of politics. The lecture
'Politics as a Vocation' closes with the prophetic words: 'Not summer's
bloom lies ahead of us, but rather a polar night of icy darkness and
hardness, no matter which group may triumph externally now' (Weber,
1948b, p. 128). For Weber, as I have suggested, the last traces of enchantment in public life are to be found in charisma, the personality of the
political leader. Like Thomas Mann, he held to the possibility of a
redemption of the self (Goldman, 1988). However, he differed from
Mann in that he believed the disenchantment of culture could not be
reversed and simply redeem modernity.

In one of this most famous works, the lecture 'Science as a Vocation',
the traces of postmodernism are to be found. In this lecture, delivered in
1917 against the backdrop of the Russian Revolution at a time when
Germany and Europe were in a state of cultural shock and political chaos
as the First World War approached its end, Weber (1948a) argued that the
modern world has not only lost the certainty of religion but may also be
losing the security of modernist science. In this lecture, Weber reminded
his audience – who included the young Karl Löwith – of the limits of
science for social and political objectives and that the disenchantment
of the modern world cannot be so easily reversed: ' "Scientific" pleading
is meaningless in principle because the various value spheres of the
world stand in irreconcilable conflict with each' (Weber, 1948a, p. 147).
He does not only appear to endorse cautiously the role of radical ideas
but also gives a very clear statement of the absence of any principle of
unity in modern society, whose condition is one of value pluralism. He

warns against the folly of the revolutionary generation and the soldiers returning from the front who 'crave a leader and not a teacher':

> Science today is a 'vocation' organized in special disciplines in the service of self-clarification and knowledge of related facts. It is not the gift of seers and prophets dispensing sacred values and revelations, nor does it partake of the contemplation of sages and philosophers about the meaning of the universe. This, to be sure, is the inescapable condition of our historical situation. (Weber, 1948a, p. 152)

Here we find one of the first announcements of the end of 'grand narratives': science has lost its ability to provide meaning; it has become a 'vocation' and demands an 'intellectual sacrifice'. In sum, Weber's theory of modernity was a mixture of cultural pessimism – a sense of modernity as decadent and exhausted – and maturity – a forward-oriented way of thinking entailing the embracing of choice as a positive attribute of modernity.[11]

The critique of modernity was also central to the work of Georg Simmel. By means of his central concept, the 'tragedy of culture', as outlined in the essays 'On the Concept and Tragedy of Culture', published in 1911, and 'The Conflict in Modern Culture', published in 1918, Simmel portrays modernity to be a conflict between life, or content, and forms.[12] In modern society the forces of life do not express themselves as unmediated content; they are expressed in cultural forms. Simmel believed that social reality is not itself visible, but is always constructed by social actors through cultural categories. His social epistemology was deeply indebted to Kant, whose cognitive categories become sociologized with Simmel: reality is mediated by the cognitive structures of culture. As a Kantian, Simmel was always interested in the relationship between content and form. For him, form is the fundamental *a priori* of all of life, and in the modern period it becomes paramount. 'Content' refers to the subjective dimension of life, the life force, and the 'Form' to the objective dimension of culture. But ultimately both are related, since form is the actualization of content. It was his central thesis that under the conditions of modernity the tragic fate of subjectivity is its objectification in the external forms of culture, which acquire an existence of their own. By the tragedy of culture Simmel meant the separation, or alienation, of content and form, subjectivity and objectivity, life and culture, the personal and the cultural, in the emergence of a tragic *a priori*, the implication of which was that there could be no possibility of unity. In *Schopenhauer and Nietzsche* (Simmel, 1986) this is particularly evident. Schopenhauer embodied for him this pessimistic view of modernity as alienation, while Nietzsche offered a possibility of individual resistance. In a way, these two thinkers represented the struggle between the victory of form and content, whereby Schopenhauer represents the failure of meaning – the negation of life – and Nietzsche its heroic recovery – the 'yes' to life.

In *The Philosophy of Money*, published in 1900, Simmel saw the tragedy of culture exemplified in money, which he understood as a cultural category through which life is mediated (Simmel, 1978). For Simmel, in, for instance, 'The Metropolis and Mental Life', published in 1903, the culture of modernity is above all characterized in metropolitan experience, where the world of objects appears as highly mediated relations (Simmel, 1971). Life is experienced through relations, and one major expression of this is the growing distance between people. For Simmel, this was the product of the differentiation of modern society. But he saw this process of differentiation more in terms of Marx's notion of commodification than in Durkheim's sense of the possibility of collective effervescence under the conditions of value pluralism since he was particularly interested in the emergence of modern forms of consumption.

The importance of Simmel with respect to the modernity–postmodernity debate is that he marks the beginning of the cultural turn in modern sociology. While this is also evident in, for example, Durkheim's theory of collective representations, and earlier, in Marx's theory of commodity fetishism, Simmel was much more concerned with the role of culture in the construction of modern society (Weinstein and Weinstein, 1993).[13] In terms of postmodern sociology, his work marked the emergence of a society characterized by consumption rather than by production, for the modern individual is more likely to be a consumer than a producer as modern urban life is producing more social roles than can be reducible to the world of work. At a deeper level, what is important is that Simmel represents the final collapse of experience as the measure of objectivity. In his interpretation of Schopenhauer, he remarks that 'rationalism – which was dethroned by Kant in the special area of epistemology and was replaced by experience as the sole bearer of the possibility of cognizing reality – loses with Schopenhauer its hold on a total view of man' (Simmel, 1986, p. 29).

A final observation is that if postmodernity is marked by the turn to culture and to a view of culture as essentially contested, one of the most elaborated statements of this is to be found in the essay by Karl Mannheim, 'Competition as a Cultural Phenomenon'. In this pivotal, but much neglected, work in the sociology of knowledge and cultural theory, originally a lecture delivered in 1928, Mannhein outlined a theory of cultural contestation by which 'public interpretations of reality' are constructed. 'Different interpretations of the world', he argued, 'for the most part correspond to the particular positions the various groups occupy in their struggle for power' (Mannheim, 1952, p. 198). With this insight, culture loses its character as a collective effervescence, as in Durkheim, or as a sterile cage, as in Weber, or synthesis of subjectivity and objectivity, as in Simmel, becoming nothing more than a process of public disputation by which different groups struggle to impose their definition of reality.

Conclusion: Contested Modernities

I began this chapter with a discussion on Kant, arguing that his epistemological system dominated the discourses of modernity. We can now see how some of the core features of postmodernism have already been present in the theory of modernity, as this unfolded as an interpretation of cultural crisis from Kant through Nietzsche and Weber to Simmel and Mannheim. The idea of modernity in Kant, Hegel, Marx, Weber, Durkheim and Simmel was far from the totalizing notion of a metanarrative or a disciplinary and rationalistic order, and as Johan Goudsblom (1980) has argued, the idea of nihilism is deeply embedded in western culture. In a seminal essay, Gerald Graff attacked the 'myth of the postmodern breakthrough', claiming it was in fact part of the logic of modernism: 'Though it looks back mockingly on the modernist tradition and professes to have got beyond it, postmodern literature remains tied to that tradition and unable to break with it' (Graff, 1979, p. 62). As William Outhwaite (1999), too, has argued, modernity cannot be reduced to the totalizing disciplinary conception of modernity of Foucault, or Lyotard's metanarratives. Rejecting Bauman's reduction of modernity to the rule of legislators, he argues for a more differentiated conception of modernity as itself embodying a reflexive dimension. This is also the thesis of Johann Arnason (1995), who sees modernity as irreducible to power, for it also entails the separate question of culture. The cultural dimension of modernity cannot be separated, he argues, from issues relating to self-transformation and reflexive critique. This is a view of modernity which is also reflected in Peter Wagner's (1994) theorization of modernity as a struggle between mastery and liberty. In this chapter I have emphasized the importance of reflexivity in the theory of modernity. As argued by Arpad Szakolczai (1998, p. 209), reflexivity, as the active work of thought when stabilities are broken up, was central to the early sociologists, and is clearly evident in the mature writings of Durkheim and Weber. In this sense, reflexivity is a contrast to 'reflectivity', which means the mirroring of structures; it entails an enhanced reconstructive activity in which personal experiences can be brought to bear on questions of method.

In sum, modernity and postmodernity can be relativized in a number of ways. If the conventional divide between modernity and postmodernity can be relativized according to one's reading of modernity, the divide between modernity and its predecessors can also be relativized. The idea of modernity can be projected back into history, producing what is in fact a series of contested modernities (see Bourricaud, 1987; Pocock, 1987; Schabert, 1986). In the next chapter this will be explored by looking at the rupture between modernity and its premodern antecedents in yet a further attempt to show that modernity is an essentially contested term.

2

MODERNITY AND SECULARIZATION
Religion and the Postmodern Challenge

The debate over modernity has been very much about the consequences of secularization. Since the beginning of the modern age, proponents of modernity have defended the modern against the dogma of religion. Modernity came to be seen as a rupture, a break from that which preceded it (Gellner, 1992, 1998). The worldviews of religion and modernity would therefore appear to be fundamentally opposed, for modernity is unconditionally posttraditional. As argued in the previous chapter, the worldview of modernity can be seen as a differentiated one and entailed a commitment to critique and self-transformation, which can be understood epistemologically as a self-conscious scepticism and reflexivity, for critique entails the transformation of both Self and Other. To be sure, as I have also argued, this was not something entirely new since much of western thought prior to the advent of modernity can also be read in precisely these terms. But, on the whole, one central dimension to modernity has been the critique of tradition, from which the modern poetics of suspicion derives. Thus many theorists, for instance Ulrich Beck and Anthony Giddens, see modernity as posttraditional, and others see this posttraditional world of modernity being overtaken by postmodernity.[1] My aim in this book is to show that this conception of modernity is a fundamentally misleading one. In this chapter I will be emphasizing the critical and reflexive appropriation of tradition within modernity, which is not posttraditional. I have called this reflexive attitude in the self-understanding of modernity the critical appropriation of tradition since it involves not the overcoming of tradition but its transformation.

In order to develop this problematic of the limits of posttraditionalism I shall discuss in this chapter one of the most important debates on the self-understanding of modernity as a product of western secularization, Hans Blumenberg's classic work *The Legitimacy of the Modern Age*. Since its publication in German in 1966, it has been the subject of extensive debate in Germany, largely because of its powerful critique of one of the most influential critiques of modernity, Karl Löwith's *Meaning in History*

(1949). Since the appearance in English in 1983 of Blumenberg's work, its status has grown and no account of the theory of modernity can ignore it. Rejecting the thesis that modernity is merely a secularized version of Christianity, an illegitimate copy of something anterior to it and therefore inauthentic, Blumenberg demonstrated that modernity can be defended in its own terms and can claim a legitimacy of its own. The significance of this argument is even more far-reaching since its offers a new inter- pretation of the premodern as itself containing a protomodernity. In this chapter I will discuss this debate in detail. My central argument is that the terms of this debate must be revised since the principal challenge to the identity of modernity is no longer the thesis of historical illegitimacy, the target of Blumenberg's work – though in some communitarian critiques, for instance Daniel Bell's, that is still present – but the post- modern challenge, which curiously has, in certain respects, rehabilitated theology as a metadiscourse on religion (Berry and Wernick, 1993; Derrida and Vattimo, 1998). Lyotard returned to his theological roots at the end of his life, in an as yet unpublished work, *La Confession d'Augustin*.[2] Other studies, for instance Gillian Rose's *Judaism and Modernity* (1993), have been important in shaping the terms of new debates on religion and modernity. Rejecting the false dichotomy of the cultures of Athens (the culture of rationality associated with modernity and philosophy) and Jerusalem (the culture of revelation associated with Judaism), she argues for their reconciliation. For Rose, both philosophy and Judaism are characterized by the loss of self-identity under the circumstances of ethical crisis. Uncertainty lies at the heart of Judaism, she argues, and in a way this expresses the predicament of modernity itself. A recent debate in the journal *Telos* was devoted to the possibility of a 'liturgical' critique of modernity.[3] From within a conservative modernism, Romano Guardini in *The End of the Modern World* (1998) has argued for the retrieval of religion in the new aesthetic modernity which offers a foundation less in nostalgia than in postmodern faith. In short, the question of postmodern- ism and religion forces us to reopen in entirely new terms the debate begun by Blumenberg. I shall attempt to argue that certain developments in postmodern conceptions of theology – in particular the idea of negative theology – suggest a blurring of the demarcation of the modern and the postmodern. Therefore the postmodern challenge is not as far- reaching as has often been believed. It is not the case that modernity surmounted the myths of religion with new ones, framed in the image of modern science and rationality, and that postmodernity subsequently demolished all myths, be they those of Christianity or the Enlighten- ment: it can be demonstrated that both modernity and postmodernity rest on a negative theology wherein a certain scepticism can be found.

The first section outlines Blumenberg's critique of Löwith, and the second section looks at conceptions of tradition and modernity, such as the communitarian positions of Alasdair MacIntyre and Charles Taylor as well as Edward Tiryakian's theory of religion and modernity. The third section discusses some recent debates on theology and postmodern social theory by John Milbank (1990), Paul Heelas (1998), Jacques Derrida and Gianni Vattimo (1998) and Areyeh Botwinick (1997).

Blumenberg and Modernity

Blumenberg's *The Legitimacy of the Modern Age* was written as a critique of the philosophy of history of Karl Löwith and Carl Schmitt.[4] Though very different politically from Schmitt and Heidegger, who supported the Nazis, Löwith shared many of their philosophical presuppositions (Löwith, 1995). A theme in the works of all these 'antimodernist' writers was the thesis that modernity is a disguised version of Christian pre-modernity and therefore an illegitimate copy of something more authentic. Authenticity for Blumenberg is not to be equated with an origin, or with a founding substance or content which gets translated into something else. This theme was explicitly developed by Karl Löwith in *Meaning in History* (1949), which is the principal target of Blumenberg's critique. A widespread notion, to which Löwith merely gave expression, is that modern ideas are merely the secular equivalents of Christian concepts, such as the longing for a redemptive final event (the Last Judgement, the Second Coming). Thus, the Marxist revolution is allegedly nothing other than a modern version of the desire for redemptive justice, and the modern quest for progress is a secularization of the Christian search for salvation. Weber's notion of the work ethic as a secularization of Christian asceticism can also be seen in this light, though for Weber secularization was itself engendered by rationalism and eventually became irrelevant once rationalism moved onto other cultural forms.

Löwith himself was principally concerned to unmask the idea of progress, and with it the very self-understanding of modernity. For him, secularization is essentially nothing more than the continuation of eschatology, which is not abated by modernity. Modernity is indeed based on a central 'idea', a narrative of progress, but this idea is not authentic since it derives from the enduring significance of Christian eschatology for historical meaning. In other words, progress is only the modern expression of salvation. Blumenberg was also directing his critique against the 'political theology' of Carl Schmitt, who argued in *Political Theology* (1970, originally 1922) that 'all significant concepts of the modern doctrine of the state are secularized theological concepts' (quoted in Blumenberg, 1983, p. 92). Though Blumenberg does not enter into a sustained reading of Heidegger and Freud, it is apparent that their critiques of modernity are also on trial. Heidegger's notion of the 'forgetfulness of being' and Freud's concept of repression have in common a view of modernity that what is past and forgotten can still have a harmful presence' (Blumenberg, 1983, pp. 116–18).

A similar position in the Anglo-Saxon world aimed at unmasking modernity can be found in a classic work by Carl Becker, *The Heavenly City of the Eighteenth-Century Philosophers* (1932). Despite the absence of historicism as an intellectual force, Becker's essays reveal a logic not unlike that of Löwith concerning the secularization thesis. The 'new heaven' of the eighteenth-century philosophers was a mirror image of the celestial heaven of Augustine, and in it posterity would replace what the past had once provided as well as also replacing God as judge and justifier; the modern city and the city of God are one and the same:

> Thus, the philosophers called in posterity to exorcise the double illusion of the Christian paradise and the golden age of antiquity. For the love of God they substituted love of humanity; for the vicarious atonement the perfectibility of man through his own efforts; and for the hope of immortality in another world the hope of living in the memory of future generations. (Becker, 1932, p. 130)

Dismissing the epochal significance of the Enlightenment, Becker says the eighteenth century was not only the age of reason but was also the age of faith. In demolishing the 'heavenly city' of the medievals, the moderns simply reproduced some of the essential structures of medieval thought: 'In a very real sense it may be said of the eighteenth century that it was the age of faith as well as reason, and of the thirteenth century it was an age of reason as well as of faith' (Becker, 1932, p. 8). Many great rationalists were also Christian thinkers who wanted to find impregnable proofs for the existence of God. If St Thomas wanted to use reason to justify faith, the moderns, he argues, wanted to restrict reason in order to make room for faith. He claims that even a sceptic like Hume was agreed that reason is incompetent in matters of faith. Becker detects a turning away in Hume's later writings from epistemological scepticism to a concern with history and the emotions:

> Hume's turning away from speculation to the study of history, economics, and politics was symptomatic of a certain change in the climate of opinion – of an increasing interest in the concrete political and social activities of men, and of the disposition to approach such matters in a more earnest temper, a mood highly charged with emotion. (Becker, 1932, p. 83)

Indicative of this turn to sentiment was Rousseau, who embodied the spirit of the Enlightenment; a spirit, which, for Becker, cannot be reduced to the celebration of reason at the cost of religion and sentiment, for no sooner had the Enlightenment discovered reason than it was found it to be inadequate and feeble.

Blumenberg can be read as a defence of the modern against those, such as Löwith, Schmitt and Becker, who would rather see it as inferior to its origin, Blumenberg rejects the very notion of a founding origin which was later corrupted by a secularized theology. His argument is that the legitimacy of the modern world resides in its concept of a self-legislating reason which must be seen as a radical break from that which preceded the modern rupture. From about the seventeenth century onwards a clear tendency can be observed that modernity is an attempt to find new answers to old questions. There was not, he argues, a simple transposition of theological arguments into secular ones, but rather a search for new answers. This ruptural event was marked by the birth of the subject and the struggle for what Blumenberg calls 'self-preservation' and 'self-assertion'. The turn to the subject was a break from the past and cannot be understood as a mere secularized copy of theological principles. This is because the concept of the transcendent in modernity does not assume the form of an outside divine force which intervenes in human history in order to bring about the end of history. Human history cannot be seen as a 'loss of substance', a 'content' that gets translated into new forms. Blumenberg argues, 'one does not achieve a historical understanding of secularization by conceiving its implied "world" as the recovery of an "original" reality that had been lost with the entry of Christianity' (Blumenberg, 1983, p. 9; all subsequent references in this section are to this work, unless otherwise stated). He objects to the reductionist logic in historicism, which in reducing the modern idea of progress to the Christian idea of salvation implies that modernity is based on the unfolding of an underlying idea and that everything is ultimately an expression of the 'alienation of a historical substance from its origin, which it carries with it only as a hidden dimension of meaning' (p. 18). He rejects a view of modernity as carrying within it a hidden dimension of meaning, 'a mere watered-down form of judgement or revolution; it is rather the continuous self-justification of the present, by means of the future that it gives itself, before the past, with which it compares itself' (p. 32). The strong emphasis on the present is central to modernity.

> Indeed the problem of legitimacy is bound up with the very concept of an epoch itself. The modern age was the first and only age that understood itself as an epoch and, in so doing, simultaneously created the other epochs. The problem of legitimacy is latent in the modern age's claim to carry out a radical break with tradition, and in the incongruity between this claim and the reality of history, which can never begin entirely anew. (p. 116; see also p. 468)

However, the lynchpin of Blumenberg's argument against the secularization thesis is that the modern world was already secularized in the early Christian era when the eschatological hopes of the early Church were abandoned. His most far-reaching argument is that the eschatological belief in salvation as a real historical possibility ceased in the early decades of the first millennium when hope turned to fear and the future became a focus of anxiety rather than redemption. Consequently, when the idea of progress eventually emerged, eschatology had already ceased to be connected to hope: 'Eschatology may have been, for a shorter or a longer moment of history, an aggregate of hopes; but when the time had come for the emergence of the idea of progress, it was more nearly an aggregate of terror and dread' (p. 31). In this period, eschatology lost its connection with historical fulfilment when it became apparent that the 'kingdom to come' would not occur in human history. In other words, eschatology was already secularized prior to the advent of modernity and therefore modernity does not derive from eschatology: the continuity, postulated by Löwith, was shattered prior to the rupture inaugurated by modernity. Blumenberg goes so far as to argue that the secularization of eschatology was already recognized in the aftermath of the Babylonian exile when the Jewish idea of the apocalypse lost some of its historical overtones, as a result of disappointed historical expectations, and took on the character of a more speculative picture of the messianic future: 'The accommodation with the facts of world that persisted in existence simply was not accomplished by projecting into the future what according to the promise should already have occurred' (p. 43). As eschatological disappointment became ever more apparent, the recognition emerged, as is evidenced in St John, that the events decisive for salvation had already occurred. Henceforth salvation became an increasingly individual achievement, divorced from cosmic salvation, which loses its significance. By the time of the Protestant reformation the turn to individual salvation is brought to completion. However, curiously, Blumenberg does not consider the survival of millenarianism in early Protestantism, which rediscovered biblical eschatology. This rediscovery of cosmic salvation was related, particularly in seventeenth-century England, to the formation of new collective identities and nation-state building.

Against the secularization thesis, Blumenberg argues the 'basic eschatological attitude of the Christian epoch could no longer be one of hope for the final events but was one of fear of judgement and the destruction of the world' (p. 44). The early Church prayed not for a second coming, but for the postponement of the end. Thus, the understanding of history that this provides is not one of an expectation of historical salvation, but one that revolved around the theological predicament of a God whose promises could not be fulfilled by a fallen humanity. The interpretation that Blumenberg draws is that the ancient Church was already secularized, and, crucially, it was secularized not by science and reason but by religion itself: secularization can be understood only as an immanent theological process. By secularization is meant the rationalization of religious belief, the process by which belief becomes more and more drawn into a doctrinal system and loses its connection with other dimensions of life.[5] In this sense, then, secularization means not the external rationalization of religion, but its self-transformation. For Blumenberg, this amounts not to the 'secularization of eschatology but rather secularization by eschatology' (p. 45). For eschatology itself brings about secularization, which is not the translation of eschatology into something essentially different, such as the idea of progress. It is not the case that eschatology is transformed, that is, secularized, into a modern idea, for the secularization of eschatology had already taken place and its motive force was eschatology itself, which had to press towards self-institutionalization in the world with which it had to reconcile itself as a result of historical disappointment. In removing the connection of eschatology to the notion of the end of the world, eschatology retains its theological meaning. If this was the first great secularizing drive, it is nonsense, in Blumenberg's eyes, to argue that modernity is merely a secularized version of what went before it. The upshot, then, of this thesis is that the premodern period must be seen in a more differentiated light and that the events decisive for modernity had already occurred before the appearance of the modern itself. There is also an important argument here on the relationship between the personal and the collective, since salvation in Christianity is almost exclusively personal, rarely having a wider political significance for society as a whole. Modernity, in contrast, while being based on the primacy of the individual, sees redemption as largely a collective political undertaking.

Thus by means of an internal critique of theology, Blumenberg (p. 126) argues that when modernity finally made its appearance from 1500 to 1800 it did so in a world which was already secularized by nothing less than Christian eschatology itself. The significance of this argument – which is not greatly different from Max Weber's thesis of disenchantment – is enormous since it not only locates the move to secularization well before the modern era, but points to a new definition of modernity, which cannot claim the mantle of secular reason.[6] Modernity, according to Blumenberg in one of his central arguments, is in fact the 'second overcoming of Gnosticism', which the early medieval period failed to bring about. Gnosticism was one of the most radical challenges to the early Church. In the second century Gnosticism postulated a radical dualism between God and world and explained evil as a creation of a malevolent God, rather than being, as Augustine was to argue in what was to be a successful attempt to overcome the Gnostic challenge, a product of human failure. The orthodox Christian view of evil is that it is due to an 'absence' rather than being a force in itself, since the God of creation did not create evil. Gnosticism held that the God of creation was responsible for evil, and that the God of salvation had to triumph over this evil demiurge (p. 129). What this amounted to was a rejection of the principle of the essential unity of the divine plan: the God of creation and the God of salvation were radically different. Moreover, and this is crucial to Blumenberg's argument, Gnosticism is conceived as a forerunner of modernity. Although it was ultimately unsuccessful in challenging Christian dogma, Gnosticism, Blumenberg argues, was the first major discourse of 'self-assertion'. By disputing the combination of creation and redemption as the work of a single God, Gnosticism was able to open a space for human redemption as a self-instituting act. Marcion, one of the principal figures in early Gnosticism, conceived of God as, in Blumenberg's words, 'free of the burden of responsibility for the world, entirely and without restriction on the side of man's salvation' (p. 130). In other words, in seeking redemption from evil, human beings are not constrained by the principle of theodicy imposed by the God of creation.

Condemned as a heresy, Gnosticism re-emerged in the modern era, which can be understood as the 'second overcoming of Gnosticism'. Philosophy won its autonomy, Blumenberg argues, precisely as a result of the renewal of the separation of the hidden God from the revealed God. In this space, the autonomy of thought and action, as well as human institutions, could be located:

> The role of the philosopher is defined by the reduction of human certainty under the pressure of the assumption that divine omnipotence cannot have placed any restrictions on itself for man's benefit. In this circumscription of the role of reason, the elimination of the traditional teleological assumptions has a prominent place. (p. 172)

Modernity is born with the recognition of the reality of uncertainty and the emergence of an augmented 'theoretical curiosity', which is not a product of the secularization of eschatology. By reducing the hold over history imposed by the God of creation, Gnosticism and modernity recognized the condition of contingency and indeterminacy in the human condition.

It is noteworthy that this argument does not entail the view that the early moderns were hostile to revealed religion. Kant, for instance, conceived his critical philosophy as an attempt to restrict the application of reason to the domains of faith. The certainty that Descartes, who Blumenberg maintains is located on the threshold of the modern, sought for human thought is not the secularization of the certainty of salvation, since that is supposed to be guaranteed not by faith, but by human autonomy, the autonomy of thought.

> The double face of the Enlightenment, on the one hand its renewal of a teleological optimism and on the other hand its inclination to atheism, loses its contradictory character if one places it in the context of the unity of the onset of human self-assertion and the rejection of its late-medieval systematic role. (p. 179)

This argument is consistent with the claim that the rise of modern science was considerably aided by the Protestant reformation and is also reflected in Weber's notion of the paradox of rationalization.

The second overcoming of Gnosticism and the superseding of Aristotelian science cannot be explained merely by secularization, Blumenberg has established, since the transcendental impulse of modernity is an immanent one: the end of history can only be achieved by humanity itself in its historical self-assertion. Central to the self-assertion of modernity is the discovery of method. 'Self-comparison with the authorities of antiquity and reflection on method, thanks to which this comparison could be evaluated positively each time in favor of the present, were the most powerful beginnings of the idea of progress' (p. 32). Modernity arises in the discovery of method in the sixteenth and seventeenth centuries with the New Science, but also arises in the debate between the ancients and moderns on the status of the classics. Blumenberg rejects the view – associated with the poststructuralist critique of modernity – that modernity merely put subjectivity in the place of God, for what was more crucial was the advocation of method, which is not a kind of planning, a transformation of the divine plan, but rather the establishment of a particular kind of disposition. According to Blumenberg, the idea of progress as the kernel of modernity derives from two events which preceded the modern age but which succeeded the secularization of eschatology: in the field of science, the discovery of method in the early modern period; and in the aesthetic field, the abandonment of ancient art and literature as models for modernity. In the first case, the discovery of method led to the rejection of scholastic and Aristotelian concepts of knowledge. In the second case, the idea of progress emerges in the context of a critique of tradition, in particular the status of the literature and art of antiquity as permanent prototypes. 'The *querelle des anciens et des modernes* is the aesthetic anologue of the detachment of theory from authority of Aristotelianism' (p. 33). What emerges in place of the ancient canon is an emphasis on the contemporary as the maker of the future. Thus, the modern notion of infinite progress derives from the consequences of actions in the present. For Blumenberg, then, eschatology or messianism is not the substantial point of departure for these developments in the genesis of modern historical consciousness: 'the modern age does not have recourse to what went before it, so much as it opposes and takes a stand against the challenge constituted by what went before it' (p. 75).

Blumenberg effectively rejects the strong continuity argument associated with the secularization thesis, namely that secularization is to be explained as the unfolding of a single and essential idea – the longing for spiritual salvation. However, he does not deny the continuation of theological questions into the modern age but insists that what is important is less these questions than the search for new answers, which cannot be explained in terms of theology. He calls this a 'reoccupation' of an older problem (p. 65). It is a question not of 'contents but one of functions' (p. 64). 'We are going to have to free ourselves from the idea that there is a firm canon of the "great questions" that throughout history and with an unchanging urgency have occupied human curiosity and motivated the pretension to world and self-interpretation' (p. 65). In essence, he rejects the idea of modernity emanating from a founding origin: 'The claim that the modern age made an absolute beginning through philosophy is no more correct than the claim that the latter half of history had an absolute beginning in the events to which the Christian era traces its origin' (p. 74). This notion of modernity as a 'reoccupation' of an older problem and yet not a secularization of it is at best obscure since the distinction ultimately hangs on the significance of the continuation of a problem in different terms. Blumenberg does in fact concede a considerable amount to Löwith, and the extent of modernity's legitimacy remains very unclear. The result of Blumenberg's position is that modernity is still tied to what preceded it rather than to an entirely different set of questions. Religion created the ground for the emergence of modernity. Whether modernity is a reoccupation or a secularization hardly matters since either position fails to address the fact that the culture of modernity stems from problems specific to modern society. In any case Blumenberg is unable to address the question of the identity of modernity from the Enlightenment onwards. His entire position is based on the crossing of the threshold of modernity from the late medieval period. The problem that this presents is that once modernity ceases to be tied to religion it loses its identity since there is nothing left to define it. At best, Blumenberg has shown how religion and tradition created the conditions for the emegence of modernity, but we are not offered a theory of modernity as such.

What is particularly interesting about Blumenberg's work is that it strikes a major blow against the poststructuralist and postmodern reading of history. Blumenberg was of course responding to the conservative critique of modernity, but his arguments are particularly pertinent to answering recent deconstructive critiques. This is evident in at least two ways. First, the argument proposed by Derrida that all of western thought is an expression of a search for a founding origin can be viewed in a more differentiated light. Blumbenberg has demonstrated that modernity was precisely a rejection of a founding origin and entails much of what postmodernism reserves for itself, namely theoretical curiosity, scepticism, a concern with uncertainty and self-assertion. Second, the reduction of modernity to a continuity thesis that does not distinguish between modernity and premodernity is no longer tenable in light of Blumenberg's work, which demonstrates that modernity was based on a rupture with what preceded it and, crucially, premodernity was itself a process which must now be seen in terms of secularization. Secularism is thus projected back onto the premodern period. In sum, Blumenberg's work is a remarkable defence of the modern turn to the subject as a self-legitimating project.[7]

In vindicating as a legitimate construction the self that lies at the centre of the modern project, Blumenberg's thesis is open to the communitarian and the postmodern critiques of the self. It is to the communitarian critique than I now turn, and in later chapters (Chapters 6 and 7) I will deal with the postmodern critique of the self, though I will touch on this in the final section of this chapter in so far as it relates to the question of theology.

Modernity and Tradition

Blumenberg's arguments are relevant to the contemporary situation since two significant conceptions of modernity challenge that epoch's claim to legitimacy: communitarianism and postmodernism. Both of these pose major questions concerning the relation of modernity and tradition, though in radically different ways. Their target is the centrality and legitimacy of the self, a challenge that has implications for politics and for knowledge. In this section I will deal with the first of these objections and in the final section of this chapter I will look at the implications of postmodernism for religion. My approach will be to take up some of Blumenberg's suggestions, arguing against, for instance, Daniel Bell and Alasdair MacIntyre with the claim that the important issue is how we conceptualize tradition. Essentially my argument is that postmodernism as well as the hermeneutic approaches of Gadamer and Taylor allow us to see tradition – including religion and community – as compatible with modernity; but this does depend on how we under- stand modernity. Modernity is already posttraditional in that it allows tradition to be endlessly reinterpreted and processed in new ways. The mistake is to see modernity as standing in a counter-position to tradition, but this does not reduce modernity, if we follow Blumenberg, to a founding event, or the unfolding of an idea.

It is useful to make a distinction between tradition and traditionalism, the former meaning the cultural values that have endured from the past and the latter being an interpretation of those values as unchanging. The distinction hinges on whether we see tradition as amenable to change or as something fixed and enduring in its timelessness.[8]

The traditionalist thesis has been eloquently stated by Daniel Bell. In *The Cultural Contradictions of Capitalism* Bell (1976) argued that modern society has generated a contradiction: on the one side, the values traditionally demanded by capitalism for its motivational basis, such as the work ethic, are being undermined by the cultural values being produced by postindustrial society, which encourages anti-achievement and hedonistic values. The result is a cultural contradiction, which in his estimation can be overcome only by a 'return of the sacred' (Bell, 1977). The upshot, then, of the neo-conservative-communitarian critique of modernity is that modernity is a fundamentally illegitimate project unable to provide morality with an enduring foundation.

Alisdair MacIntyre's *After Virtue* (1981) is an example of a com- munitarian critique of modernity, but one which is based less on tradition- alism (as in Bell) than on respect for the creative power of tradition, which in his estimation can be a source of cultural renewal. His central thesis is that the project of the Enlightenment has been largely a failure for it has not delivered its promise to provide a moral foundation for morality, which cannot be sustained by the solitary self released from tradition. Pitting Nietzsche against Aristotle, MacIntyre argues for a vindication of the premodern against the modern. In his view the aspiration of modernity for a universal and objective criterion of rationality is impossible and must be abandoned. MacIntyre's notion of tradition is complex, for he ties it to a notion of 'virtue'. By this is meant a commitment to the pursuit of human goods rather than purely individual ones. The ancient model of virtue for MacIntyre expresses the mutual relationship of the individual to the community, and it is for this reason incorrect to associate virtue simply with tradition or with religion; it is essentially a pagan republican concept and has nothing to do with organic notions of community. The virtuous life is inseparable from the 'Good Life', in the sense intended by Aristotle, by which it is tied to an understanding of citizenship as membership of a political community.

While MacIntyre is often unjustifiably portrayed as a conservative or a traditionalist, it would be more accurate to describe him as a neo-republican, and one with strong Marxist leanings (McMylor, 1994). His communitarianism is tied to Marxism, whereas Bell's communitarianism is linked to his neo-conservatism. Most of MacIntyre's early work was in fact an attempt to bring Marxism in a communitarian direction, such as that of Christianity (MacIntyre, 1953, 1967, 1968, 1971; MacIntyre and Ricoeur, 1969). For MacIntyre, Marxism could be rescued from positivism and historicism by Christianity. Nevertheless, it must be stressed that the understanding of Christianity in his works is one that is more closely associated with pre-Christian ideas, such as the ancient idea of virtue. Indeed, MacIntyre's path from Marxism to Christianity was via Aristotle. However, I do not wish to enter into a discussion of MacIntyre's philosophy here since my aim is to discuss the concept of modernity (see also MacIntyre, 1988, 1990). For MacIntyre the ethic of virtue – or, if one wishes, the ideal of commitment to community – is not to be redeemed from the culture of modernity, which he reduces to either liberal modernity or the Nietzschean modernity of avant-garde modernism. Against this interpretation, he is arguing that modernity is indeed compatible with community and tradition. The problem, however, lies not with MacIntyre's concept of tradition as such – which, as I have argued, is not conceived of in terms of traditionalism – but his model of modernity, for instance his one-sided interpretation of Nietzsche as postmodern, when in fact he can be adequately seen, as I have argued in the previous chapter, as a representative of radical modernism.

There is, however, another way of looking at the question of modernity and tradition. It is to see both as being elucidated by each other.[9] The hermeneutical approaches of Hans-Georg Gadamer (1979) and Paul Ricoeur (1974), for instance, allow us to see tradition as something akin to the act of translation. Tradition is not unchanging but neither is it something that is necessarily composed of the fabrications of elites, as Hobsbawm and Ranger (1983) claim.[10] Against the traditionalist conception of tradition, we must see tradition as a process of creative interpretation upon which modernity itself rests. The mistake is to see modernity as the successor to tradition, as posttraditional. The modern critique of tradition is more a question of cultural retrieval than of overcoming, as is illustrated not just by the survival of tradition in modernity but by the construction of tradition. The danger that modernity is likely to fall into is traditionalism – the invention of fake traditions, such as notions of heritage, by devious elites who create the illusion of permanence – rather than tradition itself.

Charles Taylor in his *Malaise of Modernity* (1991) offers an interesting interpretation of modernity from the standpoint of liberal communitarianism. Unlike MacIntyre, he does not dismiss modernity, which he sees as highly ambivalent. Arguing against those critics, like Daniel Bell (1976), Christopher Lasch (1979, 1985, 1991), Allan Bloom (1987), who see modernity in terms of decline, of irretrievable loss, and the retreat into a narcissistic self, Taylor also takes issue against the liberal version, which glorifies the achievements of modernity, and the postmodern rejection of modernity. The three great themes of modernity are those of individualism, instrumentalism and citizenship. Each of these produces a 'malaise': the loss of meaning, the eclipse of ends and the loss of freedom. The problem of modernity is to overcome these limits, for Taylor's vision of modernity allows for a trade-off between its positive and negative dimensions. Where Bell, Lasch and Bloom see nothing but the slide into the soft relativism of the culture of narcissism, the excessive preoccupation with the emotional needs of the self, the abandonment of community for a shallow individualism, Taylor sees the possibility of authenticity, or self-fulfilment. Authencity cannot be reduced to moral subjectivism; it is something peculiar to modernity and pioneered by Descartes, who made each person think self-responsibly, and by Locke, who made personhood prior to society. However, Taylor (1991, p. 26) also maintains that authencity has its roots in the romantic movement, which was critical of a disengaged rationality and an atomism that did not recognize the ties of community. The problem today, he argues, is to overcome the narcissistic and relativist kind of authenticity that elevates choice itself as the positive virtue. In order do this it is necessary to recover what he calls its dialogical character, which is inseparable from the pursuit of community.[11]

I have mentioned MacIntyre and Taylor here in order to show how, within the communitiarian critique of modernity, two different models of modernity are offered: one which rejects modernity in favour of a revitalized tradition, and one which sees tradition as compatible with modernity. In the remainder of this section I will illustrate this by reference to the question of religion and modernity.

Edward Tiryakian (1996), in an invaluable essay, provides a way of seeing modernity as a historical struggle between three interacting cultures: the Christian, the Gnostic and the Chthonic. These are interacting and interpenetrating traditions, whose contribution to western civilization has been immense. Tiryakian (1996, p. 102) sees these traditions as 'metacultures', that is, 'a set of beliefs and symbols, generated in the distant past *and renewed* by succeeding generations of actors', providing the basic and ultimate frames and symbolism of action. Christian culture favoured modernity with its emphasis on a new temporal horizon (for example, a new calendar keeping continuous time), a written text (the Bible), a universal concept of humanity going beyond ethnic boundaries, and the idea of service, as pointed out by Parsons (1935). Further aspects of the contribution of Christianity to modernity might be its emphasis on individuation and responsibility, the ground of some of the basic personality constraints. Though conscience and sin made individuals accountable not to society but to the Godhead, they were none the less significant in generating modern morality.

In an argument which recalls Blumenberg, Tiryakian argues Gnosticism has also made a major contribution to western civilization.

> The seemingly 'natural social order' is taken to be an abomination, the creation of evil powers or of the evil deity, against whom the Gnostic community wages battle to the finish, which means, that the Gnostic community seeks to replace, to overturn the social order with another, 'new' social order. (Tiryakian, 1996, p. 105)

For Tiryakian this means that Gnosticism has a potential for revolutionary action, and like all revolutionary elites the Gnostic elites are those who claim to have a superior knowledge of the hidden truths of reality with which they legitimate their pursuit of a new order. Despite their differences, Gnosticism and Christianity are similar: both struggle to free human beings from the natural order and appeal to a strong individual activism. For Gnosticism this is to be achieved through some form of institutionalized intellectualism, while for Christianity the liberation of the self comes from the teachings of the divine saviour.

The Chthonic metaculture is essentially the pagan one. It refers to a basic ontological affirmation of the earth as the primordial locus of reality, and derives from societies for which the most important questions were those of survival. Unlike the other metacultures, it is not salvation-oriented as such, and lifestyles of asceticism or world renunciation are not central to it. With a lesser emphasis on the dualism of the human and divine orders, the Chthonic culture is richer in its cultivation of tradition, but the kind of tradition that it has historically cultivated is closer to what Durkheim called 'mechanical solidarity', namely the adaptive mechanisms that allow groups to subordinate the individual's interest to the group.

Modernity is more indebted to these cultures than is often thought, argues Tirakykian. The Victorian age, for instance, as well as its succesors, was not just the age of science and progress, but was a period when Gnosticism made a recovery.

> Gnosticism had had a latent period from which it emerged during the Enlightenment; it found in the domain of scientific enquiry and scientific institutions and in the renovated university milieu of the nineteenth century major new bastions of legitimacy where the pursuit of 'gnosis' could take place practically without restriction. Besides the important public space of the university and later the research institutes . . . the Gnostic space was also enlarged by various orders and fraternal organizations, initiatory and secretive, yet flourishing in the general liberal climate of the industrial age. (Tiryakian, 1996, p. 107)

The Christian metaculture, too, greatly expanded in this period, with the geographical expansion of missionary activity in the overseas empires. As for the Chthonic culture, as a result of industrialization and urbanization it receded from any real presence in people's lives from the nineteenth century onward, but as it withdrew from the public sphere it returned to the cultural domain as a bulwark against civilization.

> The romantic movement drew a great deal of inspiration from chthonic metaculture (often inventing or reinventing various of its elements, such as themes of witchcraft and sorcery). Nietzsche drew on early Greek chthonic metaculture (the cult of Dionysos) in rejecting the Judeo-Christian moral frame of the West as embodying a 'slave mentality', while Wagner combined Christian and chthonic metacultural elements in his grand operas such as *The Ring* cycle, *Parsifal*, *Lohengrin* and others. Picasso in his post-cubist period is perhaps the most striking twentieth-century embodiment of (Mediterranean) chthonic culture in the representational arts. (Tiryakian, 1996, p. 108)

In fact, in the last few decades the Chthonic culture has made a remarkable reentry, with a new positive evaluation of the Chthonic in feminist circles, ecofeminism, alternative medicine and in a renewed interest in the occult. Mention can also be made of the discovery of African soil by the African American community, for whom it offers a new kind of counter-tradition to the dominant western white one and a challenge to that culture's Christian urban tradition. Much more profoundly, however, is the suggestion that contemporary forms of identity relating to sexual liberation, sensuality, bodily expression, may be connected with both Gnostic and Chthonic currents in twentieth-century culture.

The conclusion Tiraykian draws is that the evolutionary view of religion having been superseded by modernity seems increasingly inappropriate for our postmodern era. Not only has the secularization thesis of the 1960s been contradicted by the upsurge of new kinds of religious belonging, but also there has been the revival of the chthonic tradition.[12] I shall now turn to the question of postmodernism and religion.

Postmodernism and Negative Theology

Postmodernism and theology are not as separate as modernity and theology allegedly were. In many ways the postmodern has rediscovered

some central theological questions, such as the possibility of transcendence. In *Theology and Social Theory* (1990, p. 1) John Milbank seeks 'to
restore in postmodern terms, the possibility of theology as a metadiscourse'. He remarks on the contrast between political theology and
postmodern social theory: 'Theology accepts secularization and the
autonomy of secular reason; social theory increasingly finds secularization paradoxical, and implies that the mythic-religious can never be left
behind. Political theology is intellectually atheistic; post-Nietzschean
social theory suggests the inescapability of worship' (Milbank, 1990,
p. 3). Postmodernism, which is today post-Nietzschean, recognizes that
questions of transcendence cannot be simply abandoned, having been
unmasked by modern social science. Millbank accuses sociology and
social theory of being trapped as the secular science of the 'sublime'
and consequently unable to comprehend 'transcendence', which is irreducible to the sublime. But what is the transcendental? There is the
suggestion that it is constituted in the consciousness of negative knowledge, of difference, though this is something that ultimately Milbank
appears to reject.

> In the 'new era' of postmodernism (which is yet in some ways but an 'exacerba-
> tion' of modernity) the human has become subordinate to the infinitely many
> discourses which claim to constitute humanity, and universality can no longer
> pose as the identical, but can only be paradoxically invoked as the different.
> (Milbank, 1990, p. 260)

For Milbank the postmodern challenge to theology is one of thinking of
difference, and it is one that that arises not from social science but from a
metadiscourse, or an ontology that fixes its gaze on difference as the
condition of the possibility of thought and action.

The question of postmodernism and religion is also the subject of a
volume edited by Paul Heelas (1998). The disintegration of the certainties
of modernity has created a situation in which postmodern religion
(Gnostic or New Age spirituality) can emerge. It can also result in a
return to the premodern past. A variant on the second model is the
argument of Akbar Ahmed (1992) that postmodernity is compatible with
Islam. If modernity represented western domination, postmodernity is
the recovery of traditions prior to the modern. More generally, in the
West postmodernism and religious revival share a common cultural root
in the emphasis on choice and self-fulfilment, to which a certain kind of
relativism also belongs. Postmodern religion might be a religion that
is 'beyond belief', a pragmatic kind of spirituality, as is illustrated in
the 'consumerist' orientation to religious belonging noted by Steve Bruce
(1998). Ninian Smart (1998, p. 87) reiterates the view that the current
period is one of invention and reinvention of traditions and not one of
detraditionalization *per se*. Postmodern religion is faced with consequences of the collapse of the idea of a better future, but this now has the

consequence – after the postmodern critique – that we have also witnessed the collapse of the idea of a legitimating past, as Don Cupitt (1998, p. 218) puts it. He sees postmodern theology expressing itself in a 'poetical theology' which differs from dogmatic religion in that it is characterized by openness and interpretation rather than closure, but this entails a loss of the idea of salvation. In his contribution, Phillip Blond (1998, p. 285) makes the connection with negative theology. 'Theology has lost its object. It can no longer point to anything with ostensive certainty and the word of "God". This loss of reality has prompted theology . . . to pursue correspondence with secular words and objects.' However, like Milbank, he seeks to recover the positive moment, rather than exploit the possibilities of negative theology: 'the price of theological evacuation of any external world relation is the rise of immanentist subjectivity and its denial of any external relation whatsoever with the most high' (Blond, 1998, p. 289).

This is precisely the task that Aryeh Botwinick (1997) sets in his *Maimonides to Nietzsche: Skepticism, Belief, and the Modern*. The fundamental problem for all of theology and philosophy is to comprehend that which is totally other than man, totally different from the categories used to invoke otherness. It is a question, according to Botwinick, of the search for equivalences, that is, a language that can mediate between two domains of knowledge and experience. Three examples of such equivalences are theology (scriptural text) and philosophy (truth), authority and consent, and theory and fact. The search for equivalences is never complete since one category can never be fully translated into another, there is always a residual difference, an uncertainity, or the possibility of an infinite regress. This means for Botwinick a commitment to the sceptical delimitation of knowledge, traces of which are to be found in Maimonides, Hobbes and Nietzsche.

Botwinick argues that scepticism, liberalism and monotheism are closely related. 'Skepticism is a doctrine of radical critique that both presupposes and denies a stable subject (in any grammatical sense)' and 'Monotheism is also a doctrine of radical critique that simultaneously presupposes and denies a stable grammatical subject, namely God' (Botwinick, 1997, p. 8; the citations in the remainder of this chapter are all to this book unless otherwise stated). Liberalism, too, entails a continual replenishment and adjustment of democratic content, for no form of authority is ever complete and final but is always revisable: there is never a 'univocal political translation of its content'. The essence of liberalism is that it introduces a set of braking devices that make the equivalence of authority and consent uncertain (p. 7).[13] Liberalism and religion are closer together because liberalism as a doctrine of secularism in the public domain exists alongside religion in the private domain. In so far as religion embodies negativity – the aspiration towards radical otherness – it supports liberalism for the scepticism upon which faith rests cannot be interfered with by the liberal state. Botwinick's position is that scepticism is also built into monotheism, since the latter cannot overcome the dilemma of self-referentialism, and the need for faith to rest on radical doubt. Thus for Maimonides, God embodies absolute difference and is wholly other than man. The only form of knowledge possible, then, is that of a negative theology, which is not too far removed from poststructuralism since 'its logic reduces its theoretical formulations to exercises in linguistic constructivism' (p. 30). What Maimonides does to God (that is, introducing a destabilizing context of reference), Derrida, the culmination of the Maimonidean tradition, applies to all of language, argues Botwinick,

> According to Derrida, all one can say is that given perpetually shifting backgrounds of signifiers against which to play off one's current formulation, the meaning (and also the reference) of any given formulation is not exhausted by any particular reformulation or paraphrase. For both Maimonides and Derrida, our stance in the world is characterized by an ever expanding mystical negativity. (p. 29)

Conceiving the relationship between theology and scepticism in this way allows Botwinick to explore new links between modernity and postmodernity. The traditional western intellectual story needs to be revised, he argues: 'Western intellectual history does not consist in a dramatic supplanting of a religious sensibility and outlook by secular self-understandings and modes of being in the world. Western thought seems to move from more inchoate and less self-conscious forms of skepticism to more fully explicit and articulated versions.' This leads to a new understanding of the link between modernity and postmodernity: 'If modernity is to be theoretically and sociologically identified with the emergence of skepticism into full prominence, I believe that post-modernity can be most persuasively envisioned as the emergence of the limitations and dilemmas surrounding skepticism into an augmented consciousness' (p. 8). In other words, modernity as an awareness of scepticism, a preoccupation with the limits of knowledge, has been with us from the beginning of western intellectual history. The implications for postmodernity are

> that it highlights the incomplete and uncompletable character of what precedes it in Western thought and therefore constitutes modernity's most elevated moment of reflectiveness and self-consciousness. Beneath postmodernism's glorying in the fragmentary and the transitory lies an appreciation of the unity of Western thought that perhaps goes deeper than earlier modernist percep-tions. (p. 9)

In projecting postmodernity back on modernity itself, Botwinick is able to see tradition as not that which is retrieved from the past but what is produced and articulated in action (p. 171). In his interpretation of Nietzsche, he establishes, against the poststructuralist reinterpretation,

the basic line of continuity with modernity and its predecessors, the idea
of disclosure through action (p. 186). Consistent with his understanding
of negative theology and the search for equivalences as manifest in what
is done as opposed to what is, Botwinick shows how Nietzsche's concept
of power is essentially a theory of the possibilities of action, and like the
notion of God, which it replaces, it is a reminder of the ineradicableness
of otherness. In sum, Botwinick demonstrates how a postmodern reading of modernity and religion involves a recognition of the role of an
active kind of scepticism and one which is closely related to democracy.
This way of thinking is open to many objections, the principal one that
strikes me is that this argument may work on the level of negative
theology, as a metadiscourse on religion, but the institutionalization of
religion in the private domain has not enhanced scepticism in a way that
lends it to supporting the principle of tolerance, as advocated by
liberalism. On the contrary, religion in modernity has been a powerful
impediment to liberal values, in the wider sense of libertarian values.
The concidence of liberalism and theology is only at the level of meta-
theoretic justifications. Scepticism is the basis not of religion, but of
theological justification. This is a distinction that Botwinick does not
make sufficiently clear.

Finally, within postmodernist deconstructionist thinking it is interesting to note a revival in religion. In a recent volume Derrida and
Vattimo (1998) explore the possibility of a link between religious experience and alterity (see also Caputo, 1997). In his contribution, Derrida
seeks to find a way of thinking about religion which might be able to
relate it to the Enlightenment's critique of religion, for the essence of
religion is the experience of difference as negativity. However, this turn
to religiosity that appears to be emerging in deconstructionist thinking
must be treated with suspicion, not least for the heavy dose of obscurant-
ism that accompanies it.[14] By relocating the reflexivity in religion, these
approaches undermine the roots of reflexivity not just in scepticism,
which has its own independent history, but more importantly in the turn
to discursivity, the basis of which is not merely negativity – or postpon-
ment, in the deconstructionist sense of difference – but communication.[15]
In other words, the substantive, or positive, moment of scepticism resides
in reflexivity and communication. Derrida and proponents of negative
theology have made the mistake, in my estimation, of remaining within
the limits of scepticism, where they seek the positive moment in negativity.

Conclusion: Posttraditionalism in Question

In this chapter I have tried to show that the debate on the transition from
modernity to postmodernity can be seen in a new light if we rethink the
earlier question of the transition from premodernity to modernity. Taking

religion as a focus, I have argued that Hans Blumenberg's theory of secularization allows us to see premodernity in a differentiated way. The crucial point that emerges from this is that one sense of secularization – the rationalization of salvation – can in fact be seen as something that reached completion prior to the modern period, whose advent was marked not by a founding origin – the continuation of eschatology in new guises – but by a rupture, marked by the turn to the self, theoretical curiosity and an emphasis on method. Thus, premodernity can be seen to have achieved many of the developments often attributed to modernity. The principal consideration here is the insight that modernity did not replace one set of myths with new ones and that postmodernity subsequently demolished all myths, replacing myth with a presuppositionless and self-negating discourse. I have argued, drawing from Botwinick, that both modernity and postmodernity can to a degree be seen to rest on a common sceptical tradition, which can be extended into the realm of negative theology. Going yet further beyond Blumenberg, I have argued, following some communitarian conceptions of tradition and the idea of negative theology, that modernity – once it is freed from the secularization thesis – can be seen to entail less of a rupture from tradition than its reflexive renewal. The upshot of all of this is that the transition to postmodernity can be seen as less radical than is sometimes supposed, since much of postmodernity can be seen as already exhibited in modernity, which cannot be reduced to posttraditionalism. But this does not commit us to a theological turn, as appears to be the case with some verisions of contemporary deconstructionism, since reflexivity has come to rest on other foundations today. (By means of a reading of works by Habermas, Touraine, Castoriadis and other figures in western Marxism I will examine these foundations in Chapter 5.)

In the next chapter I will look at another version of the 'hidden agenda of modernity', the thesis of the pathogenesis of modernity, as variously stated by Horkheimer and Adorno, Koselleck and Toulmin.

3

THE PATHOGENESIS OF MODERNITY
The Limits of the Enlightenment

The focus of this chapter is a variety of debates that arose in the period immediately following the Second World War concerning the status of the Enlightenment as the defining moment in western modernity. While Blumenberg shifted much of the work of modernity from the Enlightenment to forces deep in Christianity in order to release modernity from processes of mere secularization, the resulting celebration of modernity as an act of self-fulfilment did not stop the mounting critical attitudes to modernity. The question of the Holocaust and the world-wide penetration of capitalism, posed by the liberal left, and the reaction from cultural conservatives, who sought to discredit modernity as well as the critique of the radical left, forces us to consider a wider range of debates. The central issue that is at stake in these debates is the question of the pathogenesis of modernity.

To what extent is modernity a process of pathological development? One of the best-known statements of this position is that of Zygmunt Bauman, for whom the Holocaust is a product of modernity. In *Modernity and the Holocaust* Bauman (1989) treats the Holocaust as the test of the hidden possibilities of modern society, the most complete expression of the process of rationalization as described by Weber. However, the metaphor of modernity is no longer the 'iron cage' but the 'gas chamber'. In Bauman's estimation it was the highly rational world of modern civilization that made the Holocaust thinkable, a thesis originally proposed by Hannah Arendt (1964). According to this view, bureaucratic culture is ethically blind and purely formal, devoid of any cultural content. Divested of moral content, modernity becomes sheer instrumentalist rationalism and can link up with antimodern ideologies, such as racism. What Bauman argues is that modernity became entwined with antimodernist phobias, the outcome of which was the Holocaust. I will return to Bauman in Chapter 7 in the context of postmodernism, since his aim is to separate the culture of postmodernity from that of modernity, which for him can only be pathogenesis. It will suffice to mention here that the obvious criticism of this view is not the analysis of the Holocaust but the conception of modernity as instrumental reason. Against this reduction of modernity to the dark side of modern society, I will argue that the pathogenesis that the Holocaust represented was less the product of modernity than its negation. The mistake is to reduce modernity to the rule of formal rationality or instrumental reason.[1]

I shall pursue this theme of the dark side of modernity in this chapter by examining some major works on the idea of modernity as a pathogenesis, Horkheimer and Adorno's *Dialectic of Enlightenment*, Reinhart Koselleck's *Critique and Crisis*, Stephen Toulmin's *Cosmopolis: The Hidden Agenda of Modernity* and Eric Voeglin's *New Science of Politics*. Each of these texts in different ways offers images of modernity which stress its pathogenesis, with the Enlightenment, in particular, coming in for heavy criticism. Though not a theorist of pathogeneis, the chapter also includes a discussion of Hannah Arendt's vision of modernity as a conflict between the political and the social. I shall comment on her ambivalent view of a self-denying modernity that drew its legitimacy from ancient republicanism, which supposedly contained a normativity that modernity could not provide.

Horkheimer and Adorno: Enlightenment as Mass Deception

In a way Bauman's account of modernity is anticipated by Max Horkheimer and Theodor Adorno in *Dialectic of Enlightenment* (1979), originally published in 1944. In this work, enlightenment does not refer to the age of the Enlightenment. It is less an age than an attitude, or a cultural disposition, a human condition. Enlightenment refers to the quest for knowledge, a quest which is alleged to be closely bound up with power: to seek knowledge is to wield power, first over things and then over human beings. The dialectic which Horkheimer and Adorno see inherent in human enlightenment is one of knowledge, which is potentially emancipatory, reverts to the condition of domination: 'myth is already enlightenment; and enlightenment reverts to mythology' (Horkheimer and Adorno, 1979, p. xvi). The dialectical movement is more one of regression than of progression; it is an anti-dialectic. With this insight, Horkheimer and Adorno recast Marxism, seemingly denying it any emancipatory content. Though they do not condemn the aspiration to emancipation, they see enlightenment to be potentially totalitarian.

There is a certain unclarity in the book on the status of enlightenment. In general it means knowledge, but it also signifies culture in the broad sense, including ideology. There is the claim that enlightenment, like ideology, is a form of deception: 'enlightenment becomes wholesale deception of the masses' (p. 42). The key idea in this work, and one which is also the basis of the critical theory of the Frankfurt School, is that enlightenment takes the form of domination, or deception, when it offers a 'false identity of the general and the particular' (p. 121).

Ultimately, the target of Horkheimer and Adorno's critique is the culture of identity. At a time when identity is invoked from many different quarters, it is interesting to return to the work of Horkheimer and Adorno on identity thinking and the need to give expression to non-identity, a concept which is not too far removed from Derrida's notion of 'différance'. They attack a particular kind of identity thinking, namely the reproduction of relations of equivalence. The method, which epitomizes critical theory, is a negative dialectic, one which gives greater weight to non-identity. As Adorno put it in *Negative Dialectics* (1990, p. 5): 'The name of dialectics says no more, to begin with, than that objects do not go into their concepts without leaving a remainder.' To uncover this remainder is the task of critical theory. It was of course to be a very much diminishing remainder, according to the Frankfurt philosophers.

From Hegel and Marx, Horkheimer and Adorno derived the notion of the contradictory nature of reality, the resolution of whose contradictions impels society forward. But modernity, the Frankfurt School recognized, has displaced a good deal of reality onto the level of culture, where, as a result of changes in technology and economic organization, reality may indeed be losing its contradictory nature. This was a thesis that Herbert Marcuse later took to an extreme in his *One-Dimensional Man* (1964), with the claim that late capitalism had eliminated the distance, necessary for critique, between culture and reality – for culture had itself become a reality-creating force. For the Frankfurt School in exile one of the lessons of totalitarianism and the culture industry was that reality might be losing its contradictory nature. Fascism brought about a total identification of society and state, individual and culture, ideology and knowledge. This is epitomized by positivism, they claim, which denies the separation of concepts from objects. In reducing both to the logic of equivalence, the possibility of critical thinking is removed. The logic of repetition, which sustains the rules of equivalence, is asserted over everything else. But Horkheimer and Adorno see this as residing in the very nature of society, in particular in the culture industry. All of modern culture is based on identity thinking; it simply reproduces reality and in doing so it raises itself to the status of reality, which presents itself to the individual as an objective entity and not as a subject state. But the logic of representation denies this inversion, or substitution, seeking to reenchant the world. Enlightenment may be mass deception but it is one that cannot lay claim to any notion of truth. A new kind of critique is called for in response to the changes in the nature of society. Classical Marxism presupposes that reality is itself contradictory and that the new is contained in the old. But when reality loses its contradictory nature, critique, too, must change. If the existing society no longer produces opposition, critique must find different ways of redeeming it. Immanent critique is thus replaced by the method of negative dialectics. As is well known, for Adorno the social location of negativity is in the remnants of aesthetic modernity that have survived the culture industry.

THE PATHOGENESIS OF MODERNITY

Adorno's writings, and the Frankfurt School as a whole, undoubtedly belonged to the radical current of modernity. While it is true, as critics such as Habermas, Honneth and Wellmer have pointed out, that Adorno ultimately retreated into aesthetic modernism, rejecting the other dimensions of the project of modernity, such as the political, it is important to see, as Fredric Jameson (1990, pp. 237–9) has argued, that his version of the aesthetic is sufficiently broad to include a wider modernity than is conventionally associated with the term, and in this he differs very much from Bauman's opposition of modernity and postmodernity (Habermas, 1987b, Honneth, 1993, 1995; Wellmer, 1971, 1991). Adorno's concerns were not with the specificity of aesthetic experience but with issues that relate directly to social life and historical process, as is best illustrated in the famous essay 'Cultural Criticism and Society' (1967). It is impossible to read his *Aesthetic Theory* (1984) purely as a work in aesthetic experience. But he dealt with such questions in a way that allows us to read his work in a way that is not too far from what has more recently been called poststructuralism or postmodernism (see also Zuidervaart, 1994): for instance the idea of totality as something that can be conceived only negatively as an absent present; the search for those fragmentary moments of everyday life where commodity fetishism and power can be resisted; a negatively constructed thinking. There is, however, one sense which marks Adorno off from the postmodern. This concerns the relationship of thought to language. Though he is in many ways close to poststructuralists in seeing reality as something constructed by language, the method of negative dialectics preserves a space for thought beyond language.

If the critical theory of the Frankfurt School can be reconciled to postmodernism, it can also be related to tradition, and in a way that ties in with certain developments in recent postmodernism.[2] The key question here is tradition, or memory more broadly. According to Martin Jay (1984, p. 68): 'Adorno followed Benjamin in stressing the redemptive power of *Gedächnis*, the reverential recollection of an object always prior to the remembering subject.' This does not mean the recovery of an original meaning, the reunification of a subject with its lost objectification, or the reinternalization of something externalized. In Jay's (1984, p. 68) words: 'It meant rather the restoration of difference and non-identity to their proper place in the non-hierarchical constellation of subjective and objective forces he called peace.' The overcoming of 'oblivion', of forgetting, is an essential part of critique, for as Horkheimer and Adorno (1979, p. 320) state: 'All objectification is a forgetting.' Remembering is more than nostalgia, and it is this that separates the Frankfurt School from Lukács's epic totality or Tönnies's organic community or Heidegger's ontology of a primordial Being.[3]

In sum, the Frankfurt School, and in particular the philosophy of Theodor Adorno, stands at the end of modernity, occupying a space between radical aesthetic modernism and postmodernity. Critique shifts from the Marxist critique of political economy to the critique of ideology (or cultural criticism) and in this reconception of dialectics the method of immanent critique becomes a negative dialectics. Instead of relating ideology to reality, the particular and the universal, culture and society, critique now becomes a means of expressing the struggle for negation itself. Though Adorno retained the basic Marxist belief that society can change for the better, it was never apparent from his writings how social change could be brought about. It might be said, in conclusion, that despite the pessimistic tendency in his thought, he wrote compelling of the rescue and preservation of those critical moments of opposition embodied in the culture of modernity. According to this interpretation, Adorno best exemplifies a conception of modernity as opposition.

Koselleck: Critique and Crisis

From a different perspective, Reinhart Koselleck in *Critique and Crisis: Enlightenment and the Pathogenesis of Modern Society* (1988), originally published in German in 1959, took up the theme of modernity as a crisis-ridden discourse. Coming from a more culturally conservative intellectual background than Horkheimer or Adorno, Koselleck did not set out to rescue the radical promise of modernity and the Enlightenment project. Unlike the Frankfurt School, the dialectical constitution of reality had no meaning for him and critique was denied the power of redemption. Koselleck, in fact, was heavily influenced by Heidegger and Carl Schmitt, though he was far from a reactionary thinker. Another influence on his thought was that of Löwith with whom he was intellectually closer. One of the early postwar intellectuals of the liberal right, he set out, in what was his doctoral dissertation, to examine, from the vantage point of the Cold War, the historical preconditions of German national socialism.

In a later work, *Futures Past* (1985, originally 1979), Koselleck restated his view that modernity begins in the early modern period, from 1500 to 1800. In these centuries there occurs a temporalization of history, he argues, at the end of which modernity emerges. Modernity for him is the future of this past; it is the consciousness of the future of a past period (Koselleck, 1985, p. 5). Politics emerged out of the separation of the temporal order of the world from the divine order. This temporal order releases a new understanding of the future, which ceases to be the Christian eschatology. The principal dimension to modernity concerns a relationship between what Koselleck calls the 'space of experience' and the 'horizon of experience', which are two ways of appropriating past and future. Under the conditions of modernity the future as a mode of anticipation is 'scattered among an infinity of temporal extensions' (Koselleck, 1985, p. 272). Time can be experienced only in spatial metaphors. But the presence of the past and the presence of the future are disjointed and it is in this that historical time is generated. Expectations are distancing themselves ever more from previous forms of experience.

In this section I shall confine the discussion to the systematically presented argument of *Critique and Crisis*. Koselleck's argument, in what was to become one of the classic studies on the European Enlightenment and its consequences, was that modernity became a utopian discourse and therefore a hypocritical and politically useless worldview because it saw itself excluded from politics. In his view, the enemy of peace was utopia, whether in its fascist, communist or liberal democratic forms. The danger, as he saw it, was that utopia is based on moral exclusiveness, the divorce of morality from the practical world of politics. It would appear that the task instead is to reconnect these spheres, though in a way that would assert the primacy of the latter.

Koselleck set out to explain the eighteenth-century origins of the utopian ideas of the twentieth century. In the period from the mid-seventeenth to the late eighteenth century, he argued, the nascent and potentially liberal bourgeoisie subjected the absolute state and its decadent court culture to a radical critique which led to the crisis and collapse of that political and social order in the period following the French Revolution. From the mid-seventeenth century, the structures of modernity were laid: the state – the domain of politics – and society – the realm of ethics – were shaped as two separate domains. The exception of course was England, where state and society were not quite so polarized. The Enlightenment as the radical voice of bourgeois modernity represented the challenge – the critique – of the absolute state and the political in the name of society, which became a rival to politics. But, and it is Koselleck's thesis, this ethical challenge was utopian since the model of an alternative political society announced by the Enlightenment was unrealizable for there is no escaping the constraints of the political as described by Hobbes: politics belongs to the state. These constraints lie in the nature of politics as self-preservation; it is a question not of the ethical substance of the political but of its instrumental ability to keep peace. But the origins of the Enlightenment are to be found in Hobbes, in the neutralization of moral conscience by politics.

Koselleck accuses modernity of translating into a philosophy of history something that originally made sense in the context of opposition to the absolute state. 'In the eighteenth century, history as a whole was unwittingly transformed into some sort of legal process. This occurrence, which inaugurates the Modern age, is identical with the genesis of the philosophy of history' (Koselleck, 1988, p. 9; subsequent references in this section are to this book, unless otherwise stated). Originally a critique of the absolute state, the culture of critique lived on to provide a legitimation for modernity, which had to become utopian since the bourgeoisie were divorced from power. In the eighteenth century, unlike the preceding century, civil war had mostly been eliminated by what on

the whole was a peaceful order which had secured the political neutralization of religion. The bourgeois citizen felt secure in a world which
seemed to have eliminated war. As Koselleck points out, however
exaggerated these hopes were, they were not utopian but rooted in the
reality of a political order which appeared to have made moral progress
possible. The price for such progress, of course, was the subordination of
morality to politics, which was the rule of enlightened monarchs. The
Revolution released morality from this framework of political stability
but it always remained essentially depoliticized.

The Enlightenment after the Revolution, in fact, then became preoccupied with the depoliticized ethical world, the world of the bourgeoisie:
'The dichotomy of morality and politics made morality's alienation from
political reality inevitable. The expression of this inevitability is that
morality skips the political aporia. Unable to integrate politics, moral
man stands in a void and must make a virtue of necessity' (Koselleck,
1988, p. 11). For Koselleck, this leads to a deep crisis which is carried
forward by the philosophy of history: the ethical challenge to politics can
only be utopian for critique can never realize itself in a political order.
Koselleck shows how the bourgeois conceptions of modernity set out
from the private inner space, the ethical, within which the absolute state
had confined its subjects in order to make political citizens. The carriers
of the new public or civic morality were not only the individual but
society in the sense of associations (for example, the secret and powerful
associations such as the Masonic lodges which exemplify the blending of
religious morality with critique). Modernity is constituted in the process
by which bourgeois ethics and intellectual critique emerge in the public
sphere and pit themselves against the state (pp. 53–5). However, since
the bourgeois intelligentsia were isolated from political power, their
critique was redundant, a reflection of their political impotence. Like the
secret of the Masonic lodges, it was a sublime utopia. This, for Koselleck,
is the 'pathogenesis' of the modern: the intrusion of moral critique into
the political. The foundation of modernity was not political society but
the secret interior of the bourgeois conscience: secrecy, not publicity, is
the hidden dimension of the Enlightenment. Indeed, the Freemasons
epitomized the spirit of the Enlightenment, argues Koselleck, since their
aim was to make the state superfluous, the utopian hope that morality
could make politics redundant.

> What the secret made possible was one's seclusion from the outside world,
> which in turn led to a form of social science which included the moral
> qualification to sit in judgement on that outside world. The medium of the
> secret widened the private conscience into a society; the society came to be a
> large conscience, a conscience of the world from which the society voluntary
> excluded itself by way of the secret. (p. 83)

The utopian impulse of modernity was the reflection of the dualism
under which modernity arose: the dichotomy of state and society, politics

and morality. Society developed under the aegis of the state in the early bourgeois secret associations, which kept themselves apart from the state so as to take up a position against it: 'criticism initially kept aloof from the State so that later, through that very separation it could, seemingly neutrally, extend its reach to the State and subject it to its judgement' (p. 98). The social of course did not entirely have to keep itself apart from the state for the state largely ignored it, and even at times protected it since it regarded its moral concerns as politically useless and therefore not a threat to the state. But this moral domain which was constituting itself in civil society was in fact engendering a concept of the political – the nascent culture of critique – which would eventually pit it against the state. Critique is thus the basis of the modern dualism of state and society and ultimately reflects the depoliticzation of the latter. With Voltaire criticism was eventually excluded from the sphere of the state and confined to literary, aesthetic and historical concerns. With the indirect ascension of the bourgeois to political power, the political significance of their moral and intellectual critique was lost to them. For Koselleck (p. 163), Rousseau epitomized this quest for permanent revolution and the 'pursuit of an unattainable norm'. The result: 'Bourgeois man, condemned to a non-political role, sought refuge in Utopia. It gave him security and power' (p. 184). The Enlightement, aware that it had never achieved a perfect unity of morality and politics, sought refuge in the philosophy of history, the substitution of a utopia for critique and the withdrawl from the crisis it had provoked. Koselleck's conclusion is a deeply pessimistic and cynical view of modern critique, which effectively must deny itself when faced with political responsibility for that which it itself provokes:

> The Enlightenment, compelled to camouflage itself politically, was the victim of its own mystique. The new elite lived with the certainty of a moral law whose political significance lay in its antithesis to Absolutist politics – the dichotomy of morality and politics guided the pre-eminent criticism and legitimised the indirect taking of power whose actual political significance, however, remained hidden to the protagonists precisely because of their dualistic self-understanding. To obscure this cover as cover was the historic function of the philosophy of history. It is the hypocrisy of hypocrisy to which criticism had degenerated. With this, a qualitative leap was made which prevented all participants from gaining insight into their own delusion. The political anonymity of the Enlightenment found fulfilment in the rule of Utopia. (p. 185)

What is clearly inadequate about this theory of modernity is that it misconstrues the relationship between morality and politics. Politics is equated with the sphere of the state and morality with the private. As Habermas has noted in an early critical review of Koselleck, critique properly belongs to the social domain of civil society and its public sphere, which is based on public opinion (Habermas, 1973, pp. 355–64, originally 1960; see also Strydom, 2000, Chap. 10). The implications of Koselleck's interpretation of the spirit of modernity cannot be dismissed as reactionary conservatism, however. While his view of politics is far from satisfactory and his assumption that utopia has no practical function is too narrow, he has nevertheless pointed to one of the central problems of modernity: the question of political responsibility. His suggestion is that the utopian impulse in bourgeois ideology ultimately eludes responsibility for society, which has been separated from the state, and the separated realms of morality and politics are united only in the utopias of the philosophy of history. The problem of modernity, therefore, is to bring state and society – the moral and the political – together in order to realize the normative implications of critique. Even if we do not accept Koselleck's analysis, the question remains of the normative status of critique.

Toulmin: Modernity's Hidden Agenda

Koselleck's thesis can be contrasted to another important study that characterizes modernity in terms of a pathological obsession. In *Cosmopolis: The Hidden Agenda of Modernity*, Stephen Toulmin (1990) provides a major attack on bourgeois modernity, but unlike Koselleck he hopes to recover the humanistic and utopian impulse of an earlier modernity. His book derives from a later period, and bears the influence of postmodernism – though it is far from a postmodern critique. Like Koselleck, Toulmin locates the early modern period as the formative period of modernity, and the target of his attack is also the rationalistic culture of the modernity of the Enlightenment. 'Today,' he argues, 'the program of Modernity – even the very concept – no longer carries anything like the same conviction. If an historical era is ending, it is the era of Modernity itself' (Toulmin, 1990, p. 3; subsequent references in this section are to this book). The changed situation today – the decline in the world supremacy of Europe, the collapse of positivism in the natural sciences, the rise of globalizing forces and new kinds of problems – casts doubt on the rationalistic Enlightenment and its seventeenth-century heritage.

The lynchpin of Toulmin's interpretation is that 'modernity had two distinct starting points, a humanistic one grounded in classical literature, and a scientific one rooted in seventeenth-century natural philosophy' (p. 43). It is his view that the dominance of the second starting point in the Enlightenment was at the cost of much that was valuable in the former. The cultural break with the Middle Ages did not occur in the seventeenth century, as is often assumed, for the rationalism and scientific spirit of that century was constructed on what in fact was an ethos largely defined by a modernized and triumphant Christianity. The previous century, in contrast, was relatively tolerant in comparison to the religious intolerance of the Thirty Years War and did not know the dogmas and doctrines of the era of the Council of Trent. Toulmin thus reminds us of the more tolerant and secular culture of the late Renaissance of the sixteenth century – the writings of Shakespeare, Erasmus, Leonardo, Rabelais, Montaigne, Donne, More – as an example of an alternative modernity whose distinctive characteristic was humanism, tolerance and scepticism. The writings of the late Renaissance displayed a sceptical tolerance and open-mindness which was lost in the religious fervour of the following century when modern rationalism and experimental science emerged strengthened and not weakened by the Reformation.

In suppressing the humanistic impulse of the late Renaissance, modernity imposed its hidden agenda: the pursuit of a 'Cosmopolis', a rationally organized society shaped in the image of modern science. Modernity, according to Toulmin (p. 67), unfolded around the idea of shaping the human community, the *polis*, with the regulated order of the *cosmos*: 'from the beginnings of large-scale human society, people wondered about the links between *cosmos* and *polis*, the order of nature and that of society. Many cultures dreamed of an overall harmony between the order of the heavens and the order of society.' The dream of a cosmopolis was part of the 'Quest of Certainty', as it developed from the mid-seventeenth century, which was preoccupied with the search for a 'scratch-line' or a 'clean slate' with which a new and self-justifying start could be made. Toulmin attacks this, the received conception of modernity which retrospectively defined the modern in the post-First World War period, whose intellectual frameworks were not unlike the quest for certainty in the period following the seventeenth-century wars of religion. European modernity was first constructed around the themes of stability and hierarchy in the second part of the seventeenth century and became a hidden agenda for subsequent ages. The conventional view of modernity is false or misleading, Toulmin argues, for it developed out of the late Renaissance and eventually over-reached itself. His question, then, is whether the 'humane wisdom' of the Renaissance can be recovered in order to provide an alternative normative framework for the contemporary world: 'The current task, accordingly, is to find ways of moving on from the received view of Modernity – which set the exact sciences and the humanities apart – to a reformed version, which redeems philosophy and science, reconnecting them to the humanist half of modernity' (p. 180). The task in Toulmin's vision is not to reject modernity as such but rather to rescue something lost. Modernity must be humanized, a process Toulmin believes is already occurring in certain currents today. The essence of the humanization of modernity is the shift from stability and system – the framework of the rationalistic cosmopolis – to a more pronounced emphasis on function and adaptability (p. 192). He believes this humanization is already occurring in the relinking of facts and values. Science and culture are no longer separate: morality is creeping into the autonomous discourses of science, in particular in medicine. Nature can no longer be seen as stable but is itself a changeable entity.

The collapse of the idea of a fixed cosmological order challenges the coherence of the vision of the cosmopolis which sustained so much of the project of modernity.

Toulmin's critique is an important contribution to the debate on modernity. He draws attention to the one-sided conception of modernity as it unfolded around the idea of the cosmopolis and points to the collapse of that order in the twentieth century with the emergence of new kinds of sovereignty both beyond and within the nation-state. Rejecting postmodernist alternatives, Toulmin looks to a concept of rationality that existed before the time of Descartes and which could provide a normative basis for a new modernity. Unlike Koselleck, he is not afraid of utopia for he believes modernity is in need of a humanizing dimension.

While there is much that is valuable in Toulmin's interpretation, the result is unsatisfactory. Modernity is still reduced to its historical framework, the humanism of the Renaissance. There is the sense of a historical nostalgia for a framework that has passed. Toulmin acknowledges that the sixteenth century was in many ways more rooted in the culture of the Middle Ages than the subsequent century. But on the whole, he maintains, the break with the past had occurred:

> In any event, the cultural break with the Middle Ages did not need to wait for the 17th century: it had already taken place a good 100 or 150 years earlier. When we compare the spirit of 17th-century thinkers, and the content of their ideas, with the emancipatory ideas of 16th-century writers, indeed, we may even find 17th-century innovations in science and philosophy beginning to look less like revolutionary advances, and more like a defensive counter-revolution. (p. 17)

Toulmin's view of the seventeenth century as a century of rationalist mastery serving as a hidden agenda for modernity can be disputed. The conflicts of that century were more than purely religious and concerned the struggle for rights, which is something he never acknowledges. It is indeed true that the question of religion is not crucial since many innovations were made within a broadly Christian worldview, a position that is also conceded by Blumenberg. The search of certainty can also be seen as a struggle for the democratization of knowledge (see Delanty, 1997c, esp. Chap. 1). Despite his emphasis on the historical conditions of intellectual ideas, Toulmin does not recognize the essentially democratic nature of both rationalism and empiricism, as represented by the two leading thinkers of the seventeenth century, Descartes and Locke. By affirming the consciousness of the subject as the sole source of the validity of all claims to knowledge, they in their different ways demonstrated that in principle knowledge is available to all human beings and that the sole measure of validity is the introspection of consciousness. One may characterize this as the futile search for certainty, but it was conducted in the context of opposition to dogmatism. In many ways the seventeenth century was a far less certain world than the preceding century, where the famous 'chain of being' for the greater part still dominated the worldview of most intellectuals. Indeed, at this juncture, we can suggest that modernity is an epistemic culture of uncertainty. For in removing God from the world and in substituting human cognitive powers for theological certainties, the modern age was deeply uncertain of what it stood for. Indeed, this is the central claim of Leo Strauss in his essay 'The Three Waves of Modernity' (1975).[4]

In Toulmin's sketch of the principal figures of the early modern period, little mention is made of Pascal, who does not fit into his seventeenth-century prototype, and yet he is one of the most important figures in modern scepticism. To take up an idea suggested by Pierre Bourdieu in his *Pascalian Meditations* (2000), Pascal stands on the threshold of what might be called a hitherto unacknowledged modernity, the culture of reflexivity.[5] Reducible neither to content nor to pure formalism, the seventeenth-century thinker embodied the essence of reflexivity, a sceptical attitude.

Bourdieu was not the first to draw attention to the figure of Pascal. In one of the most important studies on the seventeenth-century mind, *The Hidden God*, Lucien Goldmann wrote about an alternative modernity to the conceptualism of Cartesian rationalism, namely the tragic vision of Pascal:

> The term 'modern man', however, means something else in addition to 'scientist', for from its first manifestation dialectical thought has always refused to recognise the autonomy of conceptual thought, and, implicitly, to see the scientist as the ideal human type. (Goldmann, 1964, p. 172)

The thought of Pascal was a quest for knowledge of what was absent from the world and which only an appreciation of tragedy would provide:

> The God of tragedy is a God who is always present and always absent. Thus, while his presence takes all value and reality from the world, his equally absolute and permanent absence makes the world into the only reality which man can confront, the only sphere in and against which he can and must apply his demand for substantial and absolute values. (Goldmann, 1964, p. 50)

Pascal stands out in the intellectual history of the seventeenth century as a precursor of modernity, a reminder of the other side of the 'quest for certainity', namely the tragic vision.

There is one final point to be made. This concerns the very notion of 'cosmopolis', which Toulmin projects back to classical Greek thought. By reducing the idea of cosmopolis to a synthesis of the human order of the *polis* and the divine order of the *cosmos*, the order of society and the order of nature, he fails to see that in its genuinely modern form – for instance, as represented by Kant in 'Idea for a Universal History with a Cosmopolitan Purpose' (1970) – the quest for cosmopolis was linked to the emancipation of the social from the natural, not its harmonization. The notion of a hidden agenda, be it one of secularization as unmasked by Toulmin or the pursuit of a perfect cosmopolis, is deeply problematical since it presupposes an essence that somehow unfolds, remaining fundamentally unchanged in the actual forms it takes. I believe the modern cosmopolis which came into existence in the seventeenth century was one that is manifest in the growing discursive capacity of society. The modern cosmopolis is a discursive society in which communication becomes the medium of social integration, challenging both Church and state. The seventeenth century saw the opening of many discursive spaces – universities, coffee houses, political clubs, libraries – which were all related to the emergence of a reading public, as argued by Habermas (1989a) and Sennett (1978). The consequence of this was the introduction of a great deal of contingency into the heart of modern society.

The important point that emerges from this is that while, epistemologically speaking, the subject of modernity may have been the Cartesian *cogitio*, as a social entity the subject was nothing less than publicly structured communication, which becomes the new *a priori*. Toulmin derides the modernity of the seventeenth century and its modern embodiments for what he dismisses as an empty formalism. But this is precisely the nature of modern forms of communication, as argued by Habermas. Post-metaphysical philosophy and modern communication are characterized by the retreat of content before form. The universalistic content of modern culture, not its substantive content, is confined to its procedures.

Voeglin: Modernity as Gnosticism

Eric Voeglin's reflections on modernity are to be found in the second half of his well-known book *The New Science of Politics* (1952), in particular the chapters 'Gnosticism – The Nature of Modernity' and 'The End of Modernity'. As with many thinkers of the early to mid-twentieth century, he was preoccupied with the prospect that modernity might be 're-divination of man and society'. In an argument that recalls Karl Löwith, Voeglin claims that modern 're-divination' has its origins in Christianity, deriving from components that were suppressed as heretical (Voeglin, 1952, p. 107; all subsequent citations in this section will be to this book unless otherwise stated). He is convinced that much of modernity derives from an 'inner Christian tension', a position which is not too far removed from Blumenberg's position. For he recognizes more clearly than did Löwith that eschatological disappointment resulted very early on in the abandonment of the literal belief in the millennium, as is witnessed by Augustine and the subsequent struggle between pope and emperor, the spiritual and temporal orders. He writes: 'The history of the world was constructed in the Augustinian tradition for the last time only by Bossuet, in his *Histoire universelle*, toward the end of the seventeenth century; and the first modern who dared to write a world history in direct opposition to Bousset was Voltaire' (p. 110; see also Voeglin, 1975, esp. Chap. 1). From the eighteenth century onwards the specifically modern mode of representation emerged within the limits of profane history. Like Toulmin, Löwith, Koselleck and many other critics of modernity, Voeglin sees the modern age as deeply illegitimate: 'The attempt at constructing an eidos of history will lead into the fallacious immanentization of the Christian eschaton' (p. 121). So modernity now becomes a 'fallacious construction'.

Voeglin attributes this to Gnosticism, which, in immanentizing salvation, lost out on the experience of uncertainty which is central to Christianity, an experience which ultimately rests on faith, not reason. In short, he equates modernity with the growth of Gnosticism (p. 133). 'Gnostic speculation overcame the uncertainty of faith by receding from transcendence and endowing man and his intramundane range of action with the meaning of eschatological fulfilment' (p. 129). He sees Gnosticism, originally a Christian heresy, as reemerging in the nineteenth century with Comte and the cult of scientism, which he regards as one of the strongest expressions of Gnosticism. But the culmination of Gnosticism is totalitarianism. In Voeglin's framework, the de-divination of Christianity left in its wake the permanent need for a civil theology. This need was met by Gnosticism, which he generalizes to include virtually every modern movement, from the Reformation to German national socialism and communism. This is because he sees Gnosticism as arising at that critical point when eschatology is secularized and a political space is opened up for ideology.

> The rise of gnosticism at this critical juncture now appears in a new light as the incipient formation of a Western civil theology. The immanentization of the Christian eschaton made it possible to endow society in its natural existence with a meaning which Christianity denied to it. And the totalitarianism of our time must be understood as journey's end of the Gnostic search for a civil theology. (p. 163)

Gnosticism presents two dangers, the destruction of truth and what Voeglin claims is the self-defeating pursuit of an ideal political society which destroys human existence. Western society is not itself modern, he asserts, for 'modernity is a growth within it, in opposition to the classic and Christian tradition' (p. 176). In Voeglin's bleak account of modernity, the fate of all Gnostic critique is that of the Leviathan. It is no coincidence, he believes, that England resisted 'Gnostic totalitarianism'. The English Revolution occurred at a time when Gnosticism had not undergone its radical secularization. But when the French Revolution happened, it split the nation into those seeking to defend the Christian heritage and those who furthered the cause of the Revolution. Voeglin concludes his study by remarking that the 'German Revolution' − by which he presumably means national socialism – which occurred in a society without strong institutions to restrain its worst excesses, was 'modernity without restraint' (pp. 188–9). Bauman's thesis of the link between modernity and the Holocaust and Horkheimer and Adorno's notion of the dialectic of enlightenment finds resonances in this view which sees Germany, rather than England or France, as embodying modernity, but a modernity that has become its opposite. The only hope for civilization, in Voeglin's view, is that 'the American and English democracies' prevail and that civilization will succeed 'in repressing Gnostic corruption' (p. 189).

Taking into account that Voeglin's book was published in 1951 and was a response to the need to recover the political imagination after the Second World War without appealing too closely to history, there are still many problems with his account of Gnosticism as the inner expression of modernity.[6] There is some merit in seeing modernity as a culture of opposition, rather than reducing it to the formation of modern society. But to reduce modernity to Gnosticism, however broadly that is understood, is to make too big a claim for the role of civil theology in modern societies. It is indeed convincing to see a certain continuity in the original Gnostic challenge to early Christianity in so far as this pertains to an increasing discord between the realms of world and spirit, which was the foundation of Gnostic teaching. But to see this as the continuation of civil theology is highly misleading since much of the culture of modernity was concerned with civil society and had little to do with the search for a civil theology. More recognition must be given to the ruptures within the culture of modernity. Moreover, totalitarianism in Germany, Italy, Spain and Russia was, as Claude Lefort (1986) has shown, something which eliminated from the social its very autonomy and stood for the total domination of society by the state. The world into which the totalitarian state emerged was not one in which the authority of the Church had been simply reduced or eliminated, but one which had been highly fragmented by purely economic forces. It makes more sense to see totalitarianism as a state-led revolt against society, rather than the outcome of an intellectual tradition. If we see modernity in this way, as an expression of the rise of the social, totalitarianism was the revolt against modernity, not its outcome. Thus what Voeglin calls Gnosticism could be simply seen as the rise of the social. In other words, it is a question of the rise less of civil theology than of civil society.

Arendt: The Loss of the Political

The final theorist of modernity to be discussed in this chapter is Hannah Arendt, whose vision of modernity was a good deal more differentiated and less apocalyptic than Voeglin's. But she shares the same essentially negative view of the modern world as having destroyed the conditions of freedom which are associated with the political. Unlike Koselleck, who, like Carl Schmitt (1985), restricted the domain of the political to the state and saw the intrusion of the moral critique of society as the symptom of pathogenesis, Arendt located the political in the domain of civil society. In this way she avoids the dualism in the Schmittean philosophy which Koselleck uncritically adopted. But this broader conception of the political was at the cost of generating another dualism: the separation of the social from the political. Arendt's recasting of the political as embodying the public – as opposed to the realm of the state as in Schmitt – demanded the total commitment of this domain to the pursuit of a pure politics of participation in public life. Not only was the private banned from this, but so, too, was the social. It is not surprising, then, that this conception of the political as defined against the social would be tied to a very ambivalent view of modernity.

In one of her most famous works, *The Human Condition*, Arendt (1958, p. 6) argues how the modern age must be distinguished from the modern world: 'the modern age is not the same as the modern world. Scientifically, the modern age which began in the seventeenth century came to an end at the beginning of the twentieth century; politically, the modern world, in which we live today, was born with the first atomic explosions'. Her subject was the modern age, but it was one in which her political philosophy was ill at ease. The modern age, she says, carried with it the glorification of labour. Its vision was that of a labouring society rather than a political one. In this justly celebrated book she drew a distinction between two domains of action, the private and the public. The private is the realm of household and of work; the public is the sphere of participation in political life. The problem with modernity is that it has extended the former at the expense of the latter, which is the truly authentic domain of the human condition. Whereas the Greeks confined work and labour to the private, the modern age has extended these categories to the public, displacing it with a category that has become social but has not an essentially political nature.[7] Thus the social eats its way into the political. The social is the sphere of needs, which for Arendt are not specific to the political, whose condition is free self-government, the total participation of citizens in political life. This is not because Arendt was uncritical of capitalism but because she saw politics as having little to do with social issues. Politics is the highest expression of action and is not based on interests, which are private matters. The problem with this position of course is that it presupposes a notion of the political that has very little to do with what it is normally held to be. Politics, for Arendt, is sublimely oblivious to the social, as well as to the world of bureaucratic organization – there can be no point of mediation. Her model was that of the Greek *polis* and what she believed to be its modern equivalents, the republican model of civil society and the kibbutz. In these models the social is, allegedly, relatively compact and not based on endemic inequalities, thus allowing politics to be a purely discursive matter. But, she recognized, modernity has produced social inequalities, and thus a demise of politics. Consequently she saw modernity in terms of the struggle between the loss of the political and its recovery from the merely social – an impossible project since politics cannot solve the problem of society.

Arendt's attack on society can be seen as the continuation of the Rousseauian attack on society, but from a Kantian perspective, the republican standpoint of the public use of reason. Cohen and Arato (1992, p. 191) put it succinctly:

> Juxtaposing direct participation to representation, and federalism to unified sovereignty, she presents us with a model of pyramidally organized 'small republics', 'councils', or 'wards' capable of institutionalizing a framework of public freedom and establishing a form of government at all levels linked to the paradigm of the communicative generation of power – a veritable 'great republic'.

The political is to be identified with a strict notion of the public as a communicatively constituted body of equal citizens whose commitment to public life has nothing to do with social concerns. The origins of this interactive conception of politics, in fact, lay in Heidegger, from whom Arendt had derived some of the basic categories of human activity as being in the world but as praxis, not as being.[8] Ultimately for Arendt the political is the domain of personal immortality, not 'happiness', which belongs to the system of needs. This position led her to bizarre conclusions, such as because education is a social matter, not a political one, it cannot become organized along the lines of equality, for that is the essence of the political – the social is condemned to perpetual inequality; at least it cannot be rescued by politics. In 'The Crisis in Culture' (1961a) she expressed a similar view on the massification of culture, which leads to the destruction of the cultivated mind. The essence of culture is not unlike politics in that it is essentially public (Arendt, 1961a, p. 218). But mass culture is based on mass society, which Arendt sees, in a way that recalls Adorno's critique of the culture industry, as an extension of the private. But here an elevated notion of culture, as the life of the mind, comes closer to the patrician vision of T.S. Eliot, were it not for his view that the 'unity of culture' is European[9] – for Arendt, since the French and Russian Revolutions and national socialism were failures, only America offers a model for the recovery of the unity of ancient republicanism.

It is not too surprising, then, that the ultimate malaise of modernity for Arendt is the destruction of the political by totalitarianism, which she chooses to see as an attack on the possibility of politics rather than on the social. It is for this reason that she looked back to the American Revolution as the only authentic revolution in modern times, for all other revolutions reflected the priority of the social. The American Revolution was genuinely political while the French Revolution, which involved the entry of the masses, was too much bound up with the social question.

Arendt's book *On Revolution* (1965) was an attack on the 'social question', which effectively sealed the fate of modernity as one of the rise of the social and the loss of the political. With the French Revolution, virtue becomes terror, the social and violence are part of the same logic. Violence cannot be part of the political, for Arendt. The Russian Revolution was a more extreme expression of this process, which she associates with modernity and the discovery that poverty is not a natural trait but is socially created. Her whole conception of the political under the conditions of modernity was largely one of a logic of recovery. Modernity was seen as having destroyed a conception of politics which, in its pure form, was the ancient Greek republican one. Ancient republicanism, like the American Revolution, was an expression of a politics which was, in Arendt's controversial estimation, free of want and misery and therefore of the need for compassion for suffering (Arendt, 1965, pp. 63 and 79). Virtue, not the heart, is the essence of the political for Arendt. The problem with modernity is that it elevates the heart because it has created so much suffering (Arendt, 1965, p. 92).

Arendt was not a romantic conservative. Her political philosophy was one of radical republicanism rooted in a citizenship of discursive participation and grounded in an ontology of the political. In anchoring this in ancient republicanism, she insists that this has nothing to do with tradition, which in fact is rejected. Ancient virtue was anti-traditional for the American revolutionaries:

> When they turned to the ancients, it was because they discovered in them a dimension which had not been handed down by tradition – neither by the traditions of custom and institutions nor by the great tradition of Western thought and concept. Hence it was not tradition that bound them back to the beginnings of Western history but, on the contrary, their own experiences, for which they needed models and precedents. (Arendt, 1965, p. 198)

In 'Tradition in the Modern Age' she announced: 'The break in our tradition is now an accomplished fact' (Arendt, 1961b, p. 26). The break with tradition – by which she means the loss of the older forms of intellectual and political authority – occurred not with modernity but with totalitarianism, a phenomenon that requires entirely new moral and cognitive categories. The great critics of modernity – Marx, Kierkegaard, Nietzsche and their immediate predecessor, Hegel – foreshadowed the final break with tradition. Faced with totalitarianism, all earlier rebellions against tradition were within the confines of tradition, Arendt argued. Arendt's was, as Benhabib (1996) characterizes it, a 'reluctant modernism', one that had embraced the modern age but which could only see in it political forms that sought their legitimacy in something that was resistant to modernity. She never succeeded in mediating the dualism of political equality and social inequality that pervaded her work. Maybe this gulf could not be bridged, since she adhered not only to a strictly communicative conception of politics but also to a view of the public realm being based on an equally self-enclosed private domain, which would provide the political domain of the public sphere with a firm foundation. The problem with modernity is that the social not only transgresses into the political but also erodes the social:

> The rise of society brought about the simultaneous decline of the public as well as the private realm. But the eclipse of a common public world, so crucial to the formation of the lonely mass man and so dangerous in the formation of the worldless mentality of modern ideological mass movements, began with the much more tangible loss of a privately owned share in the world. (Arendt, 1958, p. 257)

However, though Arendt was very hostile to the modern European revolutions of 1789 and 1917, she did not see modernity as engendering totalitarianism as such. Totalitarianism, which cannot be explained by the social or by the political, is something entirely antithetical to modernity for it emanates from a thoroughly depoliticized society.

Perhaps the greatest problem with Arendt's work, as Claude Lefort argues, is that from a political point of view 'the questioning of modernity means a questioning of democracy' (Lefort, 1988, p. 55).[10] This intellectual style, which is also to be found in the work of Leo Strauss and Martin Heidegger, is reflected in a deep suspicion of modernity, which is seen as a corruption of an original and more authentic conception of the political first articulated in Greek thought. Presumably because Arendt equates democracy with representative power, which is fundamentally antithetical to her conception of politics as public participation, she tended to see modernity in extremely negative terms, with modern democracy suffering from the same malaise as totalitarianism. Her concern ultimately was the search for the political, not democracy, which was only one particular manifestation of politics.

Conclusion: Developmental Logics

In this chapter I have outlined some of the main theories of modernity as embodying a pathological component and others which have more broadly seen modernity in terms of a process of decline. Toulmin and Voelgin can be identified with a position that ultimately rejects the cultural modernity of the European Enlightenment in favour of an earlier one, while Koselleck appears to reject modernity in so far as this is reflected in the culture of critique. It is precisely this critical stream in modernity that Horkheimer and Adorno sought to preserve while rejecting modern society. What all these views have in common is that they are reactions to the disasters of the first half of the twentieth century, which is dominated by the heritage of the Holocaust. Toulmin's book dates from a later period, of course, and it is the most contemporary in its concerns, but here too the central thrust is the problem of leaving history behind. Modernity is rejected for a 'postmodernity', which will be the 'third phase of modernity', but whose inspiration comes from a humanistic early modernity (Toulmin, 1990, p. 203). However, there is no doubt that of those who attribute the problems of modernity to a hidden agenda, Toulmin's vision is the most relevant to the current situation. Finally, it can be remarked that the central problematic of the work of Hannah Arendt – the relation of the social to the political – is also of immense importance. Today the problem can no longer be posed in terms of the separation of these domains, for both the social and the political are themselves challenged by a further dimension, the cultural. In later chapters I will focus more specifically on the question of culture. Here I would like to remark as a conclusion to the present discussion that a perspective on alternative cultural patterns, or developmental logics, is important in challeging the thesis of the hidden agenda of modernity. The theorists discussed in this chapter do not recognize the contested and transformative nature of culture and consequently do not see more than one cultural pattern. Entirely missing from these perspectives is a sense of the developmental logics within cultural modernity.

The problem of pathogenesis and modernity, I would like to argue, cannot be discussed without taking into account an argument proposed by Klaus Eder (1985, 1992, 1999) and Piet Strydom (1987, 1993, 2000), following Habermas (1979). This concerns the question of evolution and learning mechanisms. Without going into the details of this, the important point is that modernity must be conceived in terms of a relationship between cultural learning and social evolution (see Delanty, 1999a). What we need to understand is how a society transfers or institutionalizes its cultural potentials in social practice. Modernity, according to this view, can be seen as a struggle between what is cognitively available on the cultural level (that is, what has been culturally 'learnt') and what has been realized in social practices. Modernity can entail both evolution and regression, the latter being a kind of 'unlearning'. The crucial point that emerges from this is that the question of modernity is essentially one about how a society cognitively selects, from available cultural resources, solutions to the problems it encounters in social practice. In the modern period, the inescapable solution is to be found in processes of communication. But the real problem of modernity is that communication is a domain of ever-increasing contingency. Postmodernity can be seen as the heightened consciousness of this.

In the next chapter I will focus on this question of modernity and contingency, with particular reference to theories of posthistory and the theories of modernity of Niklas Luhmann and Leo Strauss.

4

THE IMPOSSIBILITY OF MODERNITY
Cultural Crystallization and the Problem of Contingency

In this chapter I look at a number of positions which share a concern with the implications of the post-Enlightenment age for modernity. I concentrate on the consequences of the critique of the Enlightenment for liberal thought. In many ways modernity is an expression of liberal thought, a reflection of the possibilities of subjective freedom in dealing with the problem of contingency. Modernity is a world in which choice becomes a problem. In the absence of the certainties of natural law or notions of divine right, modernity substitutes human history for natural history. In this shift, evolution becomes more a matter of culturally shaped choices than of historical inevitability. It becomes a question of selection under the conditions of increasing cultural contingency and historical indeterminancy. As Claude Lefort (1988, p. 19) argues, contingency lies at the heart of modern democracy, for

> democracy is instituted and sustained by the dissolution of the markers of certainity. It inaugurates a history in which people experience a fundamental indeterminancy as to the basis of power, law and knowledge, and as to the basis of relations between self and other, at every level of social life.

In this chapter I want to propose the concept of cultural crystallization, originally used by Arnold Gehlen, to describe one of the central predicaments of modernity: the consequences of the fragmentation of the unity of culture and the exhaustion of ideology as a framework for political organization.[1]

The previous chapter concluded by raising the question of how cultural choices are made in the absence of a universalistic morality. Modern culture, theorists such as those to be considered here (Gehlen, Strauss, Luhmann) argue, has entered the stage of crystallization: the loss of coherence and certainty. Under these circumstances the problem of contingency has become more acute, since there is no clear cultural solution to the dilemma of choice. But views range as to how this is to be interpreted. Some theorists have denied the problem of contingency, proclaiming history to have reached its end; others still, operating within the framework of rational choice, have rehabilitated a calculative subject. For Gehlen and Fukuyma, in their visions of *posthistoire*, the solution is clear: in the case of the former it is modern institutions; in the case of the latter it is liberal democracy. The chapter begins with Arnold Gehlen's notion of cultural crystallization and 'posthistory' and goes on to discuss Francis Fukuyma's version of the end of history thesis. Second, I discuss Leo Strauss's theory of modernity, as expressed in his essay 'The Three Waves of Modernity'. Finally, I look at Niklas Luhmann's theory of modernity, outlined in his *Observations on Modernity*.

Posthistory and Cultural Crystallization

In recent times one of the most important debates on modernity centres on the idea of 'posthistory', a concept that originally meant the exhaustion of modernity, while for others it means the fulfilment of modernity. In its conservative form, it is best associated with Arnold Gehlen, whose version of the 'end of history' is not too different from Fukuyama's (1992) liberal conception. First, a few remarks on Gehlen.

One of Germany's leading social philosophers in the Adenauer period following the Second World War, Gehlen (1963) proposed the theory of 'cultural crystallization' to describe the modern situation. According to Gehlen, in a famous phrase, 'the premises of the Enlightenment are dead, only their consequences remain'. In his view the institutional complexes of modern society have separated themselves from cultural modernity, which can now be discarded. Cultural critique is redundant since post-historical society is governed not by cultural ideals but by purely functional forces: culture has been absorbed by institutions and has been routinized. Gehlen calls this situation 'cultural crystallization' because modern culture has quite literally used up its resources, and even in its radical forms it has been realized in modern institutions. Cultural ideas are no longer able to produce the 'new' that was central to modernity. The task of politics is purely to complete what has essentially been achieved by institutions.

With this argument, Gehlen denounces radicals who want to aspire to revolutionary change. They fail to see, he argues, that modernity is at an end: we have arrived at 'posthistory'. Posthistory does not mean the end of what Marx called 'prehistory', but what has been called by other conservatively inclined intellectuals the 'end of ideology'.[2] Posthistory is the routinization or normalization of newness and progress. The denial of cultural modernity and the rejection of the role of ideology sums up the posthistorical condition, in which history is denied a future. Gehlen effectively argued for cultural neutralization, a theory which was backed up by his philosophical anthropology, which held that man is essentially weak and requires institutions for protection from an unconstrained culture (see Gehlen, 1988, originally 1955). In one of his best-known books, *Man in the Age of Technology* (1980), originally published in 1949, he outlined his vision of modernity as a process of increasing indeterminancy which has led to the exhaustion of culture:

> Perhaps the whole theme of 'culture,' particularly in the German sense of the term, belongs in a certain sense to the past. Indeed, not just the theme, but rather its very referent – the period of preindustrial high culture with all its associated rhythms of existence – appears now as a unique event, lasting from 3000 BC to 1800 AD. (Gehlen, 1980, p. 125)

It may be mentioned in passing here that while Gehlen – who earlier supported the Nazis – was totally opposed to the Frankfurt School, his critique of modern culture was not too far removed from Adorno's in the superficial sense that both shared a view of culture having exhausted its possibilities for innovation. However, it is clear that they drew different conclusions from this, with Adorno rejecting the notion of cultural crystallization as a hopeless bourgeois ideology.[3] Cultural modernity for Gehlen has become something that has essentially been left behind and from which only its consequences remain. There is no future, just a timeless present.

Today the idea of posthistory is very much associated with Fukuyama's *The End of History and the Last Man* (1992), originally an essay published in 1989. According to Lutz Niethammer (1992) the idea of *posthistoire* – a French term which curiously is used only in German – derives from the mid-twentieth century and was used by a variety of intellectuals of the political right and, to a lesser exent, the left (for example, Arnold Gehlen, Carl Schmitt, Ernst Jünger, Henri de Man, Bertrand de Jouvenel). Fukuyma's American version of this idea shared with this European tradition its original use by Alexander Kojève, the reconciliation of idea and reality.[4]

The thesis of Fukuyma's book is that there is now a world-wide consensus concerning the legitimacy of liberal democracy which has conquered its rivals, first fascism and then communism, and totalitarianism more generally. This argument that liberal modermity has triumphed over disciplinary modernity is not as banal as is often claimed, and is not refuted by the upsurge in nationalism since the early 1990s because what is being asserted is simply that democracy has won world-wide acceptance in the last few decades. The opponent of democracy is totalitarianism, or at least political authoritarianism. On a more philosophical level, what has come to an end is not history but History, that is: history understood as a single, coherent, evolutionary process (Fukuyma, 1992, p. xii). The end of history is the end of the search for civilizational alternatives to liberal democracy (a term Fukuyama freely exchanges with capitalism). However, what he fails to see is that the struggle for democracy, in being part of the 'struggle for recognition' – the Hegelian term he employs – does not lead to a straightforward endorsement of liberal democracy as such, but can lead to a situation of political and cultural crystallization, to use Gehlen's expression. Democracy has crystallized today in that it does not take a unitary form; it can be expressed as much in populist forms as in liberal democracy. What Fukuyama confuses is democracy and westernization, as well as liberalism in politics (that is, liberal democracy) and liberalism in economics (that is, neo-liberalism). Democracy may have found widespread acceptance the world over, but one expression of this has been in a powerful movement against westernization (see for example, Smelser, 1997, pp. 78–9). Democracy can provide neo-traditionalist ideologies with both legitimacy and a means of institutional reproduction. It is certainly not necessarily conducive to liberal principles, something that Fukuyama (1992, pp. 42–3) acknowledges, but he insists that the liberal idea is emerging triumphant from history. The end of history, which he readily applies to everything other than the liberal ideology, also pertains to the liberal idea: there is not a unilinear evolutionary direction to history. Ideology has crystallized, or fragmented, not into democracy but into many different histories precisely because of democratization.

In order to avoid the inevitable confusion of the end of history thesis concerning exactly what is ending – and every ending is a beginning – it is necessary to distinguish liberalism in politics and economy, on the one side, from liberalism in culture, on the other.[5] The application of liberalism to culture is not conventional, since liberalism is a preeminently political ideology, and in the guise of neo-liberalism it is now applied to economics. But there is one sense in which it can be used. In the domain of culture, liberalism is best understood as libertarianism, to express the radical component of the liberal imagination cutting across the spheres of morality and culture. By libertarianism is meant radical individualism, as opposed to a political doctrine. However, libertarianism can be associated with radical democracy, which is clearly very different from liberal democracy. If we see liberalism in this way, the thesis of the end of history makes little sense, if only because these streams in modern liberalism have been much opposed to each other. Libertarianism is still a powerful force, though it is perhaps best seen today as postmodernism, in the sense of cultural pluralism.

Cultural modernity takes different forms and it can emerge as much in opposition to societal modernization as in response to it. Contrary to Fukuyama's claim, in many parts of the world cultural change is profoundly hostile to liberal principles. This incongruence between culture, on the one side, and politics and economics, on the other, may be understood in terms of the emergence of postmodernization, that is, processes of globalization that are articulated through cultural fragmentation (Jameson and Miyoshi, 1998; see Chapter 7). My concern in this chapter is to deal more specifically with the problem of contingency that arises with the emergence of cultural crystallization.

Before concluding this discussion on the end of history, attention may be drawn to another version of the posthistorical thesis, a term Lewis Mumford used from 1956 (see Hatton, 1995, Chap. 4). Mumford's whole view of modernity was one that sought to find a way of recovering the human order of the city in a world of instrumentalism. The city is to be reclaimed from capitalism and the state as a civic space. Mumford concluded his best-known work, *The City in History*, with the claim: 'we must now conceive the city, accordingly, not primarily as a place of business, but as an essential organ for expressing and actualizing the new human personality – that of "One World Man" ' (Mumford, 1961, pp. 652–3). Posthistoric Man has exhausted the possibilities of the city, which has become a victim of mechanical power and must be rejected in the name of 'World Culture' or 'One World Man'. Posthistory, in this sense, is quite different from Gehlen's use of the term; it is less a condition of completeness than one of incompleteness. But here, too, history is seen as exhausted, necessitating the recovery of something on a smaller scale. While Gehlen's work can be seen as severing the idea of modernity from posthistorical modernization, Mumford rejected both modernity and modernization.

In sum, the end of history thesis points to an important trend in the world today – the expansion in democracy – but fundamentally fails to understand the significance of this since its conflates the different levels of democracy. Above all, it fundamentally fails to understand the Hegelian concept of reconciliation with reality, which gave the idea of posthistory its original impetus.[6] For Hegel reconciliation of idea and reality was ultimately not possible on the level of politics. By eliminating the dialectical tension between idea and reality, the end of history thesis sees the condition of crystallization as an end state rather than one of heightened contingency. As argued in the last chapter, the end of History – as a single directed process – has opened up evolution. Once the break with a master trend has been made, evolution can be seen to operate through a plurality of culturally determined logics of development.

In what follows I discuss two quite different conceptions of modernity, which in different ways express the tension between cultural modernity and the dynamics of modernization: Leo Strauss's 'The Three Waves of Modernity' and Niklas Luhmann's *Observations on Modernity*. Underlying these very distinct theories of modernity is a notion of what I have been calling cultural crystallization, a concept which must be taken out of the particular sense with which Gehlen used it and applied to the expansion of contingency in contemporary society.

Leo Strauss: Modernity as a Loss of Certainty

In a pivotal essay, 'The Three Waves of Modernity', Leo Strauss (1975) outlined the crisis of modern political philosophy, which captures the more general crisis of modernity. The crisis of modernity stems from the fact that there are no longer any normative standards by which good and bad can be distinguished. For Strauss this means that political philosophy, which derives from a premodern age, has lost its power, and may even be impossible since it is unable to validate itself: 'The crisis of modernity is then primarily the crisis of modern political philosophy' (Strauss, 1975, p. 82; all references in this section are to this text). The destruction of political philosophy was brought about by the representatives of positivism and historicism, the former privileging scientific certainty in place of normative certainty and the latter precipitating the descent into relativism and away from universalism. For Strauss political philosophy is possible under the conditions of modernity only in the degenerate form of ideology. Throughout his writings, he insisted that modernity has brought about the eclipse of political philosophy, which he confines to ancient republicanism, in particular Platonism. The political philosophy of the Greeks contained a truth that no longer has any meaning because all modern thought is hostile to esoteric thinking; it is essentially public, not secret. More importantly, political philosophy was hostile to the established order; it contained a secret not available to public discourses. In this particular usage, the political transcended the social and the state. The problem of modernity for Strauss was that it obliterated the distinction between political philosophy and political ideology.

Strauss rejects the secularization thesis as unable to explain the nature of modernity and hence its crisis.[7] It is nonsense, he claims, to argue that modernity is a secularized biblical faith by which 'other-worldly' faith has become radically 'this-worldly', since this is precisely what Plato himself tried to do in the *Republic*. Clearly Plato was not secularizing biblical faith. In an argument that strongly endorses Blumenberg, he says secularization as the preservation of thoughts, feelings or habits of biblical origin after the loss or atrophy of biblical faith 'does not tell us anything as to what kind of ingredients are preserved in secularizations. Above all it does not tell us what secularization is, except negatively: loss or atrophy of biblical faith' (p. 83). Yet, he argues, modern man was guided by a 'positive project'. Strauss's whole political philosophy was an attempt to understand the nature of this positive project, aware of the impossibility of encapsulating in an academic discourse what in fact is a political practice.

Modernity for Strauss cannot be reduced to just one single project, a 'hidden agenda', in Toulmin's sense (see Chapter 3). It unfolds through the fragmentation of the unity preserved in classical political philosophy: 'By modernity we understand a radical modification of premodern political philosophy, a modification which comes to sight first as a rejection of premodern political philosophy' (p. 83). In breaking with classical political thought, modernity was surrendering the possibility of unity. This surrendering can be seen as a process of progressive crystallization – a term which Strauss does not use but which aptly captures his line of argument – which can be seen as a cautious endorsement of Nietzsche's critique of modernity.[8]

In his essay, Strauss outlines the three waves which led to the overcoming of classical political philosophy. These relate to Plato's three 'waves' in Book V of the *Republic* concerning the question of the realization of political philosophy as it is ideally conceived by the philosopher rulers. They can also be compared to the notion of modernity as a process of Gnosticism, as outlined by Eric Voeglin (see Pangle, 1991). It is to be stressed that Strauss is not arguing for the rejection of modernity, for liberal democracy, which he wants to defend, derives from the first two phases. What he wants to achieve, however, is a recovery of some of the premodern insights in order to provide liberal democracy with a stronger identity, but such a recovery is possible only if it takes account of all three of the waves of modernity, including the third, which in many ways engendered fascism. Like Hannah Arendt, he sees in ancient thought the source of inspiration for politics today, but he does not think there can be a simple return to these ideas. This ambivalence is central to his political philosophy, and like Arendt he sees politics in terms of the pursuit less of justice than of virtue.

The architects of the first wave were Machiavelli and, especially, Hobbes, for these two political thinkers rejected the classical understanding of politics which held that the best political system was one that made possible the practice of virtue. According to the former, the prince need not legitimate himself by anything other than sheer instrumentalism. More importantly, the question of how a political system comes into existence depends not on chance, as the ancients believed, but on human powers. Creativity is the essence of the political for Machiavelli, for whom politics becomes a technical matter, no longer rooted in morality. Hobbes brought to completion what Machiavelli initiated: the rejection of classical natural law. For Hobbes natural law becomes reduced to self-preservation. Now nature is no longer opposed to human will, offering a standard for judgement. The first wave of modernity can be said to be the rejection of classical natural law and the separation of politics from morality.

The second wave begins with Rousseau. He began with the modern notion of the state of nature but sought to reestablish a link with virtue. Since he could not restore the classical concept of virtue, which had been demolished by Hobbes and Machiavelli, he was forced to reinterpret it. In the state of nature man lives an asocial and inhuman existence as a result of the corrupting forces of history and society. The task for Rousseau is to recover the human dimension of nature, the central component of which is freedom. But the problem is that the republican order in which it is to be realized must be capable of bridging the divide between nature and society. It was left to the philosophy of history, in particular Kant and Hegel, to develop this paradox in Rousseau, namely how does freedom become realized in society if it derives from human nature? The second wave of modernity thus refers to the revolt against society and the appeal to natural freedom. Rousseau believed modernity could bring about the escape from society to nature, while at the same time denying the origin of republican civil society in nature. This conflict between nature and society parallels the conflict between romanticism and classicism. As Strauss puts it: 'Modernity was understood from the beginning in contradiction to antiquity; modernity could therefore include the medieval world. The difference between the modern and the medieval on the one hand, and antiquity on the other, was reinterpreted around 1800 as the difference between the romantic and the classic' (p. 93). Romanticism is more modern than classicism, a conflict which Strauss sees exemplified in Goethe's *Faust*, and notes that Spengler in the *Decline of the West* replaced 'romantic' by 'Faustian' in describing the spirit of modernity. Modernity now becomes 'unrest, infinite striving, dissatisfaction with everything finite, finished, complete, "classic" ' (p. 94). I believe what Strauss has in mind here can be related to the notion of cultural crystallization: the unravelling of an original cultural framework into its components, which then lose the normative force of the founding project. Modernity ultimately becomes a directionless project, though never illegitimate. The idea of a project is retained, but it loses any sense of purpose. But this does not invalidate the project in the way Karl Löwith and Carl Schmitt once argued.

Returning to Strauss, the first wave of modernity laid the basis of liberal democracy in separating morality from politics, whereby the latter is based on the rule of law:

> Modernity started from the dissatisfaction with the gulf between the is and the ought, the actual and the ideal; the solution suggested in the first wave was: bring the ought nearer to the is by lowering the ought, by conceiving of the ought as not making too high demands on men, or as being in agreement with man's most powerful and most common passion. (p. 91)

The second wave went one step further in releasing nature from society, which for Hobbes was dominated by the Leviathan, the symbol of state power. If the first wave is epitomized by Hobbes and the second by Rousseau, the third is related to Nietzsche.

In the words of Strauss: 'The third wave may be described as being constituted by a new understanding of the sentiments of existence: that sentiment is the experience of terror and anguish rather than of harmony and peace' (p. 94). For Nietzsche the state of nature does not promise freedom. Rejecting the Hegelian philosophy of history, which sought to solve many of the problems in, for instance, Rousseau and Kant, Nietzsche demonstrated that history is not a progressive movement in the way Hegel saw it but is one of struggle. Political action is placed to the fore in his conception of the 'will to power'. Like Marx, but differing from him in his rejection of the classless society, Nietzsche's thought 'marks the end of the rule of chance: man will be for the first time the ruler of his fate' (p. 97). The point of the third wave is to reject the idea of progress, which dominated the nineteenth century.

Strauss concludes his essay by saying modernity, having undergone these three waves, cannot be based on any notion of unity. In this there is the suggestion of a postmodern stance on modernity.[9] The three waves sought to solve the problem of political authority variously by strategies of rejection: the rejection of natural law, the rejection of society, the rejection of progress. Strauss draws a political conclusion from this:

> The theory of liberal democracy, as well as communism, originated in the first and second waves of modernity; the political implication of the third wave proved to be fascism. Yet this undeniable fact does not permit a return to the earlier forms of modern thought: the critique of modern rationalism or of the modern belief in reason by Nietzsche or Heidegger cannot be dismissed or forgotten. This is the deepest crisis of liberal democracy. (p. 98)

The upshot of Strauss's position is that in each of its three waves, the modern critique of classical political philosophy cannot be ignored, for there is no turning back. Instead of a turning back – as Heidegger argued for – Strauss's thought was closer to Nietzsche's eternal reoccurrence, the inescapability of the quest for a political philosophy. What I understand him to be saying is that modernity is condemned to contingency as a result of its uncertainty of purpose. Yet, 'liberal democracy, in contradiction to communism and fascism, derives powerful support from a way of thinking which cannot be called modern at all: the premodern thought of our western tradition' (p. 98). In another essay, 'The Crisis of Our Time', he wrote of the decline in political philosophy in terms of a loss in certainty: 'The crisis of the West consists in the fact that the West has become uncertain of its own purpose. This purpose was the universal society, a society consisting of equal nations, each consisting of free and equal men and women, with all these nations to be fully developed as regards their power of production, thanks to science' (Strauss, 1964, p. 42). He goes on to argue: 'The West was once certain of its purpose, of a purpose in which all men could be united. Hence, it had a clear vision of its future as the future of mankind. We no longer have that certainity and clarity. Some of us even despair of the future' (Strauss, 1964, p. 44). It may be concluded from this that for Strauss modernity is a condition of uncertainty, our political self-understanding cannot be self-grounding since it has been conceived in opposition to something prior to it, and even though this cannot be recovered in its original condition, we can gain some normative orientation from the recognition that modernity can only define its project by reference to a notion of moral truth.[10] This suggests that modernity is based on an aspiration towards the unattainable.[11]

I have suggested that Leo Strauss's thinking reveals a postmodernist direction. The essence of this lies in the facination with the political philosophies of Nietzsche and Plato. Nietzsche was the only modern philosopher whose thought preserved a connection with one of the core ideas of classical political philosophy: the inaccesibility of truth. For Plato truth was accessible only to the philosophical elite; for Nietzsche truth had become a matter of interpretation, beyond morality and ultimately inaccessible. Truth is present only as something that once existed in an esoteric form and of which only the trace of its secret remains.

This question of the paradoxical foundation of modernity is something I shall return to in discussing Luhmann's theory of modernity in the next section of this chapter.

Luhmann: A Self-Limiting Modernity

Luhmann's outline of modernity in *Observations on Modernity* (1998), originally published in German in 1992, in many ways can be read as an alternative to postmodern theories but one that tries to 'pull the rug out from under the contrast of modern and postmodern' (Luhmann, 1998, p. 17; all references in this section are to this work, unless otherwise stated). The reception of his work outside Germany has been considerably shaped by his debate with Habermas on the question of radical democracy and the political legitimation of power (Habermas, 1976; Habermas and Luhmann, 1971). Consequently, the two theorists have tended to be polarized in terms of left and right political positions and as a result important insights have been lost. There is now much to suggest that Luhmann's social theory can be appropriated in more useful directions.[12] With Habermas modifying his position in recent years, moving away from Western Marxism and the vision of an alternative society (see Chapter 5), the reception of Luhmann's work is pointing to something more than the old accusation of technocratic modernity, for central to his theory of modernity is a conception of contingency that is very close to postmodernist accounts of contemporary society. Reading *Observations of Modernity*, one gets a sense not of the rise of technocratic rationality but of what I would call a 'self-limiting' modernity of endless possibilities and paradoxes. The fundamental idea underlying Luhmann's conception of contemporary society – that it is differences, not identities, that provide the possibility of the functioning of society – is of great importance, particularly in the context of postmodernity and in debates on social inclusion.

Luhmann's theory of modernity is based on the recognition that everything has become contingent today and as a result it is not easy to offer a representation of society. How can society be represented, or, as he says, 'observed', when all external positions from which observation might be possible have disappeared, or have become themselves contingent. Observation must take the form of 'self-observations', or, as he also says 'self-descriptions'. When we use communication we are already operating within a particular discourse so that an observation is always 'within' and not just 'on' something, that is to say, it is as much a 'self' observation as one of an external world.

For Luhmann, modernity is a process which entails a particular kind of relationship between Self and Other, between an internal category and an external one. The essence of this is the construction of a difference, for all attempts to define the identity of the self require an other. This is also true of temporal categories. So, when

> contemporary society calls itself 'modern,' it identifies itself with the help of a differentiation from the past. It identifies itself in a temporal dimension. This is nothing particularly special at first glance. All autopoetic systems, even, for example, the consciousness of the self, can only construct identity with constant allusions to their own past. This means that self-reference and external reference must be differentiated. (p. 3)

Rather than identification, what is important is 'disidentification', through the construction of relations of difference, or otherness. Luhmann's philosophy is not unlike that of Adorno or Derrida in this respect, for all share the suspension of identity which can only be negatively stated as non-identity: 'Whether we like it or not, we are no longer what we were, and we will not be what we are now' (p. 3). This condition of postponement, or deferral, sums up modernity, which requires, in Luhmann's view, the constant creation of otherness. Unity is impossible, as is identity, at least not without the creation of other kinds of difference for every internal situation requires an external one. Another way of putting this is to say that what is becoming more important in contemporary society – a term Luhmann prefers to modern or postmodern – is that in all areas of life internal distinctions are becoming more significant than external ones. One of the implications of this is the impossibility of society, since once a distinction is made between Self and Other, subsystem and its environment, further distinctions will be made within the discourse and subsystems of the self. It is differences, not identities, that provide the possibility of the functioning of society (Luhmann, 1990a). Internal closure and the construction of structures of exclusion are inscribed in the very nature of contemporary society, which can never have recourse to real unity. Contemporary society is therefore self-limiting: openness always leads to closure. This clearly has major implications for the construction of collective identity and comprehensive forms of social exclusion. Luhmann's social theory suggests that the struggle for unity is a doomed possibility.

At the heart of Luhmann's mature social theory is the idea of autopoesis, that is, self-creating systems of meaning. Modern society is a functionally differentiated system whose subsystems have become autonomous of each other and of the social system as a whole.[13] Unlike in Parsons's system theory, where there was an overall systemic unity, in Luhmann each subsystem is self-reproducing, or autopoetic. Thus, the self-description of a subsystem is possible only within that subsystem, which alone can make sense of the distinction between self-reference and external reference. In short, this distinction can only be made from a point within the system. Luhmann, in fact, believes subsystems must make this self-observation in order for them to distinguish themselves from their environment (that is, other subsystems). The important point is the postulation of unity as only the 'unity of an imaginary space' (p. 10), for one of the features of modernity is the construction of abstract systems of meaning. The unity of a system is only possible as an imaginary unity, whereas in reality there is a radical separation of the internal and the external. 'Traditional concepts of rationality lived off the *external* presumptions of meaning, whether they were based on the copying of natural laws, given objectives, or given values for the choice of objectives' (p. 17). Modernity in contemporary society has transferred all judgements to a system-internal unity of self-reference and external reference. The postmodern is nothing more than the absence of any point of unity, by which the distinction between internal and external reference can be bridged:

> If we understand 'postmodern' to mean the lack of a unified cosmography, a universally applicable rationality, or even just a collective attitude toward the world and society, then this results from the structural conditions to which contemporary society delivers itself. It cannot abide a final word, and therefore it cannot abide authority. It knows no positions from which society could be adequately described for others within society. (p. 18)

There is of course an apparent paradox between the postmodern situation of pluralism and the dissolution of the unity of society into a multiplicity of systems and discourses, on the one side, and the inevitable emergence of 'world society', on the other, wherein capitalism and socialism have ceased to be two different world orders. Luhmann solves this by simply saying this situation is not really new: the postmodern is already contained in the modern. Every observation is itself an operation, for in a situation of extreme complexity and multiple codes of information, meaning and communication, observations make sense only if they are realized in an actual operation with which the particular subsystem is produced.

Another way of putting this is to say that contemporary society involves the proliferation of 'second-order observations' for direct observation is not an available option today. 'Beginning with Marx, it has always been a part of sociological reflection to analyze the world of social manifestations not from the perspective of the participating first-order but rather from the perspective of the observer of such observers' (p. 77). We are approaching a society that in perpetually experimenting with forms of communication is making the form of communication central to the experience of social content: content has become form. One of the central insights in Luhmann's sociology is the idea that in the movement from modernity to contemporary society there is an increase in observer positions: direct knowledge and experience is being more and more replaced by mediated processes. This is not unlike the post-structuralist notion of reality disappearing into a system of signs, but for Luhmann the subject still exists, though not as a self-contained narrator. The subject has become an observer. The contemporary observer is an observer not of an objective reality but of other observations, including, most importantly, itself, or in other words its own observations. This can be seen in the increase in self-reflexivity today, the self-monitoring of subjectivity.

> In the modern world, more and more is attributed to the observer, at least in many cases. This could be a symptom of the fact all world experiences are becoming contingent. Beyond the ever-present question of whether someone else will characterize something correctly or incorrectly, one can use the observation of one's own observation to observe, characterize, and understand the other observer. (pp. 48–9)

The increase in second-order observations is expressed in the expansion in the volume of communication, for 'society can conduct observations only in the form of communications, not in the form of conscious internal operations and above all not in the form of perceptions' (p. 57). Luhmann rejects any recourse to the priority of either the subject or the object in order to solve the problem of contingency. This can be seen in many areas of contemporary society: in politics, for instance, since the nineteenth century public opinion has functioned like a mirror for different groups in society, making power contingent (pp. 58–9). In artistic production, too, second-order observations are replacing first-order observations in that art no longer represents something outside itself, for in the aesthetic form external distinctions are replaced by internal ones. In the realm of scientific knowledge the question of methodology has become all-important, for scientific truth is a matter not of proclamations but of the observation of observations. In law, recourse to second-order observations is evident in the salience of questions of procedure. Love is a domain in which the second-order observation is particularly evident since this is a medium in which each individual must consider the observations of the other. The construction of distinctions hangs more on 'how' something is distinguished than on 'what' is being distinguished: 'We are interested not just in what is distinguished but above all in how things are distinguished and who makes those distinctions' (p. 26; see also Luhmann, 1986).

In light of these remarks we can say that for Luhmann contemporary society is self-limiting. Modernity as epitomized in the critical philosophy of Kant stood for the self-limiting nature of knowledge, but Kant's critical knowledge was guaranteed by an autonomous subject. Luhmann's modernity goes one step further: the subject as codifier and narrator is replaced by a subject as observer. In this revision of the modern idea, the subject becomes essentially just one of many positions from which observations can be made. The 'observer cannot be observed'; the observer 'disappears into "unmarked space" ' (p. 27). The implications of this are great for politics. As is apparent in Luhmann's famous debate with Habermas, politics no longer occupies a position at the centre of society, which is centreless (Habermas, 1976; Habermas and Luhmann, 1971). In contemporary society, there is no single subsystem capable of imposing its observations on other ones. Under the conditions of societal complexity, political communication has become just one mode of communication; consequently politics loses its legitimating role (see Luhmann, 1990c).

Modernity, as a European venture, according to Luhmann, was based on the search for differences, a quest that expressed itself in modes of observations. 'The history of European rationality can be described as the history of the dissolution of a rationality continuum that had connected the observer in the world with the world' (p. 23). The world disappears, like nature, into a system of observations, the origin of which may have been the nominalism of the late Middle Ages. But Luhmann's constructivism is one that has a certain regard for reality, though one which is retained as a paradox since the external is possible only by the internal, that is, in a self-referential form. The forms of contemporary society are drawing more and more into the exploration of their own possibilities. In these forms the future disappears into an extended present. The future in the age of modernity was a means of extending the present beyond itself as a self-projection. Today, the future has been replaced by risk (see Luhmann, 1993). 'We can better describe contemporary society in its consequences', Luhmann argues, for the 'continuity from past to future is broken in our time' (p. 67). The future is dependent on decision-making, and in a way it may be suggested that the future has collapsed into the very process of decision-making. The real problem of modernity lies in the time dimension. 'In the dimension of time, the present refers to a future that only exists as what is probable or improbable' (p. 69). Today the future is being experienced in the form of risk; in other words in decision-making. Risks concern possible but not determined events, or improbabilities that result from a decision. According to this conception of the future, the future becomes merely a matter of reducing complexity.

In collapsing the distinction of present and future into a future-extended present, everything becomes contingent. This is evident in the communication of knowledge. When knowledge is communicated, what is being transmitted is as much knowledge as 'ignorance' – it must be able to absorb uncertainty – since knowledge in the absence of pre-ordained authorities is always incomplete and uncertain. This raises the problem of how society copes with the removal of authority: 'it is not enough that society delegitimizes representation and consequently authority. It is not enough, to put it another way, to allow critique and protest to run amok. Society must be able to survive the communication of ignorance' (p. 90). The answer, according to Luhmann, is that the cognitive has also a normative dimension and it lies in the 'responsibility for consequences' (p. 92). However, he makes clear this has nothing to do with the 'old European ethic' or dreams of an 'ethical civil society' (p. 92) since these traditions have no place today, given the increase in complexity and contingency. Another solution is recourse to trust, which is also a normative stance to what is a cognitive problem (see Luhmann, 1979).

We can conclude this outline of Luhmann's theory of modernity by returning to the notion of crystallization with which we began. Though this concept is not used by Luhmann, it captures the general direction of his thought: modernity has entered a phase in which unity has crystallized into its components and into a multiplicity of self-thematizations. The more a society expands – the more it approaches 'world society' – the more it will become internally differentiated. The problem of integration has been replaced by the problem of differentiation, but in a way that there can be no recourse to unitary value systems. In place of privileged institutions (Gehlen) and value systems (Parsons), Luhmann stresses the contemporary salience of communication. But this is a model of communication that is very different from Habermas's, which is tied to a notion of action; in Luhmann's model of communication the actor has disappeared. Unlike virtually all other social theorists, he makes the question of contingency so central that the basic problem that it presents for social theory cannot be solved. This is the problem of choice. For Luhmann, in a world of endless crystallization, society is ultimately impossible, except, as he says, as 'world society.'

Luhmann's mature systems theory has also brought social theory close to postmodernism in one respect, namely the central importance he gives to difference.[14] While his earlier work was more concerned with the implications of differentiation, his later work is more centrally addressed to the constructivist and cognitivist question of autopoesis. Systems theory begins with the recognition that all distinctions require difference which cannot be eradicated by a model of consensus. He thus rejects, with postmodernism, the assumption of identity. There are, then, certain affinities with autopoesis and deconstruction, though Luhmann does not of course draw the same political conclusions as authors such as Derrida and Lyotard for whom these are all questions concerning the nature of struggle. However, Luhmann does not use the term 'postmodern', since he sees modernity itself as characterized by precisely the 'loss of reference' (Luhmann, 1994a). The work of Luhmann provides a good illustration of the thesis that an ethos of postmodernization already pervaded modernity.

Conclusion: Contingency and Communication

The concept of cultural crystallization that I am proposing in this chapter is one that seeks to make a positive appraisal of the contemporary situation of contingency. Whereas Gehlen used the term to mean the end of a project, the historical project of the European Enlightenment, I am using it to mean the opening up of multiple logics of development in contemporary society. The solution to the problem of contingency is not the comfort of social institutions, as Gehlen, the sociological prince of Adenauer's Germany, thought, or, as the various proponents of post-history would have it, the embracing of liberal democracy. Rather than accepting the implications of Luhmann's social theory, which rejects the possibility of solutions to a problem whose very form has become the basis of the social, in the next two chapters I will explore different solutions to the problem of contingency: the project of recovering modernity (Habermas, Touraine, Lefebvre, Heller, Castoriadis) and the postmodernism critique of modernity. What I hope to demonstrate in these debates is a conception of contingency in terms of communication. Luhmann's theory denies the underpinning of communication by agency, whereas other approaches such as those of Habermas and Touraine make agency central to social theory.

5

RESCUING MODERNITY
The Recovery of the Social

The theories of modernity discussed in the previous chapters anticipate the postmodern critique of modernity in many respects. The notion of the crystallization of culture and the coming of the posthistorical society can be seen as a prelude to postmodernism since it proclaims the demise of the unifying narratives of the great political ideologies and the emancipatory promises of modern culture. This can be traced back to Max Weber's and Georg Simmel's theories of modern culture as disenchanted and tragic, having lost its capacity to provide unity and meaning. The turn to formalism in early twentieth-century thought is of course more clearly evident in radical modernism, a movement that is often seen as the origin of postmodernism as an aesthetic discourse (see Chapter 7). The work of Luhmann, with its emphasis on the opening up of self-reflexive observer positions in contemporary society, can be seen as the most sophisticated theory of cultural fragmentation, and one coming very close to postmodernism. However, it is clear that there was an anti-modernist aminus in many of these critiques of modernity – in particular Voeglin, Strauss, Toulmin, Gehlen, Koselleck – while others – Horkheimer and Adorno – retained the aesthetic dimension of cultural modernity, rejecting all other dimensions. Hannah Arendt, in contrast, adhered to the emancipatory promise of a political modernity that drew its normative force from a still relevant ancient republicanism. Blumenberg provided the basis for a new departure, but his theory of modernity stops at the Enlightenment, and it is thus unable to explain the arrival of the postmodern caesura.

In this chapter I examine a number of theories of modernity which seek to recover the idea of modernity from the pessimistic philosophy of history that pervades many of the accounts already discussed, but accounts which are resistant to postmodernism. The central issue, I argue, is that the recovery of modernity is tied to the recovery of the idea of the social. But exactly what is the social? Is it the same as the idea of society?

In this chapter, by means of a discussion of the theories of modernity of Habermas, Lefebvre, Heller, Castoriadis and Touraine, I argue for a conception of the social defined in terms of communication. Modern societies are essentially communication societies (Strydom, 1999a). Communication can be seen as the principal medium of integration today, for unity is no longer established by any single institution or social structure. This makes modern society extremely vulnerable to fragmentation but it also makes it amenable to many possibilities for enhancing the project of human autonomy. Modernity can be seen as the gradual expansion of, what I call, discursive spaces (Delanty, 1999a, 2000b). These are the spaces in which society solves the problem of contingency, which is something that is faced by all complex societies as a result of processes of differentiation, the growing expansion of risk, the indeterminacy and uncertainty of life histories, and the pluralization and reflexivity of cultural value systems. As is already intimated in the social theory of Luhmann, contingency cannot be solved by recourse to institutions (Gehlen) or cultural value systems (Parsons) or the institution of democracy (Habermas). Accepting the premise that contingency is increasing in contemporary society and that many of the traditional solutions are becoming inadequate in dealing with the fundamental problem of choice, different readings can be made of institutions, culture and democracy than is suggested by Luhmann. It can be argued, if we take a communications theoretic approach, that communication is now the mechanism by which society reproduces itself. Institutions, culture and democracy are pervaded by communicative processes and discursive space.

Habermas: From History to Discourse

The debate between modernity and postmodernity has been central to some of Jürgen Habermas's writings since the early 1980s, when he launched a major attack, from the vantage point of modernity, on postmodernism. In an essay published in 1981 there is the suggestion – which can only be held to be untenable – that the line separating postmodernism and neo-conservatism is a thin one (Habermas, 1981).[1] Whether in literature, philosophy, social science or architecture, Habermas has been an unrelenting opponent of all kinds of postmodernism.[2] In a major work some years later, *The Philosophical Discourse of Modernity*, this theory is developed into a powerful defence of European modernity against all forms of postmodernist thinking (Habermas, 1987b). This position has been subject to a great deal of discussion and there is much to suggest that Habermas has conceded some of his earlier positions (Bernstein, 1985). While much of his interpretation of postmodernism – which equates deconstruction with destruction and the unlikely spectre of a 'new historicism' – can, and indeed must, be questioned, there is a more fundamental problem with his concept of modernity. In the next two chapters I will discuss postmodernism in detail, looking at, for instance, the shift from the French-influenced poststructuralism to American postmodernism and the emergence of postmodern conceptions of community. It will be argued that a lot of what goes under the name 'postmodernism' cannot be dismissed as a betrayal of the promises of modernity. In this section I examine a more or less unacknowledged shift in Habermas's own concept of modernity from a model based on historical completion to one based on discursive openness. Looking at the development of his work in this manner allows us to reconceptualize modernity in a way that does not simply pit it irreconcilably against the postmodern. In the following, I want to show how the recent turn in Habermas's thought allows us to disconnect the concept of modernity from the Enlightenment project and make it more relevant to understanding the current situation of multiple modernities.

No theorist more than Habermas has defended the Enlightenment project against its critics both on the right and on the left. Modernity is equated with the promises of the European Enlightenment, a project which Habermas sees as incomplete, rather than, as Gehlen would have it, completed, or, as Löwith once argued, something that in fact has never begun. Thus, rather than abandoning it for something prior to modernity (Heidegger), or accepting the current situation (Gehlen), or looking to postmodernism (Baudrillard), Habermas defends modernity as a project that is still relevant to contemporary society since the force of its normative critique still lives on in new kinds of communicative practices and social struggles: 'instead of giving up modernity and its project as a lost cause, we should learn from the mistakes of those extravagant programmes which have tried to negate modernity' (Habermas, 1981, p. 11). Rejecting, too, Foucault's designation of modernity in terms of disciplinary power and the Frankfurt School's notion of modernity as the rise of instrumental reason which gave birth to totalitarianism, Habermas, true to Marx, sees modernity as an essentially contradictory process. However, his notion of the inner conflict within modernity is reducible not to class struggle but to the conflict between two kinds of reason: communicative and instrumental. In this struggle, the materialist conception of history becomes a struggle between cultural self-reflection and power. Modernity can be reduced neither to the disciplinary state nor to purely economic forces. Nor, of course, can it be reduced to the purely aesthetic, for culture in Habermas's model is primarily communicative and to that extent it involves social reflexivity. Cultural modernity, for Habermas, embodies critical self-transformation.

By means of a theory of cultural modernity as communicatively constituted, Habermas seeks to provide the foundation for an alternative to the Marxist account, while retaining the dialectical tension of the latter. Social struggles are thus made central to modernity. In his early conceptualization of modernity, the Enlightenment plays a central role. In his first major work, *The Structural Transformation of the Public Sphere*, originally published in 1962, Habermas tied the project of modernity to the completion of the Enlightenment (Habermas, 1989a; see also Habermas, 1989d). Thus, modernity is largely defined in terms of a period, from the late seventeenth to early nineteenth century, the period roughly from the end of the wars of religion to the revolutionary wars. In this period, which is also marked by the American and French Revolutions, cultural modernity emerges around new communicative spaces in society. Habermas does not use the term 'space' as such. However, the term he uses, the public sphere, suggests a strong spatial dimension to communication.[3] It is clear that the public sphere is a space in society, since it is seen to reside in the civil domain between the private and the domain of the state, but it is also a domain of discourse. In this pathbreaking work, which even before it appeared in English in 1989 had already made a major impact, Habermas sought to link cultural production to changing social structures. The category of public opinion offered the means to achieve that very link. The public for Habermas was less a particular form of agency, though it is clearly to be identified with specific social actors, the educated bourgeoisie, than a form of discourse which is characterized by public communication:

> The bourgeois public sphere may be conceived above all as the sphere of private people come together as a public; they soon claimed the public sphere regulated from above against the public authorities themselves, to engage them in debate over the general rules governing relations in the basically privatized but publicly relevant sphere of commodity exchange and social labor. (Habermas, 1989a, p. 27)

So, it was 'critical rational debate' that characterized the early public sphere, which had the function of the political regulation of civil society as well as cultural debate. Political and aesthetic criticism constituted the two forms the public sphere took. It was institutionalized in the new public spaces that were opened in western society in the seventeenth and eighteenth centuries, with the creation of public institutions such as public libraries, museums, parks, universities, coffee houses, political clubs such as the Enlightenment societies, and above all the emergence of the press. The social basis of this was the emergence of a reading public, largely bourgeois in its composition.

According to Habermas, the early public sphere was potentially emancipatory, despite its association with the bourgeoisie, for it contained a critical component. Like the early Marx, he believed the bourgeois emancipation movement was a progressive movement in so far as it struggled to gain the recognition of the rights that constitute modern citizenship, democracy and the constitutional state, and to that extent something like immanent critique is possible, that is, a form of critique which aims to overcome contradictions in society. Such a position presupposes, of course, that the normative potential for self-transformation already exists and only needs to be realized, or the conditions be created for its realization. But even in this early work there is the suggestion that advanced capitalist society may be eliminating its contradictions, thus making immanent critique impossible. Once the absolute state, the target of the bourgeois critique, was destroyed, the public sphere lost its earlier critical thrust, which rested upon its relative autonomy. But this was not just because of the political conservatism of the post-revolutionary bourgeoisie. From the mid-ninteenth century onwards, the tension between cultural modernity and disciplinary modernity was weakened as a result of the increasing commercialization of the public sphere. The press, for instance, ceased to be an organ of autonomous political and cultural opinion formation, becoming instead a commercial activity. The public sphere, Habermas argues, loses its strictly public nature and is penetrated once again by the private. The return of a depoliticized private domain which gains access to the public sphere amounts to its 're-feudalization' (Habermas, 1989a, p. 195). This, then, is the first major structural change to the public sphere. In the twentieth century the re-feudalization of the public sphere reaches completion with the rise of mass society, where the dialectical tensions that were inherent in bourgeois society are weakened. Advertising and entertainment rob the public sphere of its critical function, and whatever public discourse is left is reduced to 'representative publicity'. Thus, in the shift from capitalist production to the emergence of a society based on mass consumption, there is no longer any space for autonomous discourse.

Working in the late 1950s, under the influence of Adorno, Habermas's image of modernity was a profoundly pessimistic one: modernity was a model of decline. His early work tried to show how modernity entailed the gradual removal of communication from the public sphere, which then becomes emptied of normative content, becoming ultimately a mechanism of domination. In mass society there can be no authentic communication, only controlled consumption and administered opinion. The promise of cultural modernity was confined to a society that has understood the social to be more or less the civic. With the destruction of this sphere by advanced capitalism, Habermas saw no possibility for a really critical public sphere. The result was a theoretical impasse: modernity entails the extension of communicative rationality from the cultural domains to all of society, but as a result of an all-pervasive capitalism which has commodified a previously autonomous cultural sphere the nature of society now makes this impossible. This theory obviously rested on a strong belief in civil society and a rejection of mass society. It did not occur to Habermas, still under the influence of the old Frankfurt School, that both of these extremes are useless. However, Habermas had already departed from the pessimistic theory of history of Adorno, for modernity was firmly located in communicative reason, whereas for Adorno it was confined to a largely self-denying aesthetic moment. Though Habermas saw modernity as the destruction of communicative reason, his version was one that demanded not the abandonment of modernity but its completion. Methodologically, this was to be realized in a reconstructive critique, rather than the negative dialectics, of the mature critical theory of Adorno. This was a position that was utterly unacceptable to Adorno, who found a moment of emancipation only in an uncomprisingly autonomous aesthetic modernity.

The completion of the project of the Enlightenment, Habermas claimed, consists of realizing the professionalized components of discourse in everyday life, not abandoning those discourses:

> The project of modernity formulated in the eighteenth century by the philos-ophers of the Enlightenment consisted in their efforts to develop objective science, universal morality and law, and autonomous art, according to their inner logic. At the same time, this project intended to release the cognitive potentials of each of these domains to set them free from their esoteric forms. The Enlightenment philosophers wanted to utilize this accumulation of special-ized culture for the enrichment of everyday life, that is to say, for the rational organization of everyday social life. (Habermas, 1981, p. 9)

The three central dimensions of cultural modernity – the moral-practical, the cognitive, the aesthetic – offer modern society potential models of emancipation, but these models are contained in professional discourses. The problem, as Habermas puts it, is that the 'twentieth century has shattered this optimism. The differentiation of science, morality and art has come to mean the autonomy of the segments treated by the specialist and at the same time letting them split off from the hermeneutics of everyday communication' (Habermas, 1981, p. 9). For Habermas this all raises the question of the negation of the culture of expertise. How can the emancipatory content of cultural modernity be released from its autonomous discourses and realized in everyday life? This has been a question that goes back to the Young Hegelians and the early Marx, with their concern for the negation of philosophy. It was later realized in a different form by the surrealist movement, which sought to abolish the institution of the autonomy of art. According to Habermas, the great mistake is to assume that by breaking open a single cultural sphere, the project of modernity could be realized. Moreover:

> A reified everyday praxis can be cured only by creating unconstrained inter-action of the cognitive with the moral-practical and the aesthetic-expressive elements. Reification cannot be overcome by forcing just one of those highly stylized cultural spheres to open up and become more accessible. Instead, we see under certain circumstances a relationship emerge between terroristic activities and the over-extension of any one of these spheres into other domains. (Habermas, 1981, p. 11)

Thus, rather than accept any attempt to negate cultural modernity in order to bring its discourses closer to everyday life, Habermas argues for their continued autonomy, but only in so far that they serve to illuminate everyday life.

There are two noteworthy aspects to this. First, the suggestion is that discourses of emancipation come from outside the social. Everyday life does not itself produce emancipatory discourse, which instead comes from the autonomous discourses of professionals. This is not unlike Habermas's position in the *Theory of Communicative Action* that those social movements that have crossed the threshold of reflexivity can redeem the life-world from reification. Second, there is the very firm belief in the emancipatory nature of the European Enlightenment with the result that modernity is conceived of in terms of a model of historical completion. We do not need here to cover the well-documented debate on the limits of this model for the contemporary situation, and Habermas has acknowledged the limits of his earlier work (Calhoun, 1993; Habermas, 1993). However, though he has recognized that the public sphere of the Enlightenment was based on exclusion on class and gender lines, he did not offer a fundamentally new theory until his work of the 1990s, when he developed a discourse theory of law and democracy (Habermas, 1996, 1998a).

In his work of the 1970s, culminating with the two-volume *Theory of Communicative Action* of 1981 (Habermas, 1984, 1987a), Habermas outlined an intermediary position: the public sphere is associated with radical social movements. Responding to the rise of new social movements from the late 1960s and building upon his more abstract work in speech acts and communication, Habermas offered the foundation of a new theory of modernity. Retaining the original insight of modernity as a struggle between communicative and instrumental action, he now sees this as a conflict between life-world and system. In this struggle, the forces of instrumental reason do not just colonize the communicative structures of the life-world but are also resisted by the latter. This connection is because Habermas in the 1970s sees modernity as being renewed by a new generation of social movements. Yet the relationship is unclear between the theory of communicative action and early notion of modernity as outlined in the work on the public sphere. This is clearly evident in that no sooner was the theory of communicative action published in 1981 than Habermas restated in very forceful terms his notion of the incompletion of modernity in the essay 'Modernity versus Postmodernity', also of 1981, in a variety of essays on postmodernism (for instance, Habermas, 1989e) and in the *Philosophical Discourse of Modernity*, originally published in 1985 (Habermas, 1987b). In view of this, we can say with some confidence that even though *The Theory of Communicative Action* broke from the theoretical and normative impasse of *The Structural Transformation of the Public Sphere*, it did not lead to a rethinking of the idea of modernity from whose shadow the new social movements are unable to escape. At a time when Nietzsche was being embraced by a form of postmodernism influenced by Heidegger, Habermas turned to Kant and his notion of reason as a self-limiting discourse split into three spheres.

> By the end of the eighteenth century, science, morality, and art were even institutionally differentiated as realms of activity in which questions of truth, of justice, and of taste were autonomously elaborated, that is, each under its

own specific aspect of validity. And these spheres of knowing were separated off from the spheres of belief, on the one hand, and from those of both legally organized everyday life, on the other. (Habermas, 1987b, p. 19)

Habermas's model of modernity can be seen as combination of Kant's notion of reason as entailing the separation of cultural modernity into its practical, cognitive and aesthetic dimensions modified by the Weberian notion of the disenchantment of the world; Hegel's conviction of 'the self-critical assurance of modernity' as a historical process and the reconciling power of intersubjectivity; and the Marxist critique of false consciousness. Kant, Hegel and Marx were the architects of a modernity destroyed by Nietzsche, Heidegger and Derrida, according to Habermas. His notion of modernity is summed up in the vision of the left-Hegelians:

> Neither Hegel nor his direct disciplines on the Left or Right ever wanted to call into question the achievements of modernity from which the modern age drew its pride and self-consciousness. Above all the modern age stood above all under the sign of subjective freedom. This was realized in society as the space secured by civil law for the rational pursuit of one's own interests; in the state, as the in principle equal rights to participation in the formation of political will; in the private sphere, as ethical autonomy and self-realization; finally, in the public sphere related to this private realm, as the formative process that takes place by means of the appropriation of a culture that has become reflective. (Habermas, 1987b, p. 83)

It seems to me that there is a contradiction in Habermas's theory of modernity. On the one hand, the theory of communicative action provided an exit out of the impasse of the earlier work on the public sphere, while, on the other hand, he still adheres to a model of historical completion. There is some recognition that the normative content of cultural modernity can be located in everyday life, and not in professionalized discourses, for 'everyday practice affords a locus for spontaneous processes of self-understanding and identity formation, even in nonstratified societies that no longer have knowledge of themselves available in the traditional forms of representation' (Habermas, 1987b, p. 359). Habermas appears to be evolving a position that is breaking the connection between the Enlightenment and modernity, with modernity now being carried forward by social actors. Modern forms of communication make possible, he argues, a highly differentiated network of public spheres:

> Within these public spheres, processes of opinion and consensus formation, which depend upon diffusion and mutual interpenetration no matter how specialized they are, get institutionalized. The boundaries are porous; each public sphere is open to other public spheres. To their discursive structures they owe a universalist tendency that is hardly concealed. All partial public spheres point to a comprehensive public sphere in which society as a whole fashions a knowledge of itself. The European Enlightenment elaborated this experience and took it up into its programmatic formulas. (Habermas, 1987b, p. 360)

In this modified position, modernity is now being equated with a reflective consciousness, which Habermas believes actually exists in contemporary society. Autonomous public spheres draw their strength from the communicative structures of the life-world. Though he concludes his book on an ambivalent note, which appears to tie modernity once again to the project of the European Enlightenment, it is clear that we now have the basis of a new model of modernity. In his later work (Habermas, 1996, 1998a) we find an even firmer basis for a new conception of modernity rooted in public discourse. This points to the abandonment of a model of historical completion. The crucial question concerning the location of reflexivity is stated in new terms. In Habermas's earlier model, it would appear that reflexivity was located outside the life-world, in professional discourses such as those of science and art. This would have been in line with his adherence to the Enlightenment model of the public sphere, a realm cut off from the private. But it is now clear that the public and the private cannot be cut off from each other in this way, for much of public discourse is pervaded by issues formally relegated to the depoliticized private spheres. In particular, identity is not confined to the private but is part of the public, as is illustrated by the importance of collective identity in new social movements. Since the 1990s Habermas has been moving towards a position that relocates reflexivity in those parts of everyday life which still preserve some degree of autonomy:

> Autonomous public spheres can draw their strength only from the resources of largely rationalized lifeworlds. This holds true especially for culture, that is to say, for science's and philosophy's potential for interpretations of self and world, for the enlightenment potential of strictly universalistic legal and moral representations, and, not last, for the radical experiential contents of aesthetic modernity. (Habermas, 1987b, p. 365)

In an address to the Spanish Parliament in 1984, Habermas (1989c, p. 54) described the current situation in terms of a 'New Obscurity': 'the New Obscurity is part of a situation in which a welfare state program that continues to be nourished by a utopia of social labor is losing its power to project future possibilities for a collectively better and less endangered way of life'. In late modernity there is a loss of certainty as a result of the declining power of political ideology, in particular the social democratic ideology of the welfare state. This argument fits comfortably with the thesis of the colonization of the life-world but ultimately undermines Habermas's concept of modernity, though he does try to reconcile both positions against postmodernity since he wants to hold on to the possibility of utopia. His reply to the postmodernist denial of utopia in general is a weak defence of utopia:

> I consider this thesis of the onset of the postmodern period to be unfounded. Neither the structure of the *Zeitgeist* nor the mode of debating future life

possibilities has changed; utopian energies as such are not withdrawing from historical consciousness. Rather, what has come to an end is a particular utopia that in the past crystallized around the potential of a society based on social labor. (Habermas, 1989c, p. 52)

Why I think this notion of obscurity undermines the idea of modernity is because it puts into question the possibility of completing a historical project. My contention is that with the increasing recognition in Habermas's work of the separation of discourse – as public communication – from communication – as dialogical – the spectre of ever greater obscurity is unavoidable. However, he does not see it in this way since he still adheres to a model of consensus.

In *Between Facts and Norms: Contributions to a Discourse Theory of Law and Democracy* (Habermas, 1996, originally 1992) and *The Inclusion of the Other: Studies in Political Theory* (Habermas, 1998a, originally 1996), the emphasis is on the institutionalization of discourse by means of law and democracy. If the early public sphere rested on exclusion, the new conception emphasizes the 'inclusion of others'. Disagreeing with John Rawls's notion of an 'overlapping consensus' as the only way of resolving conflicts, Habermas puts forward a new conception of public discourse which is far-reaching.[4] Whereas Rawls restricts the 'third perspective for the reasonable' to the existing positions of participants and therefore to an established consensus, Habermas looks to a jointly and publicly reached consensus. 'This standpoint transcends the participant's perspective, occupied by citizens who are constrained by their respective comprehensive doctrines' (Habermas, 1998a, p. 95). The advantage of this approach is that it neither accepts established traditions nor aspires to a perfect design. Speaking from the standpoint of the philosopher, Habermas defends his method of 'reflective equilibrium' as one that must find its perspective already operating in civil society.

A prior standpoint of critical evaluation is necessary in order to identify learning processes as such. Philosophy finds such a standpoint in its aspiration to objectivity and impartiality. But in so far as it draws on procedural properties of practical reason, it can find confirmation in a perspective that it encounters in society itself: by the moral point of view from which modern societies are criticized by their own social movements. Philosophy adopts an affirmative stance only toward the negatory potential embodied in the social tendencies to unstinting self-criticism. (Habermas, 1998a, pp. 97–8)

The third perspective of which Habermas speaks is an arena of contingency, since it is ultimately the perspective of open-ended public debate.

In the present context what merits attention is the implications of discourse theory for the idea of modernity. As already mentioned, the two themes fit very uneasily with each other since there is no necessary connection, other than the claim that Habermas has often reiterated that the reflexivity of discourse is something deeply embedded in European modernity.[5] My contention is that the increasingly abstract theory of discourse that Habermas has been elaborating over the last twenty years can offer a way out of the dead-end of the project of modernity thesis. In fact, the question of multiple modernities and the cosmopolitan challenge occupy much of *The Inclusion of the Other*.[6] Though Habermas has not directly addressed the issue, it may be suggested that the picture of public discourse that is emerging in his work allows us to reconceive modernity in a more open-ended way. In place of historical completion, attention must be focused on the diversity of frameworks in which public discourse unfolds. The features of cultural modernity are not specific to the European Enlightenment, though they may have been more realized there than elsewhere. These characteristics – self-transformative critique, the struggle for autonomy, and reflexivity – are today to be found in many different cultural contexts and cannot be understood as westernization.

With respect to the question of the public sphere, what is suggested now is that there is not just one public sphere but a multiplicity. These new public spheres differ in two further respects from earlier conceptions. The public sphere is located not in the allegedly neutral domain between the private and the state, but in the culturally mediated domain of the social. There is also the suggestion that what is more important is less the spatial question than the discursive. The public is neither an actor nor a particular space but a kind of discourse, public discourse. This would appear to be the conclusion of some of Habermas's arguments concerning the perspective of the public, as a third perspective, in his most recent writings (Habermas, 1998a). However, it is a position that he has not consciously advocated. What makes such a position plausible is that in abandoning the intermediary position he outlined in the *Theory of Communicative Action*, which ultimately rested on a belief in the emancipatory promises of the new social movements, Habermas in *Between Fact and Norms* provided the basis of a theory of discourse which did not rest on an actor or a spatial location, other than a communicatively integrated life-world. Thus the public sphere and cultural modernity, which were originally conceived in the *Structural Transformation of the Public Sphere* as lying outside the life-world in the neutral spaces of civil society and professional spheres, shift onto the worldviews of the new social movements to eventually come to rest in public discourse. In this shift from space to agency to discourse, cultural modernity also loses its connection with Occidental rationalism. The picture we now have is one of discourse disengaging itself from both space and agency. Communication, from the perspective of the public, is an open-ended discourse in which there can be no closure. It is this reluctance to grant a moment of closure, which marks Habermas's work off from that of Karl-Otto Apel (1980), that points to new affinities with postmodernism. Unfortunately, rather than explore these possibilities,

Habermas has too readily written postmodernists off as 'young conservatives', essentially no different from neo-liberals.

In the recent work the distinction between communication and discourse becomes much more pronounced, though this distinction was always central to Habermas's work. Discourse refers to a more critically and reflexively augmented kind of communication than that which is the basis of the life-world, while at the same time being derivative of communicative action. The suggestion appears to be that discourse is embedded in certain kinds of quasi-institutional practices and spaces in society. This situation has opened up a fundamental choice that the inheritors of critical theory will have to make: it is a choice between the possibility of the immanent critique of modernity, a possibility that is offered by the theory of communicative action, which still preserves a link with the last vestiges of revolutionary praxis and an essentially social form of integration that is capable of resisting the institutionalized form of system integration; and a position that has moved beyond the promises of immanent critique, which is abandoned in favour of a new politics of institutional mediation in which the social and the institutional are not hopelessly pitted against each other. This is a choice between a view of democracy as essentially anti-institutional and one that sees new institutional possibilities for a discursively constituted democracy. It is inevitable that the second position entails a weakening of the culture of critique. This choice is not unrelated to the two available options that have replaced the false divide between modernity and postmodernity, namely a view of modernity as one of the historical completion of the European Enlightenment project, on the one side, and one that sees modernity in terms of multiple logics of development.

It would appear that it is the second position which is becoming more influential, not least because it is able to address the relatively new question of globalization and the need that this gives rise to for a transnational civil society.[7] Democracy may have arisen in the context of the nation-state but with the growing importance of transnational processes, of which European integration is a particularly significant development, we have to rethink the whole question of democratic legitimation and the public sphere. It is evident that a purely oppositional model will be inadequate to this task, which must address the question of institutionalization. What I think this all points to is a model of discourse which, in cutting across life-world and system, is reproduced in public communication. Far from being communication free from domination, public communication is located in the very heart of conflict. Whereas Habermas tends to presuppose a relatively intact life-world based upon social integration through communication, I am arguing for a conception of the social as public communication. In the case of the transnational we must certainly abandon any notion of social integration, since there is not a global public sphere which is essentially

social in character (Delanty, 2000c). Thus contemporary society is characterized by a profound loss of any sense of unity. Habermas's work opens
up the possibility of seeing this loss of unity in positive terms as
the space in which public communication unfolds. While he retains the
possibility of unity – as a discursively achieved consensus – there is the
implication in his work that this may be impossible as a final event, for
the nature of discourse is its radical openess. It is in this that his
discourse social theory comes closest to the postmodern thesis of the end
of all narratives. In the context of an emerging global world in which
many voices surface, the fragmentation of the social and the growing
influence of communitarian politics of identity, we can no longer speak
of consensus as the practical outcome of discourse, for it is frequently the
case that it is precisely the preservation of difference that many of these
conflicts are about. Moreover, in so far as the category of the social is
being displaced by public communication, this is frequently in the context
of the fragmentation of the social, and as a result the Habermasian
presupposition of an essentially shared and communicatively integrated
life-world cannot be taken for granted. What we are in fact left with are
free-floating discourses that are not necessarily attached to concrete
forms of life. Thus one of the challenges is to link discourse to the spaces
of everyday life. To explore this I look at the work of Lefebvre and Heller,
authors who have made central to social theory the question of the everyday, a theme which is centrally linked to the confluence of modernity and
postmodernity.

Lefebvre and Heller on Everyday Life

In an early work, *Introduction to Modernity* (1995), Henri Lefebvre outlined the basis of a suggestive theory of modernity.[8] His central insight
has a direct bearing on the theme of this chapter concerning the question
of contingency and the central impulse of modernity: 'Would not the
essential characteristic of modernity be the *aleatory* which is invading
every area and penetrating consciousness in the form of questioning?'
(Lefebvre, 1995, originally published in 1962, p. 202). In this work,
Lefebvre brings a strong Marxist dimension to bear on the experience of
contingency: 'modernity – our era – brings the aleatory into the very
concept of socialism', he argues, linking chance and necessity. One of the
features of modernity is that it entails the growing consciousness of
the aleatory, which may be seen in terms of contingency. The particular
kind of critical sociology he practised was one that took the category of
the 'everyday' to be one of the central areas in which modernity is
manifest. He goes beyond Marx's attempt to understand the modern
world politically as he does Baudelaire's attempt to understand the
world aesthetically. 'Modernity is best characterized not as an already
established 'structure', nor as something which clearly has the capacity

to become structured and coherent, but rather as a fruitless attempt to achieve structure and coherence' (Lefebvre, 1995, p. 187). Rejecting the equation of modernity with culture, as in modernism, Lefebvre argues for a definition of modernity as the experience of contradictions. The suggestion is that in the everyday, social contradictions are experienced. 'Surely what is new and genuinely modern is the contradiction between individual loneliness and the bringing together of crowds or masses in gigantic cities, in massive business companies, in vast offices, in armies, in political parties' (Lefebvre, 1995, p. 189). Lefebvre's vision of modernity is one that sees fragmentation, or atomization, as the mechanism by which society becomes socialized in, to use one of his most famous concepts, 'the bureaucratic society of controlled consumption' (Lefebvre, 1984b). Despite this apparently pessimistic view of modernity, it is important to add that he did see modernity as the site of a tension, the working out of its contradictions. His concern with the 'everyday', a concept that in many ways bears the influence of Heidegger, who greatly inspired him, led Lefebvre to explore the idea of space, and in particular urban space (Lefebvre, 1991, 1996). His writings are dominated by the search for an alternative spatial imaginary to the dominant frameworks of space. The space of the everyday, rather than that of the workplace, is the subject of his writing, as was the case with other leading representatives of Western Marxism (Marcuse, the Frankfurt School, Gramsci: see Soja, 1996, Chap. 1). In looking to the urban rather than the industrial, or the ecomonic more generally, Lefebvre offered a fundamental challenge to Marxism since, in effect, he was proposing the priority of space over time. Space is a medium of everyday life but it is also productive in that it shapes social relations. With this shift from time to space, historicity breaks from any relationship with historicism and the social is accordingly open up to new interpretations. With Lefebvre we have the first suggestion that space can be conceived as a discursive construction, an idea that is fully developed in his major work *The Production of Space* (Lefebvre, 1991, originally 1974), which shifts the focus from the production of things to the production of space. In this shift the question of the everyday becomes paramount, challenging the centrality of economy and state as the site for the social struggles of modernity.

As is apparent from many recent writings, of which the best example might be Edward Soja's *ThirdSpace* (1996), which is very much indebted to Lefebvre, the idea of space has become a central dimension to contemporary society. Rejecting the two dominant kinds of space, material space, which is something that can be mapped and instrumentally regulated, and mental space, which reduced space to representations, Soja argues for a third space, the space of the social. In order to take further this connection within Western Marxism between the category of the everyday and modernity I will discuss the work of Agnes Heller.

In an early work, too, Agnes Heller (1984) made the concept of everyday life central to Western Marxism. Originally published in Hungarian in 1970, *Everyday Life* ranks with Lefebvre's work as one of the most important contributions to a phenomenology of everyday life. With its origins in Heidegger, the everyday was an anti-historicist concept, and one opposed to all kinds of dialectical critique. In the particular rendering of the concept in the Marxism of Lefebvre and Heller, a pronounced anti-Heideggerianism comes into play. The category of everyday life loses its association with the Heideggerian distaste for modernity and becomes bound up with notions of self-transformative critique, the dimension of 'being-with-others' and the derogatory category of 'the they'. The obvious phenomenological dimension to it also differs from Schütz's notion of the everyday as the life-world in that it embodies a far greater range of perspectives, including theoretical and critical reflection, as well as the incorporation of difference. But, as she pointed out in the 1984 preface to the English edition, she later abandoned the self-conscious evolutionist philosophy of history that so evidently lay behind that work (Heller, 1984).

The significance of the idea of everyday life grew in Heller's writings, to eventually be seen as the basis of modernity, for 'in modernity the human condition resides in everyday life' (Heller, 1990, p. 47). In this section I am principally concerned with her book *Can Modernity Survive?* (Heller, 1990), and in particular with the pivotal essay in it, 'Can Everyday Life be Endangered?' After outlining some of the central issues in this concerning modernity and everyday life, I will then comment on her conception of postmodernity, as outlined in this work and in others, such as *The Postmodern Political Condition*, co-authored with Ferenc Feher (Heller and Feher, 1988).

Heller's social theory of modernity is based on a complex view of modernity as a series of logics of development such as democracy, capitalism and industrialism. However, more basic is the structure of objectivations: objectivation in itself, objectivation for itself and objectivation in and for itself. These Hegelian terms, which are associated with the Hegelian Marxism of Georg Lukács, refer respectively to the domain of primary socialization in everyday life, which is pre-reflective and pluralistic, the sphere of reflective meaning, which offers something like a grasp of universality and a perspective beyond the immediacy of the everyday, and the sphere of social and economic institutions. Essentially, Heller sees the wider struggles and conflicts in modernity taking place alongside the struggles between these three domains of 'objectivations', a term which is not to be confused with objectivity, for it carries with it the connotation that 'objective' is 'manifested, re-cast, re-enacted upon by subjects, that is human beings, "the adult generation" whose living experiences have already been crystallized in everything "objective" ' (Heller, 1990, p. 49; subsequent references in this section are to this work, unless otherwise stated). Her sense of objectivations can be understood in the sense of human creativity, which entails an attitude and relation to an object, but is not dominated by the object. As she puts in another essay in her book, modernity is very much bound up with the hermeneutic experience of intersubjectivity, entailing a transformation of both Self and Other. However, modernity is not reducible to the structure of objectivations which is an underlying paradigm.

It is helpful to put this in the context of Habermas's theory, which Heller criticizes, while evidently borrowing from it. Like Habermas, she stresses the sphere of socio-cultural integration which is specific to the life-world. This more or less corresponds to what she calls objectivation in itself. It refers to pre-reflective action and the acquisition of language and the learning of the rules of communication; it is the primary sphere of socialization and learning to be with others. In this sphere meanings are acquired, and what is to be stressed here is the plurality of meanings. This is in contrast to the heightened order of the objectivation for itself, which can be compared to Habermas's notion of discourse, as an intensified kind of communicative action. In this sphere, what comes into play is not the plurality of meanings but the singularity of meaning, which cannot be generated in the everyday, which is contextually bound. This sphere requires a sense of 'human wholeness', though it is not incompatible with the possibility of multiple cultural objectivations. Now, like Habermas, for whom there is a creative tension between communication and discourse, for Heller there is also a tension between these two spheres. The first can exist without the second, but the second cannot exist without the first. But both Habermas and Heller recognize the existence of a third domain, the sphere of social and economic institutions. In Heller's terms this is objectivation in and for itself. This is not essential to the human condition, since the other two spheres can exist without it, for the second, the sphere of reflexivity and universality, can never become totally institutionalized and the first sphere, the everyday, is pre-institutional. However, 'the institutional sphere shapes the other two without ever being able to assimilate them' (p. 53). Like Habermas and the thesis of the colonization of the life-world, Heller asks the question of the destruction of the everyday by the institutional, a destruction that would also have consequences for the possibility of objectivation for itself: 'We may thus raise the question as to what would happen if the fundamental sphere of objectivation ceased to exist as a result of some systematic development and it were instead replaced by other objectivations' (p. 51).

The existence and struggle between these three spheres defines the centrality of the problematic of modernity, according to Heller. Her focus is slightly different from Habermas's: instead of fearing the destruction of discourse, her concern is with the endangering of everyday life, the sphere of objectivation in itself. The sphere of objectivation for itself has a secondary status in her theory and she does not think that everyday life has been colonized in the way Habermas describes it. In general, she wants to read everyday life as a domain of both threats and emancipatory promises. She contends, 'without everyday socialization of a certain kind, without at least the preserved vestiges of the human person as a whole, the human condition would inevitably collapse. The model of complete institutionalization seems to be the model of chaos, for a total manipulative order is chaos.' The question thus becomes: 'Under what condition then can the sphere of "objectivation in itself" prevail and remain the same socializing factor in everyday life, in life pure and simple?' (pp. 57–8). The problem is that in modernity the sphere of objectivation in itself is no longer the most important structuring level in society. One of the features of modernity is ever-increasing contingency. 'Contingency is a historical category inherent in modern contingency' (p. 54). Its significance is due to people having access to the other two dimensions, the reflexive sphere of objectivation for itself and the institutional sphere, and as a result they are not confined to the domain of primary socialization. 'In modern everyday life, men and women have direct access to the sphere of "objectivation for itself". They therefore do not need to subscribe to the meaning as it had been filtered through the primary objectivation' (p. 59). But Heller does not see this as a process having as many dangers as possibilities, since none of the three spheres actually develop in a mutually complementary manner. There is always the danger that the institutional will become omnipotent and will devour the other spheres. Heller sees the human condition residing in everyday life, the primary domain of objectivation in itself. 'If this objectivation withers, the human condition vanishes along with it' (p. 60). The institutional sphere forces individuals to be specialized, but this can be at the price of the loss of meaning, since 'the institutional sphere has the ability to learn, but it does not have the ability to create meaning' (p. 59). The challenge, as she sees it, is to preserve the fragile balance between the three spheres and to resist the 'cancerous growth' of anything at the expense of the other. However, in her later writings she has given more importance to 'objectivation for itself'. Culture thus becomes a bulwark against capitalism and identity politics.

This position is indeed a useful corrective to the Habermasian pre-occupation with the sphere of discourse – Heller's objectivation for itself – since this cannot function unless it preserves a relation not only with institutional contexts but also, more importantly, with everyday life. To be sure, this is something that Habermas recognizes – arguing increasingly for the contextualization of discourse in communication and its institutionalization in legal structures – but we do not get the same sense of the need for a balancing of these spheres. This has been a theme in all Heller's writings, and is particularly well illustrated in her A Theory of History (1982). In this work a vision of modernity was presented which stressed multiple logics of development, which are essentially contradictory, incomplete and possibly incompletable. She distinguished between two logics of civil society – capitalism and democracy – and technological industrial development (Heller, 1982, p. 284). Civil society entails the universalization of the market, that is, capitalism (private property, inequality and domination), but at the same time it establishes a certain degree of freedom in the form of negative liberty, as is manifest in human rights and the rights of citizenship, and more generally democracy, equalization and the decentralization of power. We can thus distinguish between capitalism and democracy as the two central logics of civil society. Existing alongside these contradictory logics lies the third logic of development, the development of industralism: the limitation of the market through the centralization of the allocation of resources by the state. In this instance, the state tries to provide a solution to the problems presented by the conflict between capitalism and democracy. Socialism is an expression of a fully devoloped solution of this, but in the West capitalism has had the upper hand. In Heller's later work (1990, p. 122) this three-fold conception of modernity is reiterated. However, the status of this theory of history and its relation to everyday life is at best unclear, despite the concern in *A Theory of History* with everyday historical consciousness.[9] On the one side, modernity is a framework of three logics of development – capitalism, democracy and industralism – and on the other side it is underpinned by a conflict between three kinds of objectivation – objectivation in itself, objectivation for itself and objectivation in and for itself. In the first case, the problem appears to be a concern with the theory of justice and the autonomy of civil society, while in the second case the concern is with the preservation of everyday life. It is evident that in the first model, which shows signs of waning, there is a faith in the possibilities of immanent critique and a belief that the developmental logics of modernity can offer hope for the future. This ambivalence on the question of what can be redeemed from modernity is also present, as we have seen, in Habermas. Heller, too, seems to waver between a belief in the logics of modernity offering something emancipatory and an increasing recognition that this might not be possible.[10] Now the question concerns the very survival not just of modernity but of everyday life. A note of pessimism can be detected with the older categories:

> If one gives a balanced view about our world's possibilities, one has to give voice to a degree of scepticism about the cultural potentials of the future. In all probability, no cultural surplus will be produced, only as much cultural energies will be generated that are sufficient for the spiritual well-being, or perhaps for the mere survival, of the modern world. (Heller, 1992, pp. 8–9)

Nowhere is this ambivalence with modernity more clear than in the essay 'The Concept of the Political Revisited' (in Heller, 1990). Here there is an acute tension between a view of modernity as entailing the three-fold logics of development and, on the other side, a need to go beyond these logics in the articulation of a new vision of the political. Heller defines the concept of the political in the modern world as the 'concretization of the universal value of freedom in the public domain' (p. 125). The suggestion appears to be that it is the political – which is a dynamic movement as well as a new kind of historical consciousness –

that links politics (that is, the sphere of the state) with everyday life, but this concept of the political does not appear to draw its normative impulse from modernity. Initially Heller held that one logic – democracy – could prevail but has more recently moved to the view that all that can be achieved is a balance between the logics.

In *A Theory of History* Heller discussed at length the notion of a new historical consciousness, but increasingly there is an embracing of post-modernity to describe this consciousness, a turn that undoubtedly has had a lot to do with the collapse of communism as a viable alternative to capitalism and the emergence of cultural pluralism which can no longer be subsumed under any particular narrative. Postmodernity for Heller is definitely not an epoch, but a way of historical thinking, and a politically resigned one at that: 'Postmodern consciousness turns towards itself. It is from our ways of life that the chances for the survival of modernity can be deciphered' (p. 6). For postmodern, she means nothing more than 'contemporary discourse'. One of the chief characteristics of this is its dialogical character, since what has been irredeemably lost is monological discourses: 'We all live under the spell of hermeneutics: hermeneutics and the awareness of intersubjectivity overdetermine one another' (p. 6). In her characterization, modernity, in its current phase of postmodern historical consciousness, is highly self-reflexive in that it is a conscious-ness that is constantly asking questions about itself. Postmodernity is the 'consummation of modernity' (p. 169). In *The Postmodern Political Condition*, Heller and Feher (1988) portray postmodernity as a movement within modernity and one which reaches out beyond its European origins. Modernity was an essentially European movement, and post-modernity, while having a European origin, is post-European. European culture has always been the 'hermeneutical culture' *par excellence*, they argue, but is now becoming a museum, having been superseded by the culture of postmodernism: 'the nineteenth century was in the main the century of European culture. Modernity alias the West alias Europe was then self-confident. What can be termed "European culture" thus flour-ished mainly during the period from the Napoleonic wars to the out-break of World War One' (Heller and Feher, 1988, p. 149). The decline of European modernity came with the realization that European modernity had also engendered barbarism. Their cautious embracing of post-modernism is consistent with the growing pessimism in Heller's thought concerning the immanent logics of development of modernity, which has now abandoned its European framework. As argued above, her early work emphasizes the redemptive possibilities of modernity. But what happens when modernity enters its postmodern phase? 'Redemptive politics of any kind are incompatible with the postmodern political condition' (Heller and Feher, 1988, p. 4). Instead of a redemptive or even an immanent critique of modernity, postmodernity opens up the political to new kinds of possibility. Heller and Feher cite as an example of the postmodern political condition Adorno's famous term *minima moralia*.

Moral discourse and democratic politics, which is considerably aided by cultural pluralization, one of the chief features of postmodernism, are considerably opened up in a society which is less homogeneous and which has made 'dissatisfaction' central to its very cultural self-understanding. The 'dissatisfied society is characterized by the expansion of both wants and needs' (Heller and Feher, 1988, p. 23). In a more recent work, *Biopolitics*, Feher and Heller (1994) argue that the existing forms of social agency, in particular many of the new social movements, which in their view are characterized by a pervasive concern with biopolitics, are not capable of providing solutions to the challenges of contemporary society. This is because this kind of politics gives priority to the value of life over that of freedom, or a more dialogical politics. This position belies the view that modernity is rapidly exhausting itself of its ability to generate cultural and political alternatives. The idea of a dialogical politics suggests something akin to the Habermasian notion of discursive democracy, but we are not given a detailed sense of exactly what it entails. It is evident, however, that dialogical politics is located in the spaces that are opened by postmodern developments, in particular cultural pluralization. But the problem is that our concept of politics still derives from an earlier period and we are now faced with the growing incommensurability of cultural innovation and the political imagination. Culture is embracing postmodernity, while politics is still within the horizon of modernity.

Castoriadis and Touraine on Modernity and Postmodernity

In the final section of this chapter we look at the work of two major French theorists, Alain Touraine and Cornelius Castoriadis. On the surface it would appear that they are defenders of modernity, since they are both very resistant to postmodernism. However, a reading of their work will reveal a deeper ambivalence concerning modernity, and some of their central insights point to a surmounting of both modernity and postmodernity. Let us first take Castoriadis.

In his major work *The Imaginary Institution of Society* (1987, originally 1975), Castoriadis portrays modernity as a conflict between two kinds of imaginary significations: the project of autonomy and the project of rational mastery (see also Castoriadis, 1991, 1993a). On the one side is the radical imaginary of autonomy and on the other the project that is represented by capitalism. For Castoriadis, these two projects can be related to the centrality of the imaginary. While the unity of society lies in its institutional structures, there is a more elemental unity in its imaginary constructions, which constitute, ultimately, the possibility of a model of social integration. All societies possess an imaginary which is related to, but is more than, the symbolic. The imaginary has to use the symbolic in order to express itself, and Castoriadis postulates a 'radical imaginary' as the common root of the actual imaginary and the symbolic (Castoriadis, 1987, p. 127). Institutions, he argues, cannot be understood just as symbolic networks.

> Institutions do form a symbolic network but this network, by definition, refers to something other than symbolism. Every purely symbolical interpretation of institutions immediately opens the following questions: why *this* system of symbols and not another? What are the *meanings* conveyed by the symbols, the system of signifieds to which the system of signifiers refers? Why and how do the symbolic networks become autonomous? (Castoriadis, 1987, p. 136)

For Castoriadis, every society must answer some very basic questions, such as what is it, what are its goals, what does it lack. The role of imaginary significations is to provide an answer to these questions concerning the identity of a society and the constitution of its cultural model. The modern world has come to rest upon two imaginaries: the imaginary of rational and technical control and the imaginary of autonomy. Castoriadis defends the radical imaginary of autonomy, by which he means the 'self-institution' of society, the creative and self-questioning dimension which is integral to modernity.

It is this self-questioning and transformative dimension, which is immanent in the imaginary of modernity, that is lost in postmodernity, according to Castoriadis. Modernity for him consists of a field of tensions (Arnason, 1989). It is not merely driven by disciplinary power but is inseparable from the radicality of the creative imagination and the ideal of an autonomous society. Castoriadis (1993b) sees postmodernity as a 'retreat from autonomy'. It is unable to conceive of itself as positive, hence it must be 'post-something'. In contrast to the idea of post-industrial, which does correspond to something in reality – a society that is no longer based on production to one based on consumption and leisure – postmodernity, in his view, is an empty category. The characterization 'modern' makes sense only in relation to the past, yet its imaginary signification is one of openness to the future: the Ancients came before us; but we cannot name those who will come after us. Castoriadis is unhappy with those – from Kant through Hegel to Habermas – who reduce modernity to ideas, or see it in terms of the consciousness of the historicity of an epoch. These approaches neglect the centrality of real struggles and conflicts, and it is his thesis that the

> individuality of a period is to be found in the specificity of the imaginary significations created by and dominating it, and that, without neglecting the fantastically rich and polyphonic complexity of the historical universe unfolding in Western Europe from the twelfth century onwards, the most appropriate way to grasp its specificity is to relate it to the signification and project of (social and individual) autonomy. (Castoriadis, 1993b, p. 36)

In this perspective, three periods may be distinguished: 'the emergence of the West', the 'critical modern period' and the 'postmodern retreat into conformism'.

The first is the emergence and constitution of the West from the twelfth to the eighteenth century, with the growth of cities, demands for political and intellectual autonomy and reinterpretation of tradition. With the emergence of what might be called the classical episteme of the seventeenth century an uneasy balance had been reached between a reformed traditional order and modernity. A second period emerges in the eighteenth century and continues until the second half of the twentieth century. In this period the central conflict between capitalism and the project of autonomy becomes attenuated, with the Enlightenment severing the link with theology and the older authorities. But in this period, too, capitalism becomes all-powerful and is even able to articulate a powerful new imaginary, the unlimited expansion of rational mastery. This imaginary eventually shifts from capitalism itself to the bureaucratic and technical organization of all of life. According to Castoriadis, this imaginary signification and the project of autonomy are mutually entangled and their struggle defines the modern period.

> Despite these mutual contaminations, the essential character of this epoch is the opposition and the tension between the two core significations: individual and social autonomy, on the one hand, and unlimited expansion of 'rational mastery,' on the other. The real expression of this tension is the development and the persistence of social, political, and ideological conflict. (Castoriadis, 1993b, p. 39)

We have now entered the third period, the postmodern phase. The two world wars, the collapse of the workers' movement, the decline of the idea of progress, have all paved the way for a new epoch in which ideological strife has waned. Castoriadis sees in this the loss of the project of autonomy. The growing shift to privatization, depoliticization and individualism all point to the complete atrophy of the political imagination. This is all in contrast to the ideological restlessness of the modern period and its creative outbursts in the arts and culture. If the modern period in the field of art entailed the self-conscious pursuit of new forms, 'this pursuit has now been abandoned. Eclecticism and the recombining and reprocessing of the achievements of the past have now gained pride of program' (Castoriadis, 1993b, p. 41). Thus collage becomes the central principle of all art in the period of the postmodern. Castoriadis's central objection to the postmodernist position is that it is an abandonment of the commitment to critique, which was central to modernity. For this reason the present period is best defined as 'the general retreat into conformism'. The really crucial point for him is that the hitherto embodiments of the project of autonomy – Marxist-Leninist socialism and the liberal republic – have collapsed but that project can be taken up in different ways. Postmodernism clearly is not one such way since it understands itself as a rejection of autonomy, be it the autonomy of knowledge, of the self, or of culture.

Castoriadis's work was an expression partly of a search for a principle of unity that could be capable of overcoming the fundamental contradiction of modernity between, on the one side, the imaginary of mastery and the radical imaginary of autonomy and, on the other, a great faith in the redeeming power of the radical imaginary to assert itself against the rationalizing imaginary of capitalism and bureaucratic control. Castoriadis, who died in 1997, never systematized his thought.[11] There is something unsatisfactory about his critique of postmodernism, which cannot be dismissed as a rejection of autonomy and a retreat into conformism. The project of autonomy is challenged not merely by the rational imaginary of mastery, represented by capitalism and bureaucracy, but by a whole variety of fragmentations, such as authoritarian communitarianism. In this in this context that we can briefly consider the work of Alain Touraine.

In his *Critique of Modernity* (1995, originally 1992), Touraine outlines a far-reaching theory of modernity and a critical statement on postmodernity.[12] This work marks a departure from his earlier work, which was based on a firm conviction in the role of social movements as the agents of historicity. Since the 1990s, he has turned away from a social movement perspective – that is, a perspective that places historicity in the hands of a central social actor – to a position which even rejects the idea of the social itself. For Touraine today what is more important is the need for a search for a principle of unity, for contemporary society is presented everywhere with the spectre of fragmentation. Previously the social actor was able to provide a principle of unity capable of linking the Reason and the Subject. These two dimensions can be taken to be similar to Castoriadis's two imaginaries, mastery and autonomy, or Habermas's opposition of an instrumental reason emanating from the system and a communicative reason deriving from the life-world. The project of subjectivation is as old as the Reformation and Enlightenment, and possibly is even more deeply rooted in the culture of modernity than is rationalization, in so far as the latter is an expression of instrumentalization. Unlike Castoriadis, and differing, too, from Habermas in his pre–1990s writings, Touraine sees modernity as holding out the promise of a dialogue between these two principles. It is his view that neither is viable without the other, a society cannot be based primarily on identity but nor can it be based purely on instrumental control. The challenge is to unify both. The problem today, as he sees it, is that the hope for a principle of unity is very much diminished. Yet modernity holds out a promise betrayed by postmodernity: 'The idea of modernity does not derive its strength from its positive utopia – the construction of a rational world – but from its critical function' (Touraine, 1995, p. 31; all subsequent references in this section will be to this text, unless otherwise stated). But this critical thrust increasingly has lost its momentum, largely as a result

of three historical critiques, to which we can now add the postmodern
critique. The first is the exhaustion of the bourgeois liberation movement, the second the loss of meaning in the culture of technology and
instrumental action, the third the rejection of the objectives of modernity
(p. 94). Touraine identifies four main forces which have dominated
modernity – sexuality, commodity consumption, the company and the
nation – and which correspond to the spheres of personality, culture,
economics and politics. The problem today is that these domains have
become so fragmented that there is no longer a principle of unity. For
instance, the personal order has become divorced from the collective
order. Production and consumption have lost any relationship to the
personal and the collective. 'The cultural and social field in which we
have been living since the end of the eighteenth century has no unity: it
constitutes not a new stage of modernity, but its decay' (pp. 98–9). In this
sense, he agrees the current situation can be termed 'postmodern' in so
far as this is a reminder that the twentieth century has been a century
not of progress but of crisis (p. 99). Touraine's thesis is that with the
fragmentation of modernity into four domains, disengaged from each
other, the only unity that exists is that provided by instrumental rationality. If modernity is to have any meaning it is in terms of a principle of
unity. Where can this come from? Touraine postulates the idea of the
Subject, or subjectivation, a counterforce to the rule of Reason, but he is
adamant that the Subject cannot itself unify the shattered fragments of
modernity: 'Only a combination of subject and reason can perform that
task' (p. 218). The Subject of which he speaks makes sense only if we take
seriously the critiques of Nietzsche and Freud, for there can be no going
back to the Enlightenment model of the self-contained and transparent
subject. For Touraine modernity is about the rise, eclipse and return of
the Subject. But modernity cannot be reduced to the Subject, for it is also
an expression of Reason.
    Touraine sees postmodernity as a false solution to this problem.
Postmodernism, he argues, 'takes to extremes the destruction of the
modernist representation of the world. It rejects the functional differentiation between domains of social life – art, the economy, politics – and
its corollary, namely the ability of every domain to make use of instrumental reason' (p. 190). Postmodernism is about eliminating differences
between the different orders of society, and as a result it is, as Fredric
Jameson (1990) has also argued, a culture of pastiche since it rejects any
principle of unity. Touraine is hostile to it because it rejects the principles
of both Reason and the Subject, which he believes must be retained as
the central concepts of a modernity that may be exhausted but one that is
still capable of providing a new cultural model:

Postmodernism marks the completion of the task begun by Nietzsche: the
destruction of the reign of technique and instrumental rationality. Experience
and language replace projects and values. Neither collective action nor the

meaning of history have any existence. Postmodernism reveals that contemporary hyper-industrialization does not lead to the formation of a hyper-industrial society; on the contrary, it leads to a divorce between the cultural world and the technical world. And it thus destroys the idea on which sociology has, until now, been based: the interdependence of the 'modern' economy, 'modern' politics and 'modern' culture. (p. 191)

In sum, the label 'postmodern' can be resisted in so far as contemporary societies still have a capacity to assert their historicity in the form of a search for a new principle of unity.

What Touraine in fact fears more than postmodernism, it must be pointed out, is the radical and authoritarian communitarian strand in contemporary society: 'A social totalitarianism is giving way to a cultural totalitarianism' (p. 311). There is even the suggestion that the politics of the 'next century will be dominated by the national question, just as the nineteenth century was dominated by the social question' (p. 322). This is particularly apparent from Touraine's more recent writings, which concern the widespread appeal to community (Touraine, 1997, 1998). The only solution to these problems is a kind of democracy rooted in an active citizenship which alone is capable of achieving some degree of integration. That is why Touraine resists the idea of 'society' or 'the social', since under the conditions of the fragmentation of modernity there is no unity other than what is achieved by the democratic form of communication.

> Society can no longer be defined as a set of institutions, or as an effect of a sovereign will. It is the creation of neither history nor the Prince. It is a field of conflicts, negotiations and mediations between rationalization and subjectivation, and they are the complementary and contradictory faces of modernity. (p. 358; see also Touraine, 1998b)

As Touraine says, the main aim of his book is to define the cultural field, and especially the forms of social thought that are at stake in current struggles (p. 361). While the nineteenth century was dominated by the economy, the twentieth century by politics and resistance to totalitarianism, it may be suggested that the twenty-first century will be dominated by the question of culture. Therefore it is important to be able to clarify the terms of this debate, and Touraine believes the postmodernist position, while in many ways correctly reflecting the crisis of modernity, is inadequate as an alternative. While Touraine's conclusion that modernity involves an endless dialogue between Reason and the Subject is an important corrective to the postmodernist surrendering to fragmentation, he ultimately fails to provide a convincing alternative himself. The notion of the Subject wavers between a sense of social agency which might be tied to social movements, on the one side, and a substitute for the fallen idea of the social, on the other. One detects a lingering belief in a social actor who will unify the scattered fragments of modernity. Since it never becomes clear who this will be, the rejection of the social is too abrupt.

Conclusion: Discursive Space

The theories of modernity looked at here share a common concern with rescuing modernity from the tendentially antimodernist tendencies of the theorists considered in earlier chapters. As we have seen in this chapter, the focus for many of those who retain a basic faith in the promise of modernity is the arrival of the postmodern critique. Even those who are particularly hostile to postmodernism – Habermas, Castoriadis, Touraine – accept that much of the postmodernist critique of modernity may be valid and that we are living in a society which in some respects can be said to be postmodern. However, there is widespread recognition that the postmodern political alternative is less than adequate. Thus, the framework of modernity is questionable, but in the absence of an alternative it is the best option. This would be appear to be the position that Habermas, Heller, Castoriadis and Touraine share.

Running through these accounts of the uncertain encounter of modernity with postmodernity is a recognition that the transformation of modern society might be understood in terms of a new form of social integration. The older forms of social integration presupposed, variously, a dominant institution or structure, with more radical ones asserting the priority of a social actor. The work of the theorists discussed in this chapter reflects a sense of the exhaustion of this model. A tentative conclusion might be that it is communication that is now the mechanism by which society reproduces itself. Communication has penetrated right into the very practice of democracy today, as is reflected in the theories of Habermas and Touraine. All domains of society are pervaded by communicative processes and there are ever-expanding sites of discursive space. This is something that is central to the theories of Habermas and Lefebvre. We do, however, need a stronger sense of how discursive space and social space are linked. Here I am reminded of an idea of Claude Lefort's that in modern society democracy can be defined as an empty space for the very reason that it is not inhabited by anyone. Democracy is the radically open space of discourse (Lefort, 1988, p. 17).[13]

I began this chapter by commenting on the centrality of contingency as a problem in the theory of modernity. Relating this concept to some of the ideas highlighted in the above discussion, a perspective emerges that allows us to see the divide between modernity and postmodernity as a false one, for both discourses are essentially ones that concern the centrality of contingency as it creeps into the growing spaces in society where there is no principle of integration other than that of communication.[14] With the confluence of democracy and communication becoming more and more apparent, a heightened experience of contingency comes to characterize the current situation.

6

POSTMODERNISM AND THE
POSSIBILITY OF COMMUNITY

In this chapter I move closer to a focus on postmodernism, which will be more explicitly discussed in the next chapter.[1] My concern in this chapter is to explore by means of the idea of community how we can begin to bridge the alleged divide of the modern and postmodern. Whereas modernity was allegedly constructed on the destruction of community and postmodernity on the eclipse of the social, which had characterized the age of modernity, we can see how community has in fact become a key concern of some of the more recent postmodernist approaches. Tying community to a notion of citizenship, I shall examine a variety of debates cutting across the modern and the postmodern.

The idea of community is central to a theory of citizenship, for citizenship implies in the most general sense membership of a political community. But the problem is that community has been tied to a particular discourse – the discourse of communitarianism -which reduces citizenship too much to an organic notion of cultural community. In other words, the discourses of citizenship and community, while being mutually bound up with each other, can involve a certain tension. In my view, this tension is likely to increase when it comes to issues such as post-national citizenship, in the sense of citizenship beyond the nation-state. How can the idea of community be made relevant to post-national citizenship? What is community in postmodernity?

A major challenge for citizenship theory is to explore ways in which deterritorialized forms of citizenship can be linked to an appropriate kind of global community (Urry, 2000). While citizenship, like community, has mostly been territorially specific, there is an increasing concern today with post-national citizenship as a response to the limits of nationality, both in the context of human rights and as a response to the problems of migrants, global democracy and European integration (Delanty, 2000c; Held, 1995; Jacobsen, 1997; Soysal, 1994). One of the problems, of course, is giving a deeper, substantive dimension to such kinds of citizenship. Many discussions on post-national citizenship tend to sidestep this question and fail to see that the more citizenship is globalized the more formalized it becomes, losing any connection with participation. This is where the question of community arises since the idea of community gives the deeper level of a substantive dimension to citizenship.

This is so because citizenship is about membership of a political community as much as it is about rights and responsibilities. The idea of membership of a political community suggests the salience of identity and participation (Delanty, 1997b). The question of community, which implies proximity, unity and place, is a complex one and can undermine as much as support citizenship. In general, an understanding of community as the antithesis of society has prevailed. A crucial challenge is to overcome this dualism of community versus society, tradition versus modernity. This is particularly urgent since we are witnessing today the return of community in the context of postmodern political culture. In order to understand the implications of this development we shall have to rethink radically our understanding of community in order to resist the fragmentation of the social.

From a theoretical point of view, I believe Jürgen Habermas's (1994, 1996) critique of communitarianism and his advocation of a post-national citizenship and 'constitutional patriotism' provides an important alternative to communitarian thinking, such as Amitai Etzioni's (1995) approach, while at the same time acknowledging the importance of community. However, Habermas's model needs to be supplemented by a theory of community that appreciates the uniqueness of contemporary developments, which point towards the disembedding and globalization of community around a new cultural 'imaginary' (Castoriadis, 1987). In this context, I shall draw from Michel Maffesoli's (1996a) concept of 'emotional communities' and Jean-Luc Nancy's (1991) theory of the 'inoperative community'. A further theoretical perspective is suggested by Roger Cotterrell's (1995) theory of the legal community and the more postmodern approaches of William Corlett (1993), Giorgio Agamben (1993) and Maurice Blanchot (1988), who argue for a conception of community beyond unity and identity, and Bill Readings's (1996) notion of the 'community of dissensus'. These approaches provide us with a means of seeing how community today can be seen as what Benedict Anderson (1991) terms an 'imagined community' but one which is always self-consciously incomplete.[2]

What is Community?

In sociological theory community has had a long history but one largely associated with a particular ideological worldview, namely a conservative functionalism. Though the author was a German social democrat and admirer of guild socialism, the classic work in the Anglo-American reception of German social theory is Ferdinand Tönnies's *Gemeinschaft und Gesellschaft*, published in 1887 (1963). In this work, community and society are pitted against each other to the detriment of the latter: 'community' signifies the organic and cohesive world of traditional society while 'society' refers to the fragmented world of modernity with its rationalized, intellectualized and individualized structures. Communities are culturally integrated totalities while society is essentially defined by its parts. Tönnies largely regretted the passing of community – the world of the village and the rural community – and the arrival of society – the world of the city – believing that community could supply the individual with greater moral resources. The idea of community thus suggests a strong sense of place, proximity and totality, while society suggests fragmentation, alienation and distance.

This myth of community was also perpetuated by Durkheim, for whom society is essentially a community based on common cultural values. Modernity is defined by the movement from mechanical forms of integration, characterized by ascriptive values and an immediate identi-fication of the individual with the collectivity, to organic forms of integration, which are characterized by contractual relations and require cooperation between groups. Lacking the disenchantment with modern-ity that was central to Tönnies's nostalgia for community as a lost totality, Durkheim nevertheless saw the recovery of a sense of com-munity which could be compatible with the requirements of an indi-vidualized era as the challenge for modern society. In his view society was always oscillating between integration and anomic, mechanical forms of integration, on the one hand, and the more functionalized organic forms of generalized communication, on the other. Durkheim, of course, was no romantic but a postivistically inclined liberal, and had no difficulty in accepting the burden of modernity and its individualized and differentiated social organization, which he saw as potentially liberat-ing. He believed that occupational groups and a democratic political culture could provide a foundation for community as proximity and totality.

Like many of the sociological classics, Durkheim's vision of society was dominated by the transition from tradition to modernity as an epochal movement. While he reconciled himself to society, his vision of a functionalized social order bore the imprint of a fascination with com-munity as an ontological reality and as a symbolic order. Both Spencer and Weber, too, were preoccupied with the advent of modernity and the passing of traditional society. While Weber was more ambivalent than Spencer and Durkheim on the historical process of modernity and did not see many opportunities for the recovery of community, he was also centrally concerned with understanding the transition from traditional society to modernity and his pessimistic vision of modernity did not see much room for community. It may be suggested Weber looked to charisma as an alternative to the loss of community under the conditions of modernity. The penchant for community in sociological discourse was enhanced by the rise of anthropology, which perpetuated the myth of primitive society as being a holistic fusion of culture and society around a symbolic order. The early anthropologists called primitive societies 'cultures', preferring to reserve the word 'society' for their own allegedly superior scientific society. In fact, community has been traditionally understood as precisely the fusion of culture and society – the identification of the cognitive and normative order with social institutions. Primitive societies are supposed to be totalities in which cultural values and social practices are intertwined and can be understood by reference to the category of the symbolic. Communities are supposed to be symbolic orders with a strong sense of group boundaries. This is also underlined by the idea of proximity and a sense of place which characterizes primitive societies. At a time when anthropology and sociology were not differentiated into separate disciplines, sociology – in particular the functionalist tradition – inherited this powerful myth of community as a lost totality rooted in place and proximity. The result was that sociology tended to be distrustful of modernity, which it viewed as having brought about a rupture with totality. It was not only conservative functionalists who adopted this position. The myth of community as a holistic fusion of culture and society was also behind liberal and Marxist interpretations of modernity (Nisbet, 1953, 1967). The Chicago School, too, was very much preoccupied with the idea of a tension between community and society. Their studies on the impact of industrialism and urban modernization on traditional communities greatly contributed to the myth of community. Parsons's (1966, pp. 10–11) functionalism also was guided by the belief that modernity was ultimately regulated by the moral order of what he called the 'societal community'. The search for community in the form of the utopian communist society at the end of history was also central to Marxism. Few philosophies have been more successful in advocating a notion of community than Marxism, which conceived the communist society of the future as a perfect fusion of culture and society.

The myth of community has endured throughout the twentieth century as a counterforce to society. This was particularly prevalent in conservative sociology, which contrasted 'mass society' (which had weak symbolic resources and loose boundaries) and the more cohesive world of community. The vision of a recovery of totality has been a very powerful idea and ideal and has inspired many sociological and philosophical theories, as well as political ideologies (Cohen, 1985). It may be said that the twentieth century has witnessed the triumph of the spirit of community over the spirit of society. The ideologies of modernity – socialism, liberalism, conservatism, nationalism, fascism, anarchism, kibbutz democracy – have all been inspired by the quest for community. Indeed, it may be suggested that the quest for community has been inspired precisely because of the failure of the social. While society has been associated with the negative aspects of modernity – rationalization, individualization, industrialism, disenchantment – community has been more successful in expressing the emotional demands and needs of solidarity, trust and autonomy. These characteristics may be said to be the defining components of community. Community implies: (1) solidarity, in the sense of a feeling of togetherness, a feeling of collectivity and mutual attachments; (2) trust, as opposed to the secrecy and distance that characterized life in the social; and (3) autonomy, in that community involves the recognition of the value of the person as a social being.

In my view this definition of community is more satisfactory than the ideas of totality, proximity and place with which the idea of community has also been associated. Totality suggests too much the fusion of culture and society, proximity too much personal relations, and place imposes too many restrictions on non-geographical communities. Trust, solidarity and autonomy are the most fundamental dimensions to community and are characterized by a certain emotional dimension which can be exploited by authoritarian and populist movements. I shall argue that trust, autonomy and solidarity do not have to be understood from the perspective of the symbolic.

Society, on the other hand, has been defined by reference to structural and institutional processes. The values of solidarity, trust and autonomy have not been central to the definition of the social. This is perhaps why the social has been seen in communitarian-inspired interpretations of modernity as fundamentally untrustworthy, divisive and dehumanizing. The decline and corruption of community into the social has been central to sociological theory in the twentieth century. One of the challenges today is to overcome this dualism. I am not suggesting that community is to be rejected but that the false dichotomy of community and society must be overcome. Community is an important concept for an understanding of society and many of the problems with it derive from a framework of historical time in which the two concepts are located.

In many ways the distinction between society and community parallels the distinction between structure and agency. Community implies a stronger sense of the autonomy of agency while society entails the alienation of agency by objectified and ossified societal structures. Thus the task of radical sociology was to infuse the social with a sense of agency. I shall argue against this distinction between structure and agency, society and community, proposing that the social be reinterpreted from the perspective of community. In this regard it is helpful to recall a point made by Raymond Williams (1976, pp. 65–6): the polarity between society and community was a product of the nineteenth century and overshadowed the Enlightenment polarity of state and civil society. In other words, in the eighteenth century the idea of society as civil society was seen in much the same terms as community is today imagined – as immediate and embodying direct relationships – while the state was seen as the realm of organized relations. Today we are faced with a different situation: the spectre of the return of community as a societal and global imaginary.

The Contemporary Rediscovery of Community

There is much to indicate that there has been a revival in the idea of community. The communitarian debate has been important in the perpetuation of the myth of community. Communitarianism is a diffuse category and can mean many different things, but in general it is associated with a particularly North American obsession with community as an antidote to the liberal emphasis on the individual as a member of civil society (Avineri and de-Shalit, 1992). Communitarians – such as Walzer (1983), Taylor (1989), Sandel (1982) and Selznick (1992) – can be called liberal communitarians since they do not fundamentally disagree with many of the arguments of liberals. They can also be called neo-republicans (or civic republicans) in that their particular position entails a strong emphasis on particulation in public life. The intellectual hero of the communitarians is Aristotle, whose vision of the fabled *polis* is the model of community. In modern times Rousseau and Kant provided the intellectual basis for the Enlightenment's concept of the social contract and the republican order of civil society. Thus for modern neo-republicans the self-legislating republic is essentially a political community, though in some variants, such as Charles Taylor's, there is a strong emphasis on the existence of a prior cultural community. Even in those cases where this is not so pronounced – such as more orthodox neo-republicans – communitarianism does at least presuppose the existence of cultural community. In general, community expresses a moral voice, which is held to be a contrast to liberal theory.

This fascination with community as a moral voice is not specific to communitarian philosophical circles but is also reflected in a certain tradition in sociology and political theory. Works such as those of Amitai Etzioni, Robert Nisbet, Christopher Lasch and Daniel Bell all display the enduring appeal for community as a haven from society. The idea of community has now become part of our social language and is used to describe various kinds of commonalities, from residential communities to work-related communities and from care-related communities to ethnic communities. It is used to refer to community policing, community planning, the international community, and local and national communities.

The aim of this chapter is to assess the importance of community and to ask whether community can be interpreted in a way that can make the concept appropriate to the cultural and social challenges of postmodernity and globalization. What, then, is the problem with community? I believe the myth of community in communitarian discourse is open to many objections. Rather than take up the well-rehearsed liberal critique of communitarianism (Mulhall and Swift, 1996), I wish to take the slightly different route suggested by Habermas (1996) and Frazer and Lacey (1993) in order to arrive at a reassessment of the idea of community. This will entail transcending the liberal–communitarian debate. At this juncture it is important to say that my aim is to rescue the idea of community from the political philosophy of communitarianism. It is for this reason that my position is more Habermasian than liberal, for it is Habermas's aim to transcend both liberalism and communitarianism. In other words, I believe, with Habermas, that the liberal critique of communitarianism is valid, as is the communitarian critique of liberalism, and therefore both are invalid. However, my position differs from Habermas, who does not sufficiently link his discursive alternative to the idea of community. As Gerd Baumann (1991) has demonstrated in his analysis of multi-ethnic communities, I believe the idea of community can accommodate a notion of contestation and must not be anchored in cultural consensus or a symbolic order. This is also evident in the case of movement activists, as Lichterman (1996) demonstrates in his study of community and commitment. In an important article on the idea of community, Craig Calhoun (1983) argues against the identification of community with consensual value systems, claiming that community has been an important dimension to radical popular mobilizations.

Community, then, is important even though interpretations of it may differ. Before outlining my theoretical conception of community below and explaining why I think Habermas's critique is inadequate, more needs to be said about the contemporary salience of community. The revival of community in sociological theory and political philosophy cannot be divorced from the return of community in global political culture. Indeed, it may be that community is becoming the universal ideology of our time and is usurping the idea of the social. The idea of community, after all, is more central to the social movements of the early twenty-first century than is society. The appeal to community was central to Bill Clinton's election campaign of 1992, and Tony Blair's election campaign of 1997 was very much articulated in terms of a neo-republican idea of community. The rhetoric of New Labour favours terms such as 'community' and 'nation' more than 'society'. If liberal individualism was the ideology of the 1980s, community was the ideology of the 1990s. Zygmunt Bauman (1991, p. 246) remarks that postmodernity is also the 'age of community'. While in the older sociological accounts community was associated with the rural communities of the past, it may be the case that community today is the result of the postmodernization of culture (Lash, 1994). The failure to address these issues points to a weakness in communitarian thinking. The identity politics of nationalism, religious revivalism, neofascism, new age travellers and the whole range of media cultures, such as the idea of 'virtual communities', all revolve around the idea of community. Indeed the very idea of the 'global village' is based on the idea of community. The idea of community penetrates the identity politics of many social movements, as for instance the idea of 'gay communities'. Nor must the greatest myth of community – the 'European Community' – be forgotten.[3] We might quite well ask why Europe is considered a community and not a society. Indeed, since the publication of the well-known book by Karl Deutsch

(1957) *Political Community and the North Atlantic Area*, the idea of community has been central to international relations. There is perhaps a certain suggestion that the idea of society is the realm of the nation-state, while community can refer to something more transcendent and elusive.

In recent times few books have been more influential in setting the terms of debate for community than Amitai Etzioni's *The Spirit of Community* (1995). Against liberalism and radical individualism, Etzioni argues for the need to recover a sense of community. Though he explicitly says he is not advocating a nostalgic return to the past, it is significant that he constantly uses the term a 'return' to community or a 'recovery' of community, thus making the assumption that community was a thing of the past and the present is all the poorer for letting it pass. The idea of community is expressed very much in terms of personal proximity. Community entails voice, a 'moral voice', and social responsibility rests on personal responsibility. A concern with responsibility articulates a core idea of Etzioni's communitarianism, as is clear from his quarterly, *The Responsive Community*. Etzioni's conception of responsive community is rooted in 'social virtues' and 'basic settled values' (Etzioni, 1995, pp. 1–5). The family and the school are the typical institutions which can cultivate the kind of citizenship required by responsive community.

While Etzioni recognizes that complex societies and cities with many different cultural traditions cannot easily form the basis of community, his model is ultimately based on the idea of the traditional community. He grants that modern economic structures make the return to the past impossible and that traditional communities were too homogeneous and have been too constraining and authoritarian (Etzioni, 1995, p. 122). The city, not the village, is his concern. Thus the sociologically correct response to the typical liberal critique is that:

> communities are best viewed as if they were Chinese nesting boxes, in which less encompassing communities (families, neighbourhoods) are nestled within more encompassing ones (local villages avid towns), which in turn are situated within still more encompassing, communities, the national and cross-national ones (such as the budding European Community). Moreover, there is room for non-geographic communities that crisscross the others, such as professional or work-based communities. (Etzioni, 1995, p. 32)

Yet, Etzioni's definition of community as a moral voice rooted in social virtues and personal responsibility does not square with his view of community as being also highly differentiated. His conception of community is ultimately a reappropriation of the traditional idea of community as a cohesive unity. In order to understand contemporary developments which point towards the revival of community in the world today, we must part company from the sociological and philosophical myth of community in communitarian discourse. This myth is fundamentally incapable of understanding the real significance of community today: the appeal of community cannot be explained by reference to the quest for a lost totality, a moral order or a traditional order. We need to ask whether 'community beyond tradition' (Morris, 1996), or what William Corlett (1993) calls 'community without unity', can be possible, a notion that is also proposed by Giorgio Agamben in *The Coming Community* (1993). The political philosophy of communitarianism is also limited in its understanding of the discourse of community since the terms of its debates have been almost entirely shaped by two issues: the related problems of accommodating difference and individualism. In my estimation there is little point in rehearsing the well-known liberal critique of communitarianism since most advocates of communitarianism – including Etzioni – have answered the charge of majoritarianism and intolerance of dissent. Thus communitarianism is in fact liberal communitarianism (Miller and Walzer, 1995) and I am arguing that communitarianism is unable to deal with the formation of new discourses of community which cannot be explained by reference to the conventional terms of reference. In short, the problem of community today is not a question of accommodating tolerance of cultural differences, the theme of much of communitarian political philosophy.

What the new discourses of community have in common is not the hankering after a lost totality or a concern with difference or individualism, but a search for a new cultural imaginary. It is in this context that the notion of postmodern community is important (Mellos, 1994). The postmodernized communities of the global era are highly fragmented, contested and far from holistic collectivities; they are characterized more by aesthetic codes than by a moral voice. I shall outline this in more detail in the next chapter. It will suffice here to remark that new cultural imaginaries suggest that social responsibility cannot be reduced to the sense of personal moral responsibility and that globalization involves the emergence of new kinds of proximity that cannot be reduced to a sense of place (Castells, 1996). The only adequate kind of community is one that can accommodate itself with reflexivity and an awareness of its own incompleteness (Blanchot, 1988).

Beyond Communitarianism: The Postmodernization of Community

A useful entry into new conceptions of community is to consider Habermas's critique of communitarianism. For Habermas, communitarianism emphasizes the existing community too much and reduces politics to the ethical. He criticizes these models of political community on the grounds that they see community as too holistic and do not see how community, in so far as it is to be a foundation for citizenship, involves the transcendence of particular cultural traditions. His alternative concept of discursive democracy has the merit, he believes, of incorporating the strengths of the liberal and communitarian perspectives while rejecting their disadvantages. Discursive democracy, as we have seen in the previous chapter, resides not in the ethical substance of a particular community, nor in universal human rights or compromised interests as in liberalism, but in the rules of discourse and forms of argumentation whose normative content derives from the structures of linguistic communication which can always in principle be redeemed. Discursive democracy is rooted in the public sphere, which provides it with an informal institutional reality in civil society. Habermas is centrally concerned with the social conditions of critical debate in society and how such public discourse can shape democracy, which involves a relationship to legal institutionalization. Law is rooted in democracy, which in turn is rooted in public debate. Habermas is less concerned with actual participation in decision-making than in decision-making mediated by communication. In his model communication is essentially about contestation.

Habermas also breaks from communitarianism in another crucial respect: he strongly defends the possibility of a post-national society whose collective identity is defined by reference to the normative principles of the constitution rather than by reference to a cultural tradition, territory or loyalty to the state. Only what he calls a 'patriotism of the constitution' can guarantee a minimal collective identity today (Habermas, 1994, 1996). This idea may be generalized from the specifically German context in which he developed the idea to all modern societies, and is especially pertinent to such transnational polities as the European Union.

While Habermas has established the basis of a non-communitarian theory of community, his own alternative runs the risk of being too decontextualized. We need to see how community actually operates in the sense of real and lived communities. Habermas speaks from the perspective of the observer, a position he insists is available to everybody. In other words, cultural traditions are not so constraining as to prevent people from critically reflecting on their otherwise taken-for-granted assumptions. But, in general, community is a problem for Habermas, for whom the discourse ethic is modelled on face-to-face dialogue (Delanty, 1997a). Operating largely within the same paradigm of critical hermeneutics, Karl-Otto Apel (1980) argues for a concept of community as being central to a discursive concept of ethics, politics and science. The idea of community refers to the very process of communication itself as a self-transcending community of those engaged in critical reflection. Apel's emphasis on community as communication points to a new and non-communitarian notion of community. Though Apel does not attempt to develop his concept of community, I would argue that one way it differs from the conventional sociological and philosophical accounts is that community is essentially a transcendental and cognitive concept. The existing literature overemphasizes the symbolic nature of community as a cultural category (Cohen, 1985), to the neglect of the possibility that community might express a deeper level of the cognitive (Strydom, 1999a). In order to develop this possibility, I shall examine some new accounts of community which I think point to a deeper sense of community as a cognitive order or the basis of the cultural model of society. To move in this direction is to recognize the postmodernization of community.

An alternative conception of community is suggested by one of the leading postmodern theorists, Michel Maffesoli. Under the conditions of postmodern complexity, according to Maffesoli in *The Time of the Tribes* (1996a), the age of the masses is giving way to new social relationships and as a result we have entered the age of the 'tribes'. The idea of the tribe suggests for Maffesoli an 'emotional community' which is defined by an affectual and aesthetic aura. Community mediated experience of everyday life, which, according to Maffesoli, involves the constant flow of images and situations. Unlike the communities of the past, which were spatial and fixed, emotional community is unstable and open, a product of the fragmentation of the social and the disintegration of mass culture. People are increasingly finding themselves in temporary networks, or 'tribes', organized around lifestyles and images. Maffesoli sees community extrapolating a sense of 'sociability' from the 'social'. Community still involves proximity but this is something temporary and has no fixed purpose; it is characterized by 'fluidity, occasional gatherings and dispersal' (Maffesoli, 1996a, p. 76). Community serves to 'reenchant' the world and to provide a sense of solidarity that draws its strength from proximity. But the new proximity is located in urban-metropolitan spaces and is an expression of what Maffesoli calls the vitality and creativity of action. For Maffesoli (1996a, p. 104) this all amounts to the end of modernity: 'While modernity has been obsessed with politics, it may be equally true that postmodernity is possessed by the idea of clan, a phenomenon which is not without its effect on the relationship to the Other and, more specifically, to the stranger.' Community is then something radically open and unconstraining.

In another recent work, *The Contemplation of the World* (1996b), Maffesoli has developed the postmodernization of community. The communitarian ideal, which may be challenging the democratic ideal, has been too much neglected in contemporary theory, he argues. In his estimation it is part of a new 'culture of sentiment', a desire to reenchant the world. If modernity was about the disenchantment of the world, the postmodern age is an expression of the reenchantment of the world (Maffesoli, 1996b, p. xiv). Far from being a hankering back to a premodern age, community today is something that challenges the modern from a point beyond. Maffesoli (1996b, p. 26) refers to this as the 'transfiguration of the political. It gives way to the domestic, with the culture of sentiment as its most visible style.'

Two ideas stand out in the new conceptions of community: the contrast with the social and the idea of community existing in a 'non-place'. Community is an expression of fragmentation of society and is forever in tension with it but at the same cannot exist without it. This is evident in Maffesoli's work and, for instance, Jacques Rancière's (1995) *On the Shores of the Political*. Community is the province of equality, while society remains in thrall to inequality: 'A community of equals can never become coextensive with a society of the unequal, but nor can either exist without the other' (Rancière, 1995, p. 84). Marc Augé (1995) also writes about the increased salience of 'non-places' in the age of what he calls 'supera-modernity'. Non-places differ from places in that our experience of them is fragmentary and transitory. Supermodernity involves the production of more and more spaces through which we travel (super-markets and other non-places of consumption, transit lounges, leisure spaces, holiday resorts, cashpoints, the spatial images of TV and virtual realities of cyberspace). Supermodernity and its manifold of space is also characterized by the increased production of meaning that comes with ever more possibilities for agency to interpret its surroundings. It may be argued that community is increasingly being located in a world dominated by such non-places and the kind of aesthetic hermeneutics it involves for its participants. These hermeneutics have little to do with the symbolic order or a sense of proximity based on exclusion. Indeed the 'other' is not central to their definition. The kind of community that is suggested by writers such as Maffesoli is something more aesthetic and emotional and refers ultimately to the wider cognitive order of society.

A work of significance on the idea of community is Jean-Luc Nancy's (1991) *The Inoperative Community*. Nancy defends the idea of community as relevant not only to modern but also to postmodern society. Community is the basis of human experience and the identity of the self as a social being. However, his notion of identity is more that of non-identity: the experience of otherness as an absence. His approach is far from that of communitarianism in that he does not hanker after a lost community and insists that community is always based on the individual and the experience of the 'other': 'Community is what takes place always through others and for others' (Nancy, 1991, p. 15). Stressing finitude or present time as the key to community, Nancy opposes the attempt to locate community in the past or as a project for the future. Community cannot be reduced to an organic concept of social relations or to a place; it is something that always negates itself and is constituted in the differential relations of human beings. The 'inoperative community' is the tendency of community to undermine or 'interrupt' itself in the self-assertion of its members and in the struggle to define community: community is itself the experience of the loss of community. Nancy's idea of community is not unlike that of Maurice Blanchot (1988) in *The*

Unavowable Community, community as an incomplete project, a shared absence. Yet, for all his attempt to render community compatible with postmodernity (in the sense of the experience of difference), Nancy ultimately retreats into a kind of communitarianism for his conception of community, which is very much influenced by Heideggerian hermeneutics and a postmodernized and secularized Christianity, reflecting a concern with community as ontological in the sense of the expression of a human essence.

An example of a postmodern approach to community that avoids the dangers of essentialism and recognizes the political nature of community is William Corlett's (1993) *Community without Unity.* Corlett aims to apply the deconstructionist philosophy of Derrida to community, arguing that difference is the essence of community. Community, he argues, must be understood as something more than the problem of collective unity versus individualism; it is the mutual appreciation of differences and does not require a holistic notion of culture, for there is always an excess of meaning which cannot be reduced to a particular moment.

Roger Cotterrell's *Law's Community* (1995) is also a major contribution to the idea of community, though not from a postmodern perspective. The essential characteristic of community for Cotterrell is mutual interpersonal trust, for without trust a society cannot function. Trust is an important dimension to social cohesion and is increasingly becoming a major theme in social, legal and political theory (Misztal, 1996; Sztompka, 1998). Cotterrell argues that geographical proximity is not an essential characteristic of community; he also rejects the communitarian emphasis on shared values. In his view, communities can be very varied in size and character. Drawing from Luhmann, Cotterrell elucidates how social complexity makes proximity impossible and ultimately shifts the burden of trust from culture onto law. Thus, law is placed in the foreground in the contemporary conceptualization of community. Community also has a connection with communication and it is this which makes trust possible. Trust does not exist in a vacuum outside social interaction. Since social interaction is essentially communicative, we must view trust as a process of social communication. In Cotterrell's view this entails the need for a regulatory structure that fosters and supports relations of mutual trust in society. He argues (Cotterrell, 1995, p. 332) that this will involve collective participation and public altruism (the provision of the necessary material and cultural resources): 'Collective Participation – the opportunity and freedom for all members to be involved fully and actively in determining the nature and projects of the community as a whole – is a means of stabilizing and reinforcing mutual trust through the continuous ongoing negotiation of its consequences and it conditions of existence.'

Finally, we can mention Bill Readings's (1996, pp. 180–93) notion of the 'community of dissensus'. For Readings this is best exemplified in the postmodern university. A dissensual community would be one that has abandoned any attempt to find a unified point of legitimation: 'the university will have to become one place, among others, where the attempt is made to think the social bond without recourse to a unifying idea, whether of culture or of the state' (Readings, 1996, p. 191). This is in contrast, he argues, to modernity, where the abstract idea of the nation underpins the very possibility of community. This notion of community is very much opposed to the Habermasian notion of a communication community:

> A distinction must be drawn between the political horizon of consensus that aims at a self-legitimating, autonomous society and the heteronomous horizon of dissensus. In the horizon of dissensus, no consensual answer can take away the question mark that the social bond (the fact of other people, of languages) raises. (Readings, 1996, p. 187)

We thus have here a very important notion of community as a discursive entity that can never be reduced to identity or to unity.

My argument so far is that recent literature on the idea of community points to a notion of community as a cognitive structure rooted in processes of communication, law and democracy. Postmodern conceptions emphasize community in various ways as the experience of difference, whereas legal theorists stress issues such as trust. Others, such as Habermas and Apel, speak of community in terms of the reflexivity of communication. These approaches make the traditional notion of community as a symbolic order redundant, for they allow us to see community as a contested cultural imaginary. In order to develop further this understanding of community, I shall extend the idea of the cognitive into a theory of the cultural imaginary and relate this to the new idea of community as a postmodernized discourse beyond unity.

Community as a Cultural Imaginary

Following Cornelius Castoriadis (1987), as we have seen in the previous chapter, the 'imaginary' refers to the ability of a society to imagine itself; it is the cultural model of society in its cognitive, normative and aesthetic dimensions. The idea of community being advocated here sees it as part of the cultural dimension of society in its capacity to reflect upon itself. As Maffesoli (1996d, p. 118) argues, the 'imaginary is increasingly granted a role in structuring society'. Benedict Anderson (1991), too, has stressed the importance of community as an imaginary in the making of the nation-state. With the creation of large-scale nations organized around a state, community had to be reinvented around an imaginary community. The nation became the focus of this imaginary community, its cultural codes being greatly aided by print cultures. Thus physical proximity was replaced by an imaginary proximity in the creation of a wider national community. In the global age we are witnessing an extension of this imaginary community. If print cultures facilitated the rise of the national community, the computer age and cybersociety may be accompanying the rise of a new kind of community compatible with transnational governance and postmodern fragmentation.

The emergence of what I would prefer to call a neo-communitarian cultural imaginary must be seen in the context of the deterritorializing and globalizing of community. The new discourses of community are not those of the traditional peasant communities about which the founding fathers of sociology wrote: community is decentred, contested and is thereby open to new interpretations. Nor is it a moral order based on cultural consensus, or a moral voice, as the communitarian philosophers would have it. The return of community today is a response to the failure of society to provide a basis for the three core components of community: solidarity, trust and autonomy. To appreciate this we do not need a notion of the holistic fusion of culture and society around a symbolic order. In fact the contrary is the case: community today is a product of the uncoupling of culture and society. Culture is separating from society, whose institutional complexes are unable to constrain cultural value systems. Anthony Giddens (1994) refers to this as a process of disembedding, by which tradition loses its force, and agency, transformed by reflexivity, becomes emancipated. However, I would argue the reflexivity brought about by late modernity can be explained not by agency's emancipating itself from structures, as Beck and Giddens (1994) believe, but by the formation of new cultural systems of meaning.

The contemporary discourse of community, then, must be located in this new cultural context, which provides a basis for a cultural imaginary built around the idea of community. The attraction of community is that it offers a focus for the reappropriation of the cultural symbols of identity and ideology. Under the conditions of globalization, community can be taken out of its existing context and given new meaning. Thus many groups appeal in one way or the other to community. It is no coincidence that the idea of community has particular appeal to global cultures, such as the deterrorialized discourses of academia, the European Union, migrants and technology cultures such as those of the cybersociety (Jones, 1995; Meyrowitz, 1986). In the past community was shaped by the symbolic practices of tradition and custom; today it is shaped by a variety of forces of which the most important are the global processes of technology, knowledge and images (Castells, 1996). It must be noted that these have the characteristic of being strikingly non-communicative; they are primarily non-verbal and products of the postmodernization of culture. In disembedding community from its traditional sediment of morality and cultural consensus, the danger facing a postmodernized community is that it will fail to provide a basis for trust, solidarity and autonomy, the core components of community. This is the problem with cyberspace communities. In surmounting space and time, computer-mediated communication is primarily conceptual and deverbalized.

The nation-state and the national society failed to provide community with a firm foundation; the question, then, is whether the deterritorialization and globalization of community will be able to solve the problem of community – adaptation to the increasing conditions of complexity in the social environment. At this point the final dimension to community can be introduced: communication. Both community and communication are mutually implied in each other's definition. A community involves the flow of communication. Without a notion of communication, the ideas of solidarity, trust and autonomy would be meaningless, or at least would be reduced to the symbolic. The problem of community can thus be seen to be the problem of adapting flows of communication to the societal context. Thus we can see how, with the change in the wider societal environment towards greater globalization – in particular in communications systems – on the one side, and social fragmentation, on the other, community returns to provide fragmented societies with a cultural imaginary capable of compensating for the loss of the social and at the same time providing the new globalized systems of communication with a basis in the life-world. But the reception of the new discourse of community is problematic, for two reasons.

The first, as already suggested, is that the postmodernization of community runs the risk of emptying community of its relationship to communication and, second, there is the risk that community will degenerate into an authoritarian neo-communitarianism. In the first case the discourse of community loses its connection with communication and the core components of trust, solidarity and autonomy. Postmodern community – such as the European Union – is neither a *demos* nor an *ethnos*, but a globalized and deterritorialized cultural imaginary which runs the risks of reducing communication to incoherence. In the second case, as the examples of nationalism and neo-fascism attest, the idea of community reduces political community to cultural community and, moreover, involves an aestheticization of community. In both cases the idea of community is seen as the antithesis of the idea of society. In this sense, community and society are still two fundamentally opposed discourses.

In order to bring these domains closer together, and thereby overcome the false dichotomy of community and society, we need to see how they require each other. While community involves relationships of trust, autonomy and solidarity, an important dimension to the social is the sphere of institutionalized action. Taking up some themes in the theory of citizenship, I should like to claim that community and the social are linked by virtue of requirements of the ethic of responsibility to find an institutional foothold (Strydom, 1999c). Democracy and the institutions of civil society such as the public sphere are the means by which the spirit of community and the idea of the social are linked. However, in order for this to be a realistic prospect today in the global era, the ethic of responsibility must be modified to accommodate co-responsibility and the role of collective actors. We must therefore modify our concept of community accordingly.

Conclusion: Towards a Reflexive Community

My contention is that the idea of community is important and the challenge is to rescue community from either of the two tendencies – postmodernized incoherence or neo-communitarian authoritarianism – and to relink it to the idea of society and citizenship. The idea of community is relevant to postmodern society and is capable of articulating a cultural imaginary appropriate to our global age, but it is important for it to be related to processes of communication and the social life-world. The tremendous popularity of nationalism and various kinds of populist neo-communitarianism is precisely that they have been able to monopolize the discourse of community. In short, then, I am suggesting that the idea of community must be linked to the idea of the social and not seen as its antithesis. The social must not be fused with the idea of community – for this would only be to prolong the myth of total communities – but it must be mediated with it in the institutionalizing of spaces for trust, solidarity and autonomy. Community, in other words, could become the reflective dimension of society, as Scott Lash (1994, p. 162) has also argued. I believe that the idea of discursive democracy is the most appropriate means of conceiving of this, a notion that is related to Bill Readings's community of dissensus. A reflexive community is a discursive community, a self-questioning one for whom dissensus rather than consensus is the central characteristic. Only in this way can we rescue the discourse of community from either its absorption into meaningless semiotic global communities or the dangers of the symbolic as represented in authoritarian neo-communitarianism. The aesthetic and emotional dimension to community may have a role to play in this, in so far as it is capable of articulating a new sensibility.

7

FROM MODERNITY TO
POSTMODERNITY
Post-dialectics and the Aestheticization
of the Social

Most discussions on postmodernity agree that it is not a phase beyond modernity but represents the most advanced, and possibly final, stage of modernity. It might be said that if modernity entailed a strong sense of a beginning, as expressed in an emphasis on the 'new' and the 'now', postmodernity, in the closing decade of the twentieth century, signaled a sense of an ending, the ending of a century and millennium. Yet, at the present time the cultural mood suggests a certain sense of newness and beginning once again and which is reflected in the recovery of the ethos of modernity. I have been arguing in this book that postmodernity is deeply rooted in the culture of modernity, just as modernity itself was rooted in the premodern worldview. Underlying these movements is a particular set of problems relating to knowledge, power and the self.
  Much of the history of western culture can be seen as the gradual distanciation of subject from object. In the spaces that are opened up in this distanciation, new cultural logics emerge. In the beginning subjectivity rebels against objectivity, forcing it to accept the rule of the subject; at the end of this development, in the age of the postmodern, this subjectivity itself goes into decline, as the distancing, decentring and relativizing logic reaches completion. As argued earlier, the roots of post-modernism go back to premodern scepticism, which transformed knowledge and prepared the ground for the next step in the distanciation of subjectivity and objectivity, the modern turn to discursivity, and the final step to postmodernity was taken with the recognition of the reflexivity of the self. In these cultural shifts – from scepticism to discursivity to reflexivity – the distanciation of subject and object runs its course from transforming the model of knowledge to the radicalization of political practice to, in the postmodern period, the deconstruction of the identity of the self. The postmodern is merely the bringing to completion of what had already taken place in the spheres of knowledge and politics, for its

greatest impact has been on the self. The deconstruction of the self then is turned back on knowledge and politics, transforming the discourses of scepticism and discursivity, too, by reflexivity. But in this movement two logics of reflexivity can be discerned, one of deconstructionism and one of constructivism. Deconstructionism – the dissolution of the self – represents the first stage in postmodernity, with constructivism coming into its own today, as new selves are constructed.

What is called postmodernism is a diffuse set of ideas, ranging from the strictly aesthetic dimension of culture to its normative and cognitive dimensions. Under the rubric of the aesthetic lies a conception of culture that stresses the symbolic, and in postmodernism this is pronouncedly present in the confluence of capitalism and cultural production whereby symbolic capital becomes all-pervasive. The normative dimension of culture in the discourses of postmodernism relates to the question of political practice and the dissolution of the self. If the symbolic led to the entry of the aesthetic into everyday life in the rise of symbolic consumption, the normative stance of postmodernity occupied the ground of resistance, for the political practice of postmodernism was one that located the normative as the transgressive. This assumes a distinction, which will be clarified below, between resistance, which is political, and transgression, which is symbolic and relates to the confluence of the political and the aesthetic in postmodernity. The cognitive dimension is relatively neglected by postmodernism – which can be seen as the rule of the symbolic – and it is in this context that I shall discuss in Chapter 8 the work of Pierre Bourdieu, whose sociology points to an exit from postmodernity, an exit which is also a returning to a modernity that has been revitalized by the possibility of reflexivity. Modernity was organized as the separation of the normative, the aesthetic and the cognitive; postmodernity comes about as these domains undergo de-differentiation, for the blurring of the borders between these orders of discourse is commonly held to be the chief feature of the postmodern. But postmodernity accords primacy to the aesthetic, which forces itself into the normative and the cognitive, bringing about an aestheticization of everyday life.[1]

In the following discussion, I look at the four main movements which constitute postmodern culture: (1) the question of the aesthetic, (2) the theoretical turn to poststructuralism and the method of deconstructionism, (3) the sociological and cultural analysis of postmodernity in terms of postmodernization, that is, as a social condition, (4) and postmodernity as a political practice. It will be argued that all these dimensions of postmodernity share a sense of postmodern culture as one that prioritizes the symbolic, and that this leads to the over-determination of the normative and cognitive dimensions by the aesthetic, which becomes the central category of everyday life. Finally, by way of conclusion I will look at the possibility that postmodernization may be detaching itself from the framework of European/western modernity and suggest that the genuinely postmodern world is now in Japan and much of the Islamic world.

Postmodern Aesthetics

It is not my aim to give a comprehensive outline of the origins of post-modernism, since there are already several good overviews of this.[2] Instead I wish to demonstrate that the postmodern turn had its roots in late modern aestheticism, in particular the avant-garde, and that it inherited from this movement a preoccupation with a symbolic politics of transgression, the chief feature of which was the attempt to overcome the autonomy of cultural spheres and their separation from everyday life. This, in effect, neutralization of politics by postmodernism made possible a symbolic politics of transgression as opposed to a dialectical politics of resistance. Postmodernism in the arts and in questions of aesthetic style is a continuation of early twentieth-century radical modern-ism in its intensification of the symbolic domain, which is no longer confined to the aesthetic but includes the wider category of the social, or everyday life, and reaches beyond to include history and myth. When the term 'postmodern' entered common circulation in the 1970s in literary studies and the arts more generally, it was held to refer to some of the key features of late modernism – anti-representationalism, the subversion of narrative, a self-referential style, abstract formalism – but an aesthetic form which could now be capable of appropriating social content, as attempted earlier by the avant-garde (Dadaism, surrealism, futurism). That is to say, postmodernism emerged out of a new tension with form and content, a tension which could also be described as 'post-dialectical', making possible a kind of transgression that would be devoid of the power of critique and negativity that was held to be central to modernity and the culture of modernism. In the most general sense, then, postmodernism can be understood as post-dialectical thinking.

With radical modernism the aesthetic rebelled against the other dimen-sions of modernity, inspired by a belief in the emancipatory power of technology: 'the shock of the new'. Modernity imprisoned the aesthetic in the autonomous institution of art, which, to be sure, was intended to be advantageous for art since it emancipated it from the court and patronage, giving it the freedom to discover in its own form new creative possibilities and ones which could no longer be dictated by social content. In the age of totalitarianism the autonomy of art allowed it to remain free of censorship and in the age of mass culture – which roughly paralleled totalitarianism – it was protected from the 'false sublimation' of the culture industry. As an autonomous institution, the aesthetic could enter everyday life only either as a radical politics or as a depoliticized popular culture. The avant-garde represented the former strategy, and eventually ended up as popular culture when the 'shock of the new' was normalized in an age when everything was new and one that was immune to shock after the Holocaust.[3] With its cultural contents released into everyday life and negated of their radicality, the modernist impulse survived on a different level – as represented by Eliot, Joyce, Kafka,

Pound, James, Woolf, Yeats and Beckett, for instance – by preserving the autonomy of form it inherited from the modern age and allowing social content to enter form only in a highly mediated manner. In the movement from impressionism to expressionism to abstract formalism, art, too, externalized every trace of social content, retreating into pure form. If history and everyday life entered the aesthetic form, it did so only as myth. The two great literary works that mark the end of the modern era, and which are comments on the European metropolis, *Ulysses* and *The Waste Land*, delve into myth which merges with everyday life in the modern urban world. In the fragmentation of experience that metropolitan life brings, universality is possible only by the redemptive power of myth, in a consciousness that transcends the individual. In Proust's *Remembrance of Things Past*, too, the modernist aesthetic binds the consciousness of the present to the quest for an unretrieval past. It is evident, then, that this aesthetic appropriation of history and of the past in Eliot, Joyce, Proust and Yeats is essentially mythical and anthropological; it is not historical. In this way, then, modernism, while rejecting tradition, creatively appropriated myth. In a curious way, even in the thinking of Horkheimer and Adorno in *Dialectic of Enlightenment* and the work of Lévi-Strauss, modernity is constantly reverting to the condition of myth, which can be renounced only in the embracing of an extreme formalism available solely to the few. One of the most evocative images of modernity and myth is contained in Walter Benjamin's 'Theses on the Philosophy of History', in particular the reference to Paul Klee's painting *Angelus Novus*, whose face is turned towards the past as if to find in it a moment to redeem the present and resist the future, against which his back is turned. History, for Benjamin, was a source of hope and despair: 'There is no document of civilization which is not at the same time a document of barbarism' (Benjamin, 1970, pp. 258–60).

The threshold of the postmodern was reached when the promise of a political moment was finally abandoned and history could manifest itself not as myth but as everyday life. As Adorno (1984) argued, modernism had preserved a link – mediated through the aesthetic form – with political modernity, above all the promise of redemption through politics. The utopia of a society that could be reconstructed by a rational and political imagination lay at the heart of the modernist venture, the belief that the aesthetic dimension, though autonomous, could offer a symbolic transformation of social content by the aesthetic form. The postmodern turn retained this sense of symbolic transformation of social content by the aesthetic form but severed its connection with politics. Postmodernity is modernity devoid of its political project. Aesthetic modernity abolished itself with the *fin-de-siècle* avant-garde, leaving what remained for postmodernism to continue but without any project. Transgression now becomes the blurring of the spheres of cultural modernity and the loss of autonomy that comes with this weakening of what earlier would have been understood to be resistance to domination.

In the 1970s the late modernist aesthetic loses its earlier preoccupation with the autonomy of form and enters other discourses, but without any particular sense of purpose. As such it can be seen as post-avant-gardism and a product of the postindustrial society. Modernism had been an expression of a society that was experiencing the social transformation brought about by rapid industralization, and the cities where it flourished – *fin-de-siècle* Vienna, Berlin, Paris, Dublin – had undergone a recent history of turbulence as a result of social unrest, war and industrialization. In contrast, postmodernism, as it emerged in North America in the 1960s and 1970s, was facing a world that was relatively stable and in which middle-class values had become the norm. The 1970s saw a turn to eclecticism and social content, which did not have a political association, in contrast to the counter-culture of the 1960s, as Andreas Huyssen (1984) argues, when an avant-garde did resurface with experiments in cultural anarchy, of which the emergence of American pop art was the most significant. But as Huyssen (1984, pp. 18–9) points out, this experiment – that all is art – was conducted from within modernism, particularly in Europe, and can be seen as a search for alternative traditions within modernism which might be able to block out the memories of the fascist period.[4] Postmodernism emerged out of an attempt to recover the earlier avant-garde in the 1960s; it can be seen as an American appropriation of a failed European revolt. However, the genuinely postmodern turn was one that, in the aftermath of the historical avant-garde movement and other attempts from the vantage point of modernism to express a political relation between the aesthetic dimension and everyday life, between form and content, failed at least to sustain its political significance. What was abandoned was a politics of resistance and the culture of critique, thus allowing art to retrieve social content. Undoubtedly one contributing factor in the loss of a political mission was the declining significance of the totalitarian period as a watershed. The Cold War and the age of social welfare democracies was a period which neutralized the fears that animated an earlier modernity; and history and tradition, banished from earlier modernities as the source of all tyrannies, could now be readmitted to the aesthetic domain. Thus with the postmodern turn, history, everyday life, tradition, all entered the aesthetic dimension, which is transformed from the domain of resistance to one of consumption. Transgression is now a cultural logic of recombination, discontinuities, fragmentation and the loss of the autonomy that characterized cultural modernity. It is symbolic rather than political. With the political neutralization of social content, the earlier emphasis on a self-referential and anti-representational aesthetic form – in, say, the late modernism of Beckett – could now give way to a new relationship with social content, which was more affirmative than negative. The need for a denial of the past and the rejection of the everyday ceased to be basis of the aesthetic. Past and present were no longer engaged in the confrontation that was inaugurated by the

American and French Revolutions and which gave to modernity its animus; consequently they could be recombined in a new and creative way, with tradition reinvented by a modernity which could never entirely derive its legitimations and cultural resources from itself. Moreover, the earlier need to negate high bourgeois art is weakened in an age of postindustrial-postbourgeois consumption, for the tension between high and low art is less pivotal to the identity of the postmodern than it was to the modern for high art can be consumed in much the same way as popular art, for instance the reduction of classical music to 'easy listening'.

The postmodern aesthetic can thus be seen as a combination of two moments of modernism, represented by Duchamp and Beckett: on the one side, the avant-gardist negation of form and the autonomy of art, and, on the other, the reluctance to engage in politics that characterized modernism in its final, and often decadent, phase of pure form. Post-modernism allows the aesthetic to enter everyday life without political implications. This is particularly apparent in the case of postmodern architecture, which differs from modernist architecture in that it rests more easily with everyday life. Modernist architecture was essentially minimalist, seeking to reduce beauty to a pure functionalism of form, as was exemplified in the Bauhaus or the designs of Le Corbusier. Like the logical positivism of the Vienna Circle or the music of Schoenberg, it tried to remove all extraneous meaning in a retreat into a pure formalism. The symbolic domain was eradicated in a devotion to function. Postmodern architecture, by contrast, is the return of the symbolic to the aesthetic form, which is also an opening up of form to history and the social environment. Rejecting abstraction and embracing pluralism in meaning and style, postmodern architecture is communicative rather than formalistic; it is symbolic rather than self-referential, and allows space for meaning which is always more than a function.[5] Russian postmodernism in the 1980s is an exception in this respect. According to one of its major interpretors, Mikhail Epstein, it was animated by the confrontation with history and the sudden encounter with the whole of western culture (Epstein, 1995, p. 295). It embraced not multicultural and the celebration of difference, as in the United States, but the subversion of Soviet ideology by means of 'transculture'. In striving to be total, society ideology was itself a postmodern pastiche not unlike the penetration of capitalism into cultural reproduction, as described by Jameson.

In sum, then, the postmodern aesthetic was essentially a recovery of the European historical avant-garde which had been neutralized of its political project and thus could be reintroduced into the new culture of consumption in an aestheticization of everyday life. As such it can be called a 'post-avant-garde', not least because of its unleashing of the symbolic. Twice in the twentieth century – first with the European *fin-de-siècle* avant-garde and in the 1960s with American pop art – art attempted to enter the social in order to realize the historical link of art with politics; each time it failed, but the second time there was not a retreat into modernist form and a recovery of autonomy in order to protect art from its false realization in mass culture, for by the 1970s the political promise of modernity had itself been abandoned and art began to lose its sense of resistance to the social. Consequently the aesthetic enters everyday life in an ethos more of fragmentation of cultural spheres and forms than of autonomy. This development was undoubtedly connected to the fact that earlier pessimism concerning mass society, as expressed in the writings of Adorno and Marcuse, on the left, the writings of T.S. Eliot and Ortega y Gasset, on the right, had been superseded by a new understanding of mass culture as more multifaceted and hermeneutically open. The left critics had seen the danger to be the aestheticization of violence that comes with the equation of art and politics; while the right saw the problem to be a loss of spiritual and political leadership. By the 1970s those fears had given way to optimism in the cultural creativity of a new age whose preoccupations were no longer political: civil society, which had been the container of all the earlier forms of aesthetic modernity, including those attempts to realize art in life, was now being slowly absorbed by the category of everyday life.

Postmodernism as Deconstructive Theory

If aesthetic postmodernism is characterized by a relationship to the social that has been defused of political tensions, the theoretical side of post-modernism – deconstructionism – is a rejection of the social altogether in the name of a politics that can have no social content. For this reason deconstructionism has some similarities with modernism, for instance its retreat from any direct kind of politics. However, deconstruction is more decidedly postmodern in its rejection of dialectical critique and in its abandonment of the emancipatory moment which was central to modernity. Even in the philosophy of Adorno dialectics was preserved in the form of negativity.

Deconstruction, the method of poststructuralism, emerged as a specifically French theoretical stance on existentialism, phenomenology and Marxism in the 1960s. Postmodernism, as an aesthetic mode, was primarily an American development in the 1960s and 1970s, and at this time the new criticism in France was more interested in radical modernism – Flaubert, Mallarmé, Proust, Beckett, Bataille – than postmodernism as such in the American sense of a pop counter-cultural revitalization of the historical avant-garde or the new eclectism of the 1970s. What in fact happened in the 1970s was a confluence of postmodern aesthetics and French deconstructionism in American intellectual circles, for the reception of deconstruction was greatest in North America, where its impact was more literary than philosophical, as is evidenced by the impact of

Roland Barthes's *The Pleasure of the Text* (1975). In France, in contrast, the deconstructive turn was part of the reorientation of Marxist-Hegelian thinking, and many of the most influential advocates of deconstruction were members of the French Communist Party, or at least closely identified with Marxism, such as Jean-François Lyotard and Jean Baudrillard, who wanted to recast Marxism-Leninism as a 'Marxism-Nietzscheanism'. It would not be an exaggeration to say that it was Nietzsche and his notion of the 'eternal reoccurrence' that offered a way of rethinking the Marxist concept of 'permanent revolution' (Trotsky, 1931). In France deconstruction did not have the same impact on literary thinking, where a kind of modernism continued. Indeed, the intellectual figures of the French poststructuralists were the German late modernists, Nietzsche, Heidegger and Freud. These figures opened up two routes out of Marxism. For the more politically radical, for example Lyotard and Baudrillard, Nietzsche provided an alternative to the Hegelianism of Marx and a new conception of permanent revolution; for figures less concerned with the politics of Marxism, such as Derrida and Lacan, Heidegger, read through the eyes of Freud, allowed for new readings of language as a source of creativity and desire.

It is remarkable that for the German tradition, Nietzsche and Heidegger, and, to an extent, Freud, too, offered a means of recovering the project of modernity, while for the French – Foucault, Derrida, Lyotard – they offered an exit from an allegedly disciplinarian and exclusionary modernity. For Gadamer, for instance, Heidegger provided the means of a recovery of tradition and a hermeneutical conception of modernity; for Weber the disenchantment of modernity was perfectly expressed by Nietzsche, who, far from abandoning modernity, stood for a heroic individualism of spirit which Weber admired and located in the high tradition of Kant and Tolstoy; for Arendt and Marcuse, before their American exile, Heidegger provided the basis of social ontology, a being-with-others, and though they went on to other projects – Arendt in neo-republican liberalism and Marcuse in critical Marxism – they never fully renounced their belief in the importance of Heidegger as a philosophical thinker for the late modern age; for Adorno and Horkheimer, Nietzsche's critique of the Enlightenment offered the basis of a critical theory of modernity, but one that did not relinquish the possibility of emancipation; and for Marcuse and Habermas the significance of Freud was the possibility of a therapeutic social science and emancipation from distorted consciousness. The French use of Nietzsche, Freud and Heidegger was different from, one might say unrecognizable in comparison to, the German use. Where for the Germans modernity begins with Kant and the project of the Enlightenment, which was primarily a French development for it was the French Revolution that most of the great German thinkers, from Kant to Heine to Habermas, admired and wished for Germany, which had no democratic tradition of its own, the French tradition was to look more to the German late modernists in order to repudiate their own rationalist tradition. Thus, as Huyssen (1984, p. 33) remarks, the French vision of modernity was closer to literary modernism, and was very much identified with figures such as Mallarmé and Nietzsche, even Brecht. For Habermas, for instance, modernity also entails the political dimension and goes back to the Enlightenment and the French Revolution.

It is impossible to understand poststructuralism without considering it in light of structuralism. Though poststructuralism is identified with a major onslaught against modernity, it was directly a development from, and reaction to, structuralism, which was deployed against the three dominant philosophies in France in the 1960s: existentialism (Jean-Paul Sartre), phenomenology (Maurice Merleau-Ponty) and the various schools of Marxism. The structuralists – such as Claude Lévi-Strauss – made language central to social and cultural analysis, which must concern itself with uncovering the deep structures of linguistic signification. For Lévi-Strauss, following Saussure, language is a system of closed signs which can be analysed as a system of logical structures. The poststructuralists wanted to radicalize this insight, which required rejecting the existence of closed structures, for the sign was dominated not by the signified but by the signifier. By seeing the signifier as essentially dynamic and relational, the system of signs was far from being the stable, structured framework that it was for Lévi-Strauss and the signified was itself a signifier depending on its position in the system of signs. Deconstructionism was the analysis of the system of signs. One of its implications was the rejection of the subject, for structuralism – at least in Lévi-Strauss, though not for Althusserian structuralism – held to an underlying human essence, arguing that only the combination of signs changes in history, thus tying modernity to the condition of myth.

Poststructuralist thought, as associated with Derrida and Foucault, interpreted nihilism to be a form of deconstructionism, or, as Foucault called it, an 'archaeology', and later the more transgressive notion of 'genealogy'. With Foucault there was a strong commitment to the anti-humanism of Althusser. There could be no alienation because there was no self to be alienated. Alienation was possible only in a society that was erected on the foundations of a contradiction. After 1968 the idea dawned that postindustrial society might not be based on a contradiction: the signifier had rebelled against the signified and became disengaged from it. It is a curious feature of French radical thinking from this period that May 1968 was a failure, necessitating the abandoment of dialectics, whereas elsewhere, for instance in Germany and North America, the late-sixties counter-culture was considered to be a step in the direction of emancipation.

In Derrida's writings, with which poststructuralism was most closely identified, deconstructionism was an interpretative strategy which was neither critical nor hermeneutical as such (Derrida, 1977, 1978). His aim was to destroy all attempts to reduce meaningful discourse to a founding origin. The first casualty in this exercise was meaning itself, and the very possibility of meaning was ultimately called into question. Meaning and language undermine each other for Derrida, for language is not the vehicle of meaning but its destroyer. Reality – which Derrida falsely associates with meaning – is obscured by language, which creates its own levels of reality. While Derrida certainly understood his approach to have radical political implications, at some obscure level, he was not addressing explicitly social issues and it was not at all apparent how deconstructionism might be taken up in a public form since it denied any moment of closure: meaning cannot be communicated, only disseminated. The tendentially affirmative dimension in his method became more apparent in the impact his work had on American thinking, though it would be incorrect to call it a new conservatism, as Habermas termed it in 1981. Deconstructionism was essentially a method of textual interpretation which greatly stressed the impossibility of closure. With its growing influence, the poststructuralist movement became associated with a denial of the possibility of politics and of the social, for it rejected the possibility of social action and above all of identity, for action and identity require closure.

Where, for an earlier modernism animated by the possibility of politics, all was art, for poststructuralism all was language. This is more apparent in Foucault than Derrida, who after all was more concerned with the analysis of literary and philosophical texts. The approach adopted by Foucault, who wrote explicitly on power and the institutions of modernity, saw everything in terms of discourse. Discourses are all-inclusive language-games which are 'productive' of knowledge, which does not have a privileged position outside of discourses. Discourse does not offer the possibility of communication as in Habermas, for whom it contains unredeemed validity claims and the ever-present problem of legitimation; it is a closed system and is associated with power. This can be contrasted to Hannah Arendt's famous notion of power as public discourse, or the ability 'to act in concert'. In Foucault's vision of modernity, which is almost entirely disciplinary, the subject is condemned to discourse and therefore to power, which is coeval with discourse, its rules and forms of knowledge. Unlike for Habermas, discourse does not lead to reflexivity.

Despite the association of Foucault with postmodernity – though there is no explicit connection and he never used the term to characterize his approach – he was in fact primarily a theorist of modernity in its bleakest form. To be sure, his genealogical method is close to the deconstructionism of early postmodern theory, but his substantive studies were on disciplinary modernity, and were in a similar vein to Weber (O'Neill, 1986). Where he broke from modernity was his rejection of the possibility of emancipation as a collective possibility, though there is the tendency in his later thought to emphasize the other face of power: resistance, for where there is power there is resistance.[6] By the time of his untimely death in 1984, he was certainly embracing a slightly less disciplinary conception of power. At this point, when the deconstructive approach of Foucault was showing signs of waning, the American reception was turning away from an exclusive concern with disciplinarity to a concern with 'governmentality' as the site of resistance. Before commenting on this and the recovery of the political project of the subject, mention must be made of another strand in the theory of postmodernity, the cultural and sociological theory of postmodernization.

Postmodernization

Postmodernism is more than a question of aesthetic style and a theoretical methodology; it is also a theory of society, entailing a notion of postmodern times. In this sense postmodernity refers to a historical period which roughly corresponds to postindustrial society. An early use of this was by C. Wright Mills in 1959 in *The Sociological Imagination*:

> We are living at the end of what is called The Modern Age. Just as Antiquity was followed by several centuries of Oriental ascendancy, which Westerns provincially call the Dark Ages, so now The Modern Age is being succeeded by a postmodern period. Perhaps we may call it: The Fourth Epoch. (Mill, 1970, p. 184)

The ideological mark of this epoch, he goes on to argue, is that the idea of the freedom of reason, the foundation of modernity, has been called into question with the recognition that rationality may not be assumed to make for increased freedom. One of the first uses of the term as a designation of a particular phase in history goes back to Arnold Toynbee. In 1954, Toynbee gave the term 'post-Modern age' to the period that began at the end of the nineteenth century when the middle-class or bourgeois society which dominated the modern age was challenged by the rise of an industrial working class in the West and beyond in non-western intelligentsias.

In volume 8 of his monumental work *A Study of History* he wrote:

> the word 'modern' in the term 'Modern Western Civilization' can, without inaccuracy, be given a more precise and connotation by being translated as 'middle-class'. Western became 'modern', in the accepted Modern Western meaning of the word, just as soon as they had succeeded in producing a bourgeoisie that was both numerous enough and competent enough to become the predominant element in Society. We think of the new chapter of Western history that opened at the turn of the fifteenth and sixteenth centuries as being 'modern' *par excellence* because for the next four centuries and more, until the opening of a 'post-Modern Age' at the turn of the nineteenth and twentieth centuries, the middle class was in the saddle in the larger and more prominent part of the Western World as a whole. (Toynbee, 1954, p. 338)

These notions of the postmodern age can of course be called simply 'late modern', and in any case they have been overshadowed by Lyotard's definition, which tied the concept more closely to postmodernism in its other forms, in the arts, theory and politics.

Since the publication of Lyotard's *The Postmodern Condition* in 1979 (Lyotard, 1984), postmodernity came to be seen as a particular condition of society itself, and it thus becomes possible to speak of the 'postmodern condition'. This designates less an actual historical phase than a social condition, a climate of opinion, or a cultural mood entailing both an epistemic shift and an aesthetic style. Lyotard of course was advocating both a deconstructive epistemology and a theory of society. The postmodern condition was a thesis relating both to the latest phase of postindustrialism and to the epistemological rejection of modernity. Though there is much to suggest that he saw postmodernity as a new phase in society, he stated in a later essay that 'we should consider postmodernity as either an increase of skepticism or, at least, a greater reservation with regard to the Grand Narratives and their goals, rather than a new period in human history' (Lyotard, 1994, p. 189).

What I would call postmodernization refers to a wider concept of the aesthetic and the epistemological as cultural categories.[7] The debate on postmodernism thus shifted onto a broader notion of culture than the older concerns with the aesthetic in the 1970s. By the 1980s the American reception of French poststructuralism had made its greatest impact in literary studies, and about this time the relatively new discipline of cultural studies had emerged, largely associated with literature, though spanning across sociology. These developments created an opening for a new conception of culture capable of responding to the new postmodernism of aesthetic style and deconstruction theory. It might be suggested that postmodernism was an expression of the confluence of culture and relativism. This development differs from the historicism of the nineteenth century and modern anthropological theories of culture, such as Ruth Benedict's classic work *Patterns of Culture* (1934), in that the postmodern celebration of cultural relativism referred less to the socially determined nature of meaning than to the collapse of meaning as the basis of social integration.

I see two broad tendencies in the cultural theory of postmodernization; one still tied to deconstructionism and predominantly continental European – represented by Lyotard, Baudrillard and Vattimo – and a later and more Anglo-American version which had a more pronounced critical edge to it (in the conclusion to this chapter I will uncover the uncertain contours of a third, non-western postmodernization). Fredric Jameson's theory of postmodernism as the latest phase of capitalism is the best example of this version, as is the important work by David Harvey, *The Condition of Postmodernity* (1990).[9] Though both Lyotard and Jameson were highly critical of capitalism, they differed notably in their stance towards postmodernism as a cultural form. Jameson's theory of postmodernism was not remarkably different from that of Adorno, a critic he greatly admires for his negative attitude to the culture industry, and it might also be compared to the essay by Lefebvre, 'The Bureaucratic Society of Controlled Consumption' (1984a). In his well-known work *Postmodernism, or, the Cultural Logic of Late Capitalism* (1991), Jameson argues that postmoderism is the extension of capitalism into the cultural sphere – it is a 'cultural logic'. Postmodernism is nothing other than commodity fetishism. In contrast to Lyotard, who rejected all metanarratives of emancipation, he was defending the continued importance of Marxism in the age of postmodernism, a thesis also developed in *The Political Unconsciousness* (1983).[10] American critics, such as Harvey and Jameson, thus represented a break from the deconstructive postmodernism of the French authors. As Perry Anderson (1998, p. 55) wrote in one of the most perceptive of studies on the origins of postmodernism, and largely endorsing Jameson: 'Where modernism drew its purpose and energies from the persistence of what was not yet modern, the legacy of a still pre-industrial past, postmodernism signifies the closure of that distance, the saturation of every pore of the world in the serum of capital.'

It must be remarked that Lyotard was not actually concerned with culture itself, at least not in the sense of Jameson. His focus was in fact knowledge and it was his thesis that in the postmodern age – which is more or less the period of postindustrial society – knowledge has entered the mode of production and consequently it has lost its former position where it was located in a particular space, the space of the university. Knowledge has become productive and as a result it has lost its emancipatory power, which, in his view, characterized modernity and rested on its stature as a metanarrative. With the loss of these outside positions from which social reality can be judged, there is only a plurality of language-games. For Lyotard, legitimation has been replaced by performance, or performativity as subversion of the rules of discourse. Jameson in contrast was less concerned about the transformation of the cognitive as such than with the commodification of the aesthetic. While these different concerns – production and consumption – may have led them to different conclusions regarding the appraisal of postmodernism, the underlying difference remained one of the status of critique and the possibility of legitimation.

The postmodern theories of Jean Baudrillard are more centrally addressed to cultural transformation.[11] His position is marked by a rejection of the category of the social in favour of what might be termed the cultural, though he would prefer to call it metaphysical (quoted in Gane, 1993, p. 106). In this he is partly ironic, but what he means is that the social has been replaced by a world of signs, which are themselves real (see Baudrillard, 1975, 1981, 1983). This position allows him to equate the end of the social with the loss of reality in what might be called a 'metaphysical society'. The only kind of reality that is left is a metaphysical hyperreality, for contemporary society is characterized by the production and consumption of signs.[12] In this world of signs meaning is entirely relational, having lost any connection to reality. The political implication that Baudrillard draws is one that looks to the power of symbolic exchange to challenge the system of signs under capitalism. In symbolic exchange there is a deconstruction of the sign (Baudrillard, 1993). For Baudrillard postmodernity is epitomized by America, in contrast to Europe, which typified modernity. In his book *America* he describes the loss of meaning that America represents; it is a cultural desert of appearances beneath which lies no reality of any substance, no past and no future, just an endless present, a simulacrum (Baudrillard, 1989). There is even the suggestion of the elimination of difference in a return to a meaningless sameness. This position commits him to some notion of an alternative reality. Lyotard thus distinguishes his approach from Baudrillard's:

> Unlike Jean Baudrillard, I don't think that this shift results in a wide range of simulation (or simulacra), a term still too close to the belief that reality exists in itself. Rather, I guess that this development entails a move away from traditionally modern values such as truth, justice, long-term finality, and the hope of legitimation. (Lyotard, 1994, p. 191)

Mention, too, can be made of the contribution to the debate on postmodernism by the Italian philosopher Gianni Vattimo. Like Derrida, he is very influenced by Heidegger and in a significant collection of essays, *The End of Modernity* (1998), has advanced a postmodernist position that draws on Nietzsche and Heidegger and seeks to link nihilism and hermeneutics. In another work, *The Transparent Society* (1992), he discusses postmodern society as a society of 'generalized communication' that has ceased to be transparent to itself. The loss of transparency goes with the 'loss of reality' that modernity itself brought about. But this is an ambivalent development, since the uncertainty that it brings about can be the basis of a new kind of emancipation, one of a liberation of difference:

> Emancipation, here, consists in disorientation, which is at the same time also the liberation of differences, of local elements, of what could be called dialect. With the demise of the idea of a central rationality of history, the world of generalized communication explodes like a multiplicity of 'local' rationalities – ethnic, sexual, religious, cultural or aesthetic minorities – that finally speak for themselves. (Vattimo, 1992, pp. 8–9)

For Vattimo, unlike Baudrillard, postmodern society offers more possibilities for emancipation, which for him lie in 'the continual oscillation between belonging and disorientation' (Vattimo, 1992, p. 10).

With the declining influence of Lyotard's model of postmodernism, which was closely linked with his particular version of French deconstructionism, the wider and more distinctively American approach, which I am calling postmodernization, became more influential. This is the most sociological version of postmodernization and can be divided into two further perspectives. On the one side, there are the more sociological approaches which are also broadly critical of postmodern tendencies in contemporary society, and, on the other side, there are those writing largely from the discipline of cultural studies who view the postmodern condition in positive terms.[13] The latter category is likely to be still influenced by French deconstructionism, and affinities can be found with the work of Baudrillard and Lyotard, though it must be mentioned that these authors were writing from the stance of permanent revolution (by the 1980s this became a fading memory). Examples of this more affirmative stance on postmodernization are Scott Lash and John Urry's *Economies of Signs and Space* (1994), Lash's *Sociology of Postmodernism* (1990) and Mike Featherstone's *Consumer Culture and Postmodernism* (1991). In these approaches postmodernity is associated with developments towards virtual reality and cybersociety. An extreme version of the affirmative approach to postmodernism is the thesis of Bartos (1996, p. 315) that in postmodern society we are witnessing a shift from system to life-world: the 'postmodern life-world will be free from domination by the system, . . . in fact it will absorb the system'. In this fascinating but ultimately untenable reversal of Habermasian theory, the emergent postmodern society will have some of the properties of preindustrial *Gemeinschafts*, such as a decentralization of power and segmentation into smaller groups. The dominant feature, according to this view, will be the aestheticization of everyday life. This affirmative stance on postmodernization is also reflected in the writings of Serge Maffesoli, for instance his well-known *The Time of the Tribes* (1996a).

The critical use of postmodernization as a sociological category is best represented by David Harvey (1990), for whom postmodernism is the cultural side of what is more sociologically known as postfordism. His most far-reaching argument is that postmodernism is part of the rise of neo-liberalism, also a product of 1980s political culture, and serves to legitimate, while claiming that legitimations are no longer possible, the ruthless face of capitalism: 'A rhetoric that justifies homelessness, unemployment, increasing improvishment, disempowerment, and the like by appeal to supposedly traditional values of self-reliance and entrepreneuralism will just as freely laud the shift from ethics to aestheticism as its dominant value system' (Harvey, 1990, p. 336). Postmodernism is dangerous, he argues, because it avoids confronting the realities of the postfordist economy and new forms of global power; it tells us merely to accept the fragmentation of the social and the decline of political alternatives. 'Worst of all, while it opens up a radical prospect by acknowledging the authencity of other voices, postmodernist thinking immediately shuts off those other voices from access to more universal sources of power by ghettoizing them within an opaque otherness, the specificity of this or that language game' (Harvey, 1990, p. 117). Harshly critical of postmodernism as an anaesthetization of poverty, ghetto-ization and homelessness, as a retreat from ethics to aesthetics, Harvey also recognizes its positive contribution. He praises it for its concern for difference, in acknowledging the multiplicities of identities and the openness of culture, for recognizing the difficulties in communication and the limits of modernity, which was based on just one cultural value system.

In Harvey's view postmodernists present a false picture of the modern:

> The metanarratives that the postmodernists decry (Marx, Freud, and even later figures like Althusser) were much more open, nuanced, and sophisticated than the critics admit. Marx and many of the Marxists (I think of Benjamin, Thompson, and Anderson, as diverse examples) have an eye for detail, fragmentation, and disjunction that is often caricatured out of existence in postmodern polemics. (Harvey, 1990, p. 115)

It thus makes more sense to see postmodernism as a reflection of a cultural crisis in late capitalism than a step beyond it. Perry Anderson (1998, pp. 80–1) sees postmodernism as 'a product of the political defeat of the radical generation of the 1960s. Revolutionary hopes disappointed, this cohort had found compensation in a cynical hedonism that found lavish outlet in the overconsumption boom of the eighties'.

This more critical edge to notions of postmodernization is well represented in the writings of Stjepan Meštrović. In *The Coming Fin de Siècle* he applies Durkheim's sociology, which for him is a sociology of anomic cultural crisis, to the current situation: postmodernism is the institutionalization of anomie (Meštrović, 1991, p. 204). What we have in common with Durkheims's time is the experience of a century coming to an end, he argues. The mood is different today; for is not just one of anxiety and cultural crisis but one of happiness: 'The credo of post-modern culture seems to be captured by the words of the popular song, Don't Worry, Be Happy' (Meštrović, 1991, p. 202). In a more recent work, *The Balkanization of the West: The Confluence of Postmodernism and Post-communism* (1994), he looks at postmodernism as the fragmentation, that is, 'balkanization', of the West into smaller units driven by violent ethnic nationalisms and communitarian movements. Thus the collapse of com-munism and the end of the Cold War signalled not cosmopolitanism but the arrival of a postmodern world in which the lines separating friend and foe, Self and Other, would become obscure.[14]

Postmodern Politics

There is no doubt that postmodernism, along with neo-liberalism, was the most influential theoretical development of the 1980s, when, possibly because of the victory of neo-liberalism in politics and economics, it expressed that decade's disenchantment with the social. While neo-liberalism rejected the social for the economic, postmodernism expressed the other side of the demise of the social: the turn to culture. Jeffrey Alexander in an insightful essay has summarized these developments:

> By the end of the 1970s, the energy of the radical social movements of the preceding period had dissipated. Some of their radical demands became institutionalized; others were blocked by massive backlash movements that generated conservative publics and brought right-wing governments to power. The cultural-cum-political shift was so rapid as to seem, once again, to represent some kind of historical-cum-epistemological break. Materialism replaced idealism among political influentials, and surveys reported increasingly conservative views among young people and university students. (Alexander, 1995, p. 23)

Postmodernism can be seen as an expression of political disappointment, akin to the disenchantment that inspired French intellectuals to turn to poststructuralism after 1968. In America this disappointment, which coupled with declining university career opportunities, came later. In the 1990s, after the fall of communism, the world-wide turn to nationalism and a neo-communitarian politics of identity replaced the previous decade's obsession with neo-liberalism, thus lending further to the decline in available political alternatives. It was perfectly fitted to embody neo-liberalism's advocation of a philosophy without values.

The question of the politics of postmodernism has been the source of its greatest controversy. Postmodernism has now been attacked from several sides, ranging from Marxism (Callinicos, 1989; Laclau and Mouffe, 1985) to phenomenology (O'Neill, 1995) and critical hermeneutics (Habermas, 1987b), to social movement theory (Touraine, 1995) and the critical sociology of Pierre Bourdieu (1999). It would appear that there is today, after two decades of political and cultural disappointment, an opening up of new theoretical positions. In the following I will discuss some rejoinders to postmodernism which suggest increasing commonalities between postmoderism and other approaches which do not see as suspect every attempt to find an ethical or political foundation or closure. Elsewhere I have argued that these developments might be due to the fact that it is now widely perceived that the project of deconstruction has achieved its aims and new challenges are coming to the fore, such as relativism (Delanty, 1999a). At a time when Marxism, existentialism and various schools of structuralism offered an uncritical notion of the self, the deconstructive project – which was essentially one of relativism – had a legitimate target. Three decades later new problems are emerging, calling for different kinds of responses, one of which is the need for a notion of closure.

I have already argued that there is much to indicate that Foucault became increasingly interested in the possibility of a recovery of the subject. In his later writings there is a shift from power to resistance, away from the idea of disciplinary modernity. Also his stance on

modernity is more differentiated than is often thought. In his essay
'What is Enlightenment?' he writes: 'I have been seeking to stress that
the thread which may connect us to with the Enlightenment is not
faithfulness to doctrinal elements but, rather, the permanent reactivation
of an attitude – that is, of a philosophical ethos that could be described as
a permanent critique of our historical era' (Foucault, 1997, p. 312). In this,
one of his last essays, he rejects the idea of the postmodern in favour of
a more differentiated view of the modern as also containing countermodernities: 'rather than seeking to distinguish the "modern era" from
the "pre-modern" or "postmodern", I think it would be more useful
to try to find out how the attitude of modernity, ever since its formation, has found itself struggling with attitudes of "countermodernity" '
(Foucault, 1997, pp. 309–10). What Foucault rejects in the Enlightenment
discourse of modernity is the doctrine of the self; he wants to extend the
'permanent critique' of the Enlightenment to the self. It is clear that
Foucault never fully resolved the question of a normative foundation of
politics and ethics, retreating into an obscure politics of resistance. For
him the fundamental struggle was between power and resistance. This
might be contrasted to Habermas's perspective, which portrayed modernity in terms of a conflict between communication and domination,
democracy and capitalism.

   As noted above, Foucault never used the term 'postmodern' and
understood his approach to be an interrogation of modernity from a
point that never quite became clear, though, as the above quote indicates,
he did begin to embrace a notion of countermodernities.[15] There is no
evidence to suggest that he seriously considered relating the possibility
of a countermodernity to civil society or democracy, as Habermas has
proposed. The Habermas–Foucault debate was also decidedly one-sided
since Foucault never had an opportunity to reply to the extensive
Habermasian critique.[16] One might speculate that had he lived longer the
differences between the two approaches might be less confrontational.
Yet, there is no denying the fundamental difference between a perspective based on power and one based on communication. This ambivalence in Foucault has lent his thought open to so many different
interpretations. Thus Richard Rorty (1983) is able to reconcile the postmodernism he sees in Foucault with liberalism, styling his variety as
'postmodernist bourgeois liberalism'.[17] The postmodern pragmatism –
liberal bourgeois postmodernism – that he advocates is attracted to the
irony of deconstructionism, which is not too far removed from liberalism
in that it is a sceptical position which does not dictate what one should
do; like classic liberalism it is negatively conceived. What liberalism and
postmodernism share is a strong privatism and a scepticism about the
possibility of universal validity and of foundations. But there are differences between Foucault and Rorty on the question of universalism and
foundationalism: for Foucault it is impossible; for Rorty it is irrelevant.[18]
For Rorty liberalism and postmodernism share a pragmatic view on

politics and ethics. It is possible for him to make this connection because pragmatism, as represented for instance by John Dewey, is a kind of irony which thrives not just in a public or civic culture but also in a 'poeticized culture', and Foucault, who he acknowledges was not a liberal, was an ironist – unlike Habermas, who is a liberal but not an ironist (Rorty, 1989, p. 65). While I think it is true that Foucault failed to clarify the normative foundations of his position, the claim that there is a latent pragmatic liberalism in his thought seems to me to be a domestication of its central insights, which relate to power and the possibility of its subversion. Foucault stood for a far deeper critique of the self than is permissible in any identifiable liberal philosophy. The absence of a sense of collective politics and universalistic morality should not detract from his central concern to provide the basis for a theory of the transformation of subjectivity. The unclear position on politics in Foucault can be contrasted to the work of Gilles Deleuze and Félix Guattari. Their joint work *Anti-Oedipus* (1983), published in 1972, was more addressed to the political possibilities within modernity, though the politics of desire which they compared to schizophrenia had more affinities with deconstructionism and the encounter of Nietzsche and Freud. This work in fact offered Foucault a means of reconceiving his earlier notion of power as disciplinary, arriving instead at the position of seeing power as productive, generative of desire and of resistance.

Lyotard, in contrast to Foucault, addressed his postmodern approach to Habermas as early as 1979 when he attacked his notion of legitimation as an unrealistic possibility and a residue of the metanarratives of the Enlightenment.[19] In a later essay in 1982, Lyotard reiterates his objection to Habermas, claiming that it is no longer possible to regain a lost principle of unity (Lyotard, 1992, p. 3). Justice, for him, is merely the recognition of heterogeneous language-games, and it is possible to have justice without truth. Habermas, it would appear, is more concerned with locating justice in truth, so long as truth is seen as discursively constituted. Habermas, too, it will be recalled, believed, with Kant, that the aesthetic dimension, though autonomous, could provide a kind of bridge over the gap between knowledge, ethics and morality. For Lyotard that is too much to expect. Politics is rooted less in communication than in something more libidinal which he also associates with the 'sublime', whereas Habermas, he holds, has remained on the level of the 'beautiful'.[20] In contrast to the beautiful – which seeks a false unity between nature and society – the sublime is indeterminate, and ultimately lies beyond language.

In recent times the earlier antagonism between deconstructionism and other forms of modernist thinking has been waning. As deconstructionism loses its connection with poststructuralism, affinities are emerging with other schools of thought. The most significant in this context is the encounter between Gadamer and Derrida in 1981. This dialogue, collected in a volume entitled *Dialogue and Deconstruction* (Michelfelder and

Palmer, 1989), is one of the major pointers of an epistemological shift to the subject and to a hermeneutic version of deconstruction. Though less known that the Gadamer–Habermas and Foucault–Habermas debates, it had a more productive outcome, with both sides modifying their positions and exploring common purposes. In this debate Gadamer acknowledged that the act of understanding is always understanding differently, for the 'fusion of horizons', the theme of his major work *Truth and Method* in 1960 (Gadamer, 1979), is never complete and every arrival at a unity is incomplete. It is this awareness of the incompleteness of interpretation that has brought Derrida and Gadamer closer. The importance of Derrida's deconstruction to Gadamer is its highlighting of rupture and otherness.

It might be put like this: if modernity was about the centrality of the Self, postmodernity reflects a turning to the Other. From a concern with equality – a struggle for the recognition of the sameness of the Self and Other – postmodernity is about the struggle for the recognition of difference.[21] This can take the form of the discovery of the Other in the Self, or an 'ethos of pluralization', to use William Connolly's term (1995). The writings of Levinas, Blanchot and Derrida on the politics of friendship is indicative of a concern with precisely this question of the Other in the Self. In Derrida's own work there is a turning away from the deconstruction of false origins to a search for the Other, or the Other in the Self. According to Simon Critchley (1999), who has commented on this debate, Derrida's recent work – on the gift, on friendship, on Marxism – is an attempt to repoliticize Marxism (Derrida, 1994, 1997). With its origin in Levinas's notion of an ethical relationship to the Other and taken up by Blanchot in his theory of friendship, Derrida suggests a possible link between friendship and democracy. Derrida attempts to translate Blanchot's understanding of friendship, which is an ethical intersubjective relationship, into an ethical and political responsibility. It is an attempt to deduce politics from ethics. In Critchley's words: 'Ethics is defined as the infinite responsibility of unconditional hospitality, while the political can be defined as the taking of a decision without determinate transcendental guarantees' (Critchley, 1999, p. 271). If Levinas established the primacy of ethics, the essence of politics is indeterminacy; it is a realm of risk and danger. Critchley argues how for Derrida politics cannot be founded because such a foundation would limit the freedom of the decision, which can never be limited by guarantees. With this argument, Derrida establishes his notion of 'democracy to come', which might be understood as a moment between ethics and politics. The notion of 'democracy to come', elaborated in his *Spectres of Marx* (Derrida, 1994), refers, too, to the difference between present and future. Critchley relates this to a rediscovery, within deconstructionist thinking, of the idea of autonomy and claims it is an attempt to recover the 'emancipatory promise of modernity'. Leledakis (2000) detects in Derrida's recent work a shift to a concern with 'the social' as an opening of the field of meaning. The social is always a field of meaning that is necessarily always open. In this it might be argued that Derrida's early notion of *différance* – the double condition of deferring and differing – has been given what it previously lacked, a substantial social content.

Not everyone will be convinced that Derrida has made a conversion to the social. John O'Neill (1999) has taken Derrida to task for offering what is essentially a neo-liberal model of the gift: we give only to get something back. The act of giving for Derrida is a purely reciprocal relationship of absolute equality. 'One gives only what one expects to get back. One has nothing to give that one has not borrowed' (O'Neill, 1999, p. 134). Drawing from Mauss, O'Neill criticizes this on the grounds that the gift entails a relationship of inequality which is essential to social life. What Derrida in effect does is assume the absolute equality of members of society and thus accommodates the crisis of the gift in welfare societies. Pierre Bourdieu (1997, p. 95) has also pointed out what he sees as Derrida's reliance 'on the free choice of an isolated individual'.

This criticism, then, suggests that underlying Derrida's esoteric language lie some decontextualized notions of the social. Notwithstanding this objection, I would like to suggest that the increasing concern with the possibility of the social and the political ties in with developments in postmodernist thinking more generally.[22] One dimension to this is the relation between identity as a relation of responsibility between Self and Other. Derrida has explored the theme of otherness in a work on the cultural identity of Europe (Derrida, 1992). While his earlier work banished questions of identity as logocentric, in this work he addresses the question of what kind of identity can Europe have given its many origins. He argues for a notion of identity 'instituted in responsibility' (Derrida, 1992, p. 52), for identity is possible only as a responsibility for the Other. In an argument which is not too far removed from Habermas's (1994) call for a 'constitutional patriotism', Derrida argues Europe must rediscover the difference within itself, for a culture never has a single origin. 'There is no culture or cultural identity without this difference with itself' (Derrida, 1992, pp. 9–10).

Critchley reflects a movement within deconstructionism to move beyond its earlier association with poststructuralism, which was based on a repudiation of Marxism. Derrida has always deliberately left open the question of the political implications of deconstruction, for this was never to be a programme with a positive intention. It was merely a method of reading texts. It did not negate the possibility of meaning, but showed that within the sign there is always a tension or difference between the signified and the signifier, a difference that opened up limitless possibilities for the signifier, and therefore of meaning. Rejecting its reliance on the signified was one of the central aims of deconstruction in its early stages. Today there is some attempt to relink the signifier and signified without recourse to a foundationalism. But can this be more than the positive celebration of difference? Derrida's work has lent itself to American postmodernist attempts to rethink identity and the Other. Along with Foucault, deconstruction and genealogy have given expression to the socially excluded other. As Mark Lilla (1998, p. 37) put it:

> As the Sixties progressed, the children of structuralism came to forget Lévi-Strauss's skepticism about the French revolutionary myth as an honary *sans culottes*. All that that was marginal within Western societies could now be justified and even celebrated philosophically. Some followed Michel Foucault in portraying the development of European civilization as a process of marginalizing domestic misfits – the mentally ill, sexual and political deviants – who were branded and kept under surveillance through the cooperation of social 'power' and 'knowledge'. Others turned to psychology, searching for the repressed Other in the libido or the unconsciousness.

It is this fascination with the other and with difference that has made Derrida famous in America, rather than in France, where deconstruction has been overshadowed by other debates (Judt, 1992, p. 229). Nevertheless, I remain unconvinced that Derrida has developed a serious politics. The growing presence of the social in his recent work only has a superficial connection with politics, and one of the principal outcomes of the Gadamer–Derrida encounter has been a volume on religion for postmodern times (Derrida and Vattimo, 1998).

In American debates on postmodernism and politics there has already been a move beyond deconstructionist postmodernism. In this spirit Nicholson and Seidman (1995) defend postmodernism as a 'social postmodernism', by which they mean a more politically sensitive approach capable of integrating the achievements of social movements into its analysis. In their view postmodernism need not be an abandonment of the social and is not exhausted by deconstructionism. They say a deconstructionist approach was necessary in the context of overcoming modernist forms of power, but with the waning of this framework postmodernism must reconceptualize its aims. Social postmodernism is a type of 'social thinking which integrates deconstruction while simultaneously incorporating some of the analytically synthesizing and expansive political hopes of the modernist tradition of social theorizing' (Nicholson and Seidman, 1995, p. 35).[23] This position can also be clearly seen in the work of Bauman, who has written extensively on postmodern ethics (Bauman, 1992, 1993, 1995). As I have discussed his work elsewhere (Delanty, 1999a), it will suffice to mention here that his main contribution to postmodernism is the attempt to link the theme of the Other to an ethics of responsibility. The hallmark of postmodernity is the existential situation of having to make choices in a world of ever greater possibilities. Modernity reduced the burden of choice in privileging the legislator; postmodernity is characterized by the interpreter, as Bauman argued in *Legislators and Interpreters* (1987). In postmodernity the problem of choice cannot be so easily solved by recourse to established authorities, and as a result the individual must be more morally self-reliant. Postmodern ethics is an ethics of proximity, of responsibility for the Other. However, what Bauman has to offer is an ethics, not a politics. The tendency in his thinking is to reduce politics to the world of instrumentality, and whatever connection there is between the ethical and the political can only be deeply personal.

Perhaps one of the most fruitful ways to appropriate the postmodernist-deconstructionist heritage is that advocated by theorists such as Craig Calhoun (1995) and Chantal Mouffe (1993) for whom radical democracy can learn a lot about pluralism and the politics of difference from postmodernism. For Mouffe, for instance, radical democracy is neither modern nor postmodern. What emerges from the encounter of modernity and postmodernity is the recasting of universalism as a 'particularized universalism'.

Conclusion: Postmodernity beyond the West

There is much to suggest that postmodernism has taken an explicitly political turn. This is evident within the French deconstructionist tradition, where there has been a new interest in the possibility of a self lying beyond deconstructionism, but is more clearly represented in American developments, were the encounter of Self and Other has been more central to debates on social transformation.[24] My overall conclusion is that the term 'postmodernism/postmodernity' has today become normalized. It makes little sense to be 'for it' or 'against' it. It has become like modernity, capitalism, feminism, class, a part of our conceptual vocabulary. Postmodernity refers to a particular phase in modern society, which can be called postindustrial, the information age. It is neither good nor bad but an expression of the current situation. As Edward Soja (1996, pp. 3–5) has argued, it is futile to chose between two hostile camps, modernity or postmodernity, since this can only be to opt for a reductionist position. It seems sensible, instead, to look for a creative combination of both modernity and postmodernity.[25] As Friese and Wagner (1999b) argue, if the move from modernity to postmodernity was an expression of the tendency to make 'all that is solid melt into air', the current situation seems to point to a certain recovery of solidity.

I will conclude this chapter by pointing to two features of contemporary society which justify the use of the term 'postmodernity' in a specific sense. One dimension is the reinvention of tradition and history in the present. Modernity was essentially posttraditional in that one of its central driving forces was the critique of tradition by secular rationality. Postmodernity, as we have seen, does not involve this rejection of the past by a triumphant present, but is an expression of the creative appropriation of the past and present. The reinvention of the past is part of the aestheticization of everyday life which, as we have seen, is one of the main markers of postmodernism. This relates directly to the second dimension I want to stress: postmodernity as postwestern, in the sense of non-western and possibly anti-western.

Modernity was European and later American, with its roots deep in the aesthetic and political movements that animated the West since the Enlightenment. By the late twentieth century, modernity lost much of its Europeanness, not least because it has now become necessary to speak of modernities rather than any one particular model of modernity (Mouzelis, 1999; Taylor, 1999; Therborn, 1995). Postmodernity, too, began as an American cultural innovation and had its roots in late European modernism, which it never quite severed. Today the genuinely postmodern impulse comes not from the still late modern and postmodernistically inclined West but from non-western societies where the aestheticization of everyday life, history and even of politics has been more far-reaching, and where modernism and modernity had not prepared the ground for postmodernism. The European/western world is still tied to the worldview of the European Enlightenment where the two most powerful movements are those of capitalism and democracy. Cultural modernity emerged out of European civil society, and in the global world in which we now live these struggles have not abated, however much their forms may have changed.

In recent times many authors have observed the emergence of a postmodern ethos in non-western societies (Ahmed, 1992; Al-Azmeh, 1993; Arnason, 1997; Clarke, 1997; Dallmayr, 1996; Fisher and Abedi, 1990; Miyoshi and Harootunian, 1989; Sugimoto and Arnason, 1995; Turner, 1994). What is distinctive about this is the reintegration of tradition and modernity. Some have argued that postmodernism has preceded western modernity and is best exemplified in ancient China (Hall, 1991). Islam and Japan, to mention two civilizations whose encounter with the West occurred only after a long and self-formative historical process, are based on a creative revitalization of tradition and modernity. They cannot be considered posttraditional, for modernity in these societies – which should be considered civilizational frameworks – did not occur via the critique of religion – since there was no reformation or enlightenment in the western sense – but occurred through the adapation of tradition to modernity.[26] It is is not just this mix of tradition and modernity, religion and rationality, that qualifies the application of the term 'postmodern' to these societies, since there is nothing new in this, and, as Max Weber recognized, that was also the paradox of western rationalism. The postmodern moment comes from the aestheticization of an everyday life that has seen a far greater confluence of tradition and modernity than in the West.

This thesis can be taken one step further. The postmodernization of non-western societies, such as Japan and much of the Islamic world, is very much connected to processes of globalization (Jameson and Miyoshi, 1998). While globalization can be seen as the latest stage in westernization/Americanization, it cannot be reduced to modernization, for, as is well known, there are multiple logics of development. In the case of Japan postmodernization came only after a self-formative period of an autonomously developed modernity. The western impact, and in particular the American influence, is of course crucial to this, but it has been increasingly recognized that processes of globalization unleash multiple responses, which can never be reduced to the imperatives of the core (Featherstone et al., 1995; Smelser, 1997, pp. 73–98; Wilson and Dissanayake, 1996). Given that the various dimensions of globalization – in finance, in communications, in popular culture, in science – are articulated through the medium of information, as Manuel Castells (1996, 1997, 1998) argues, the possibilities for unpredictable outcomes are great. This possibily points to a final dimension to postmodernization: the growing experience of contingency. Postmodernization is no longer underpinned by European/western modernity; it is not reducible to Americanization, which is only the latest stage in modernization; rather it should be seen as kind of cultural fragmentation, a crystallization of modernity. The postmodern world is one that has been transformed by globalization and is composed of not one civilizational model, but many, for instance the European Union, North America, Japan, the Islamic world, Latin America, South East Asia. Postmodernization, ultimately, then, is the condition of postwesternization. This characterization of postmodernization is also postcommunism, for the Soviet experiment with communism can be seen as the last great experiment within organized modernity. With the collapse of this experiment, organized modernity, in crisis in the West for a longer period but sustained by the Cold War, has come to a final end.

The implications that this has for knowledge and for power may be apparent in the universal crisis of modernity as a framework of reference, but whether postmodernization will result in a new conception of the self is less clear. In one sense it is true that postmodernization, in the sense of the creative appropriation of tradition, may be more apparent in the non-western world, but this may be at the cost of some of the most cherished ideas that lie behind the western understanding of the self.

8

FURTHER REFLECTIONS
Constructivism Beyond Postmodernity

In a much discussed work, *Baroque Reason*, originally published in French in 1984, Christine Buci-Glucksmann gave a fascinating reading of modernity that in some ways resembles my intentions in this book, and which can be called a postmodernization of modernity, or a dissolution of the distinction between modernity and postmodernity (Buci-Glucksmann, 1994; subsequent references are to this unless otherwise stated).[1] There is, however, a major difference. Her search for a counter-modernity, which might reflect what was to become postmodernism, is based on an interpretation of baroque culture. 'Benjamin, Baudelaire, Lacan, Barthes something like a *baroque paradigm* asserts and establishes itself within "modernity"' (p. 141). The baroque is contrasted to the Cartesian tradition and is held to represent an alternative modernity to the alleged perspectivalism of the latter. The baroque represents a truly subversive kind of aesthetic vision: 'The baroque region of modernity derives from the labour of a plural, hetrogeneous negativity, post-Hegelian and non-Hegelian, which Adorno detected in the music of Schönberg: "a chaotic anarchy, the precedence of disorder over order"' (p. 151). But Buci-Glucksmann's reading of the baroque is through the lens not of high modernism but of poststructuralist deconstructionism: the baroque is the culture of desire and of unreason: 'baroque reason brings into play the infinite materality of images and bodies. And this being so, it always has to do with otherness as desire' (p. 139).The connection to modernity that it involves is its visuality, and she quotes approvingly Walter Benjamin's optical understanding of modernity as a 'face or look' which is exemplified in the visual arcade: 'The modern therefore takes the form of baroque phenomenology internal to the phantasmagoric display-form of the market, which can be seen in museums, salons, collections, world exhibitions, and arcades' (p. 164).[2] But this kind of visuality is an embodied one; it is not the cold eye of calculated reason but the bodily world of desire.

The philosophical basis of Buci-Glucksmann's argument might be summed up as this: there are two aesthetics of visions in modernity, one based on madness or unreason and one based on reason; the former, expressed in the baroque, aspires to express the sublime, and the latter, the Enlightenment model, is confined to the beautiful. The beautiful seeks a harmony between nature and society; the sublime seeks to express the unrepresentable, the unreachable, and must therefore be melancholic since it can never succeed. The first is a disembodied visuality; the second an embodied one. Lying behind these polarities is a more elemental conflict between the body (represented by the baroque) and the mind (represented by the Enlightenment).

What it is interesting about this argument is that it attempts to locate postmodernist conceptions of anti-Enlightenment reason within modernity, which is held to contain a counter-logic. The problem, however, with this approach to modernity is that it is based on a dualism of the baroque versus Cartesianism/Enlightenment thinking, and one which fails to understand the multifaceted nature of either culture. First, the connection between the baroque and radical modernism is exaggerated. The former was specific to the seventeenth century and was an expression of the Catholic counter-reformation. The culture of the baroque was indeed an early popular culture but one that could be used for hegemonic purposes (Maravall, 1986). It was in many respects an affirmative culture, and was far from the negativity of modernism. On the other side, Cartesianism cannot be reduced to a culture of 'the gaze', a mere mirroring of nature, as Rorty (1979) argued in his *Philosophy and the Mirror of Nature*. Martin Jay (1992), in a study on these 'scopic regimes of modernity', has correctly, in my view, assessed the shortcomings of seeing modernity in terms of the dominance of the sense of sight, in particular in so far as this is unreflexive. Thus, notions such as Foucault's apparatus of surveillance, or Rorty's image of the mirror, or Debord's (1994) society of the spectacle, or Heidegger's age of the world picture, reduce modernity to a regime of visual power, which might be called the culture of the gaze. As Jay (1992, p. 184) has pointed out: 'the Cartesian perspectivalist tradition contained a potential for internal contestation in the possible uncoupling of the painter's view of the scene from that of the presumed beholder'. In any event, and it is Jay's point, it is not evident why the 'madness of vision' of the baroque, or the casual glance of the *flâneur*, is better than the alleged culture of 'the gaze': 'Glancing is not somehow innately superior to gazing; vision hostage to desire is not necessarily always better than casting a cold eye' (Jay, 1992, p. 189). The latter can be seen as more than a strategy of control, and in any case the two scopic regimes are not so entirely separated as is often suggested in conventional accounts of modernity.

Another way to see modernity is as a culture dominated less by the eye than by the voice. As already argued, an important tradition in modernity is also the power of discourse. By focusing on voice – or discourse – we can get a better sense of the conflict between the two kinds of self lying behind the modern aesthetic, as described by Buci-

Glucksmann. Modernity can be seen as a struggle between the voice and
the eye, whereby these refer to the self as embodied in the world of lived
experience and the self as a disembodied scopic regime. In the second,
the self is essentially abstract and epitomized in the Cartesian ego, a
purely thinking and perceiving being. This conception of the self is the
basis of the modern understanding of knowledge and is also related to
the modern practice of politics, liberalism, the possibility of which is the
autonomous individual. In this book I have tried to relativize some of the
postmodernist critiques of modernity in the key domains of knowledge,
power and the self. I have done this by showing that many of these
conceptions were themselves rooted in a deep scepticism and reflexivity
which derived from modernity's awareness of its limits and the bounds
of possibility. Yet, it is clear that this was more firmly established in the
domains of knowledge and power than in the conception of the self
where a powerful visual conception of the self, as a disembodied eye has
prevailed.

****

In the alternative model of the self mentioned above – the self as
embodied in voice – we have a more reflexive relation between Self,
Other and world. If we see this relation as a discursively mediated one,
some of the problems with the postmodernist deconstructive position
can be avoided. Thus it is a question not of one scopic regime being
replaced by another, but of a radicalization of the discursive component
in modernity. The distinctive feature of modernity is not the eye of
power but the surfacing of voices of protest in the formation of the
discursive spaces that modern society created in the domain between
the state and the household.

In modernity the revolution begun within the sphere of knowledge
extended into the domain of power with the formation of a discursive
understanding of politics, and this revolution was finally extended into
the domain of the identity of the self in the postmodern period when
scepticism and discursivity were applied to the self. In modernity the self
had been transformed by the new understanding of politics and by the
extension of scepticism beyond the model of knowledge. However,
modernity did not transform the self to the same extent as it did the
model of knowledge and politics. In the postmodern, or late modern age,
roughly the latter decades of the twentieth century, one of the most far-
reaching changes has been in the identity of the self. For scepticism as
self-doubt and uncertainty has penetrated into the very identity of the
self, as is argued by Anthony Giddens (1991).

This transformation of the self – as well as knowledge and power – has
been widely understood to be an expression of reflexivity (Beck, 1992;
Beck et al., 1994; Giddens, 1990, 1991; Melucci, 1996), a theme that is also

associated with the sociology of Pierre Bourdieu (1984, 1990, 1996a, 1996b, 1996c), with earlier conceptions in the well-known works of John O'Neill (1972) and Alvin Gouldner (1970). Hans Joas (1996), too, pursues a similar line of inquiry with his notion of the creativity of action. Rather than seeing the self as abolished, as in the early writings of Foucault, the idea of reflexivity offers a better grasp of the constitution of the self in the postmodern age.[3] The available theories of the self – postmodernist deconstructionism, Habermasian social theory, communitarianism, liberalism, rational choice, Bourdieu's sociology – are unable to provide an adequate understanding of it. Briefly: as we have seen in the last chapter, postmodernist deconstruction has undermined the possibility of the self; Habermas has assumed the existence of a stable and coherent self which is the basis of the background consensus without which the discourse ethic would not function; communitarianism assumes a too strict fit between political identity and cultural identity, for the problem is not the self but the realization of the self in the political order; liberalism, like rational choice, is based on the assumption of a socially and culturally decontextualized self; and the sociology of Bourdieu, while innovative in matters relating to culture, suffers from an overly power-oriented conception of agency, neglecting the dimension of creativity and autommomy.

Authors such as Beck, Giddens, Joas, Harré and Melucci have written extensively on the emergence of a reflexive self in late modernity, a term they prefer to use than postmodernity. This is because reflexivity is connected to one of the cultural legacies of modernity, namely individualism, but now understood as 'individuation', by which is meant the process by which the self is constructed. Reflexivity refers to a relationship between subjectivity – the Self – and Objectivity – the Other, the world – in which both are articulated alongside each other. Reflexivity is essentially a category of mediation, relating subjective and objective domains, and, in the sociology of Pierre Bourdieu, science and society. Reflexivity, in so far as it is a category of mediation, has been systematically explored by Anthony Giddens. Though he did not use this term in his theory of structuration (Giddens, 1984), this work can be seen as providing the foundation for his latter work on reflexivity and the self in late modernity. By means of the concept 'structuration', Giddens tries to show the essential 'duality' of agency and structure. This is a duality rather than a dualism, because neither can be separated. Structures are rule systems which must be interpreted by social actors, who are also 'knowledgeable'. In late modernity the capacity for social actors to be able to interpret is greater than ever, since they have access to ever more cultural resources, such as knowledge, including sociological knowledge. I have criticized this elsewhere on the grounds that the theory of structuration, as well as Giddens's mature theory of late modernity, does not make more of the mediatory nature of reflexivity as a cultural category (Delanty, 1999a, Chap. 6), for Giddens tends too easily to reduce agency and structure to each other, with the mediatory dimension of culture reduced to mere knowledge. This neglects the wider cognitive dimension of culture in the sense of cultural models of interpretation and, moreover, Giddens operates with a very transparent sense of culture as something that social actors can simply manipulate. The problem with this is that it undermines the autonomy of culture as the mediatory domain between structure and agency. In other words, mediation is not quite the same as what Giddens calls 'duality' – it allows the autonomy of both structure and agency to be preserved as well as granting a central role to culture.

If culture were granted more autonomy than Giddens allows, the concept of reflexivity could also be seen in somewhat broader terms to refer to a category of human experience than is culturally constructed. Self, Other and world, as dimensions of human experience, are embodied in culturally mediated forms. Experience is not a just a property of the self but is also an expression of cultural categories. Alberto Melucci and Rom Harré have a more cultural understanding of the self as symbolically mediated and relational, for one dimension to culture is the experience of difference – between oneself and another and between the many identities of the self – which is likely to be enhanced in late modern societies. The self has been dissolved as a result of the fragmentation of experience in what is a highly differentiated and complex society, in terms of the production of meaning, information and cultural possibilities. The self belongs to numerous systems of meaning and moves through many different systems of relations in the course of a lifetime. As a result, the possibility of an identity crisis is very great, and it is likely that this will be more significant than a cultural crisis as such. Anxiety today is thus more likely to be a personal problem, rather than a cultural one as such (see Wilkinson, 1999). Under these circumstances, 'identity is in the process of being redefined as a pure self-reflexive capacity or self-awareness' (Melucci, 1996, p. 36).

Reflexivity is a cultural feature of contemporary society and is very much related to the capacity of individuals to learn to cope with cultural choices and uncertainty. The problem of choice cannot be solved by reference to a set of stable cultural norms or by recourse to a permanently constructed identity. Identity is becoming more fluid and reflexively constructed in the recognition that the only thing that makes continuity in one's biographical narrative possible is the capacity for action, the ability to make cultural choices. The following passage sums up succinctly the relation between reflexivity and cultural construction:

> In information societies our consciousness attains new levels of reflexivity. What matters today is no longer mere learning, but rather learning how to learn – how to control our cognitive and motivational processes and to adapt them to new problems. Technological power has been accompanied by an exponential growth of symbolic possibilities, by an increase in self-reflective activity: by the heightened capacity to reflect and represent reality through a

multitude of languages. This capacity seems to be gradually replacing reality itself, so that we are in a process of coming to inhabit a world constructed out of the images that we ourselves have created, a world where we no longer can distinguish reality from the reality of the image. (Melucci, 1996, pp. 42–3)

Reflexivity has become more important today as a result of the multiple bonds of belonging, roles and identities. Communication is the means of dealing with situations which are multiple and discontinuous. In other words, in contemporary societies the problem of choice is solved increasingly by the individual, whose capacity to act is coming to rest more and more on a reflexive relationship between experience and cultural options. But these options are as much restraints as possibilities. Learning to live with cultural uncertainty defines the reflexive situation of the self. This is more than a question of the cultural choices of the life-world but is also the central dimension in the encounter of Self and Other. The identity of the self is not a self-creation but depends on the recognition of others (Honneth, 1996). The autonomy of the self and recognition by others are closely related. It may be said that the self is constructed in processes of recognition and autonomy. Viewed in the broader sense, reflexivity is manifest in what might be called experience, that is, a kind of action that is not reducible to its social context, be it culture or structure. Nor is it reducible to the identity of self. By experience I mean the process – which is a learning process – by which the self is embodied in the other and in a world. This is a learning process because in order to survive in a world of a high degree of contingency and accelerated change and without cultural certainty the actor must constantly be able to learn to learn, that is, to learn to make choices. It is no longer merely a matter of making choices but of learning how to make a choice.

It is important to see that one of the implications of this view of reflexivity is that it gives a central place to communication. Contemporary societies are increasingly being integrated through communication, rather than by ideology, dominant value systems, elites or institutions. In order for the self – be it the individual or the collective actor – to make sense of its situation and make cultural choices it needs to have access to information and participation in communication. Because of their complexity and differentiated nature, contemporary societies are necessarily highly mediated, for reality is rarely directly experienced, just as it is not always a matter of making straight-forward choices. The cultural mechanism by which reality, as well as action options, is mediated is communication. It is for this reason that I have stressed the centrality of voice in the making of modernity. Today in the age of contentious action, the salience of voice has not decreased. We can say, with Jürgen Habermas, that the reflexive capacity of modern societies to engage in critique and the contestation of power rests on the expansion of their discursive powers. If we see modernity as the opening up of discursive spaces in society – as the extension of scepticism into the world of power – the contemporary challenge of cultural reflexivity can be seen as the extension of communication in the deeper domains of human experience, as in the encounter between Self and Other. New critiques of the self, which go back to Levinas, have taught us that the other is also to be found within the self (Critchley, 1999; Ricoeur, 1994).

It is clear, then, that reflexivity is not something harmonious, or even necessarily emancipatory. For Luhmann, who takes to an extreme the loss of the promise of emancipation, reflexivity is related to a total separation of communication from agency and meaning. In his sense of the term it is a matter of self-observations by subjectless discourses. For Beck reflexivity is induced by risk; for Giddens it is related to the growing abstractness of late modern society and the need for trust in expert systems. However, both Beck and Giddens, in their different ways, see reflexivity as essentially a product of changed relations between structures and agency, with agency emancipating itself from structures in Beck and with new patterns of institutionalization emerging in Giddens. Against these somewhat reductionist views on reflexivity – as a property of social actors or of institutional systems – I am arguing for a sense of reflexivity as culturally reproduced, reducible neither to agency nor to structure, and manifest in many domains of human experience, such as those of Self, Other and world. But what must be stressed is not just the category of experience as the medium through which it unfolds, namely communication: experience is today more and more reproduced in communicative forms. Thus the enhanced reflexivity in late modern societies can be seen as articulated in the vast expansion of communicative spaces which today extend into the cultural fabric of society.

This emphasis on communication is not to be understood in terms of a model of consensus, as might be suggested by some of Habermas's work, which has been too much concerned with the possibility of 'communication free of domination' as a normal ideal which is presupposed in all of communication. From the perspective of normative philosophy there might be some point in pursuing this line of inquiry, but from the more empirically oriented view of sociology what becomes important is the openness of communication. This is precisely what best characterizes the contemporary situation. The impossibility of closure has been one of the most important contributions of deconstructionist thinking. In light of the constructivist turn in social theory and the increase in action positions, we can now see how this notion of indeterminacy has become more relevant than ever before. Indeterminacy is not a matter of deconstructionist interventions but, on the contrary, is one of the enhanced capacity of social actors for creative action. But because the field of action cannot itself be chosen or rendered determinate, the possibility of closure is always postponed. Since much of action is expressed in the form of communicatively mediated relations, which exists in different and incommensurable contexts, there can only be a proliferation of discourses.

****

Where does this leave us? Are there any limits to the essential indeterminacy of discourses of communication? For it can be simply concluded that contemporary societies are experiencing something like a radicalization of the Kantian indeterminacy of the absolute in so far as this is now manifest in the cognitive structures of society. Even in Habermas's recent work there is an increasing recognition of the indeterminacy of the discursive ethic, which, in separating itself off from the communicative action of the life-world, no longer has a moment of closure. If the Habermasian discourse ethic does not offer the final moment of closure, the impossibility of which was always denied by deconstructionist approaches, the question still remains as to whether there are limits to the apparent contingency that was always contained in the discourses of scepticism, discursivity and reflexivity. Can scepticism have a positive moment? Can it be linked more closely to reflexivity? To pose the question like this is to open up the prospect of a new constructivism capable of reversing the descent into endless deconstructionism.

It would appear that there are two contemporary perspectives on this question of constructivism. These concern the relationship between science and experience. One perspective can be attributed to Pierre Bourdieu. This relates to the ability of social science to redeem the reflexive moment, and thereby preserve a link with the tradition of modernity. The other perspective is a more radical abandonment of the promise of science and the seeking of the reflexive moment in forms of human experience in which certain cognitive traits share some of the aspirations of science. A contemporary example of this is cognitive theory, as represented in Francesco Varela, Evan Thompson and Eleanor Rosch's, *The Embodied Mind: Cognitive Science and Human Experience* (1991). From a different perspective, the work of Boltanski and Thévenot can be seen in this light, too.

Bourdieu's sociology is based on a search for reflexive links between the standpoint of the social scientist and the social world. In order for social science to study the social world it must first of all withdraw from it, but once it does so it loses its direct relationship to society and is in danger of retreating into the scholastic point of view. By means of reflexivity the social scientist can withdraw from the social world and at the same time be conscious of the social context of all science, for the scholastic point of view is inseparable from the scholastic situation, the *skhole*. The recognition of the distance and the simultaneous desire to overcome it is the paradoxical situation of social science, a paradox that is better understood as one of reflexivity:

On double truth and the right distance. How to avoid seeming complicitous with the object analyzed (notably in the eyes of those who are foreign to it) or, conversely, reductive and hostile (especially to those who are caught up in the object and who are inclined to refuse the very principle of objectivation)? How to reconcile the objectivation of belief (religious, literary, artistic, scientific, etc.) and of its social conditions of production, and the sensible and faithful evocation of the experience of belief that is inherent to being inserted and involved in a social game? Only at the cost of a very long and very difficult work – and one that is the more invisible the more successful it is – to put oneself at a distance from the object and then to surmount this very distance, a work that bears inseparably on the object and on the relationship to the object, thus on the subject of the scientific work. (Bourdieu, 1999, p. 334)

It seems that for Bourdieu reflexivity is not something intellectuals and social scientists can achieve. Social actors, from the perspective of the habitus, do not appear to be capable of the same degree of reflexivity. To assume otherwise is to commit the 'scholastic fallacy'; it is to confuse the distinction between scientific and ordinary knowledge (Bourdieu, 1997, p. 130). Bourdieu's notion of social actors is not too far removed from Giddens's emphasis on the knowledgeability of the actor, for they have a 'practical sense' (*sens practique*) and it is this that enables social actors to be both determined and capable of constructing their world:

In fact, 'subjects' are active and knowing agents endowed with a practical sense, that is, an acquired system of preferences, of principles of vision and division (what is usually called taste), and also a system of durable cognitive structures (which are essentially the product of the internalization of objective structures) and of schemes of action which orient the perception of the situation and the appropriate response. (Bourdieu, 1997, p. 25)

But this practical sense is too much a product of concrete situations to be able to achieve the universality of science. The objectivity of science ultimately rests on its autonomy, as is also the case for art and literature, which along with science undergo increasing autonomy with modernity; in art as a result of the aesthetic form and in science as a result of its methodology. In *The Rules of Art*, Bourdieu (1996b, p. 242) writes:

The evolution of the field of cultural production towards a greater autonomy is thus accompanied by a greater reflexivity, which leads each of the 'genres' to a sort of critical turning in on itself, on its own principle, on its own premises: and it becomes more and more frequent that the work of art, a *vanitas* which betrays itself as such, closes in on itself. (Bourdieu, 1996b, p. 242)

Clearly Bourdieu thinks that a reflexive social science can allow something like a rational subject to emerge from the habitus (Bourdieu and Wacquant, 1992). Yet it never becomes clear how reflexivity in science and in the discourses of intellectuals and artists becomes linked to practical sense. This is comparable to the problem in Habermas's work of discourse and communication: communication can be redeemed in the discourse ethic but at the price of the separation of the latter from the context of its application.

While Bourdieu's concerns lie with reflexivity in science and the intellectual's field of art and literature, or a 'corporatism of the universal' as he has called it,[4] other constructivist approaches look more closely at the embodiment of science in the social world and its orders of justification. One might consider in this context the work of Boltanski and Thévenot, which has been recognized as one of the main alternatives to Bourdieu's sociology in France (Benatouil, 1999; Boltanski and Thévenot, 1999; Wagner, 1999). This approach, which prefers to call itself 'pragmatic' rather than 'critical', as in Bourdieu, does not see social science as being able to offer an independent 'order of justification'. From an entirely different perspective, Francesco Varela and his associates seek to heal the rift between science and other forms of human experience (Varela et al., 1991). Their version of cognitive science is based on the assumption that science must embrace the truths of human experience, thereby encompassing the possibilities for transformation inherent in experience. The cognitive human being is the starting point for their approach, which aims to explore the implications for traditional western science of the self as embodied in experience. What is being questioned in this way of thinking, and which has been reflected in other constructivist approaches, such as Sousa Santos (1995), Unger (1987) and Wallerstein et al. (1996), is the separation of experience and science, which has been presupposed in all western science, be it that of modernity or postmodernity.

****

The history of modern social thought, so often portrayed as a history of failed attempts at a synthesis, can be seen in terms of three major epistemic shifts, defined with respect to the political question, the social question and the cultural question. In the early modern period and extending well into the eighteenth century, the idea of civil society emerged with the new science of politics, or political economy. This concern with civil society formed the basis of modern social theory, whose origins can be said to lie in political philosophy (Wagner, 1998). The concern with political theory shifted to a concern with the social question in the nineteenth century, and it is this that forms the second major epistemic shift. From Marx onwards, the political question – which was largely a matter of rights – becomes overshadowed with the recognition that civil society is also a bourgeois-capitalist society devoted to material accumulation. The question now becomes one of social justice, as is also exemplified in T.H. Marshall's theory of citizenship. Sociology was born with the recognition that civil society constituted more than a purely public realm, but was preeminently social, and whose other face was national. A wider interest in the social as the domain of work, power, values, community and organization animated social theory from the first quarter of the nineteenth century, as is reflected in classical sociology, from the Scottish moral philosophers to Comte through Spencer to Durkheim, Weber, Simmel and Parsons. Sheldon Wolin (1961, p. 361) has called this turn to 'society' the 'sublimation of politics'.

The social theory of the last half of the twentieth century has been the story of the decline of the social, as understood in classical social theory, be it national, capitalist or industrial society. Under the aegis of post-modernism this decline of the social can be described as the passing of modernity, which was formed out of the supplanting of the political question concerning civil society by the social question of capitalist society, or what for some was industrial society. The demise of the social was accompanied by the rise of the cultural question in the closing decades of the twentieth century. Thus, the question of culture constitutes the third epistemic shift. Of course the first intimations of the rise of the cultural can be found as early as the work of Veblen and Simmel, Kracauer and later the Frankfurt School on the rise of mass society based on consumption rather than production, but the cultural turn did not become decisive until postmodernism became widely accepted. These early accounts were still based on the reality of industrial society, which had separated work and leisure. Undoubtedly the postmodernist obscuring of the social has been aided by the theory of postindustrial society and the double impact of globalization – which undermined the idea of national societies – and the demise of the political ideologies of modernity, which still greatly underpined classical social theory.

The current situation can be said to be one characterized by the prevalence of the question of culture, whether what is at issue is democracy, politics or science (Castells, 1997; Fuller, 1997; Trend, 1997). In power, in identity, in community, in social movements, lifestyles and consumption, in science, in nature and gender, the question of culture has become central. Depending on one's approach, this can either lead to the exclusion of the social or the political, or it can reflect an attempt to reintegrate the social and the political into a wider cultural understanding of society. Baudrillard and contemporary cultural studies can be cited as an example of the former approach, which has marginalized the social and the political; Touraine seeks to link the cultural to the political, denying the validity of the social; while Jeffrey Alexander's (1998) neofunctionalism aims to link the cultural to the social, seemingly marginalizing the political. Bourdieu would appear to have offered the most elaborate attempt to integrate the question of culture into a socially and politically sensitive approach.[5] It would not be an unrepresentative claim to make that in social science today the 'all is culture' view has gained widespread acceptance, even to the extent that science itself has become culturalized.[6] This situation has plunged social science into the deepest waters of uncertainty as to its epistemological foundations.[7]

I have referred above to the view expressed by many authors that one of the main challenges today is to relink science and experience. The cultural turn – and constructivist epistemology that accompanies it – certainly offers a basis from which to approach this question, though the notion of culture at the moment is too hotly contested for it to be immediately apparent how science and experience might be connected.[8] The concept of constructivism is also extremely varied, ranging from the approach of Luhmann to that of Bourdieu. However, this situation is not altogether unique, as the previous epistemic dominance of the political and the social question was also highly contested, between, for instance, liberal and Marxist social theory. Some suggestions can be made by way of conclusion. Taking up the notion of reflexivity and constructivist thinking more generally, we can begin to see how science and experience might be linked. If contemporary societies are seen as integrated through communication, as argued through this book, the dependence of society on science for its survival will be great, as will the reverse. Both science and society are linked because science has lost its ability to legitimate itself by reference to an independent criterion of legitimacy, such as a grand narrative. Science now depends on society for its legitimation to an extent never before imaginable, and society, in turn, needs science to survive in an age of information and communication. The model of knowledge today is inseparable from cultural reproduction since the reflexivity that is central to culture cannot be understood without reference to cognitive structures.[9] This is so because reflexivity is essentially a learning mechanism, and therefore cuts across the domains of knowledge, power and the self. What is called the postmodern turn is nothing more than the extension of reflexivity from the field of knowledge into the domains of power and the self. In this deepening of the discourses of scepticism and discursivity into a heightened reflexivity, the central problematic of modernity becomes the question of cultural constructivism, the articulation of new cultural models. The ideas of 'society as artifact' or 'knowledge as power' or 'communication as action' grasp in different ways the cultural constructivism of postmodernity.

NOTES

Introduction: Knowledge, Power and the Self

1. According to Latour, modernity is a discourse of purification which cuts across discourses of translation, or hybridization. We are not modern because these have always been present in premodern times.
2. On the history of scepticism, see Hookway (1990).

1 The Discourses of Modernity: Enlightenment, Modernism and *Fin de Siècle* Sociology

1. On the crisis of organized modernity, see Wagner (1994). On the concept of organized modernity, see also Law (1994).
2. Other works include Perrault's *Parallele des anciens et des modernes*, published in 1688–96, and Fontenelle's *Les anciens et les modernes*, published in 1688. See Jones (1961).
3. See also Walter Benjamin's famous study on the origin of German tragic drama, Benjamin (1977). See also Buci-Glucksmann (1994) and Chapter 8 of this book.
4. On the origins of modernity in Kant, Hegel and Marx, see Rundell (1987).
5. On Marx and modernism, see also Love (1988).
6. A third strand can also be mentioned, namely the conservative or 'anti-modernist' critique of modernity, with which the names of Löwith and Gehlen can be associated. Since much of this will be the subject of the next chapter, I will not consider it here.
7. For a discussion on the status of Nietzsche and Heidegger as modern or postmodern thinkers, see Smith (1996). On the impact of Nietzsche in Germany, see Ashheim (1992). See also Allison (1985) and Antonio (1995).
8. On Ortega y Gasset as a theorist of modernity, see Gray (1989).
9. In Nietzsche, it should be noted that the strong create their own values, for which they are resisted by the weak.
10. On Weber and Nietzsche, see Stauth (1992).
11. On maturity and modernity, see Owen (1994).
12. See the invaluable collection of Simmel's essays on culture, Frisby and Featherstone (1997).
13. I have concentrated here on Simmel but mention must be made of Veblen's work (1970) and Siegfried Kracauer's Weimar writings, for instance his *The Mass Ornament* (Kracauer, 1995).

2 Modernity and Secularization: Religion and the Postmodern Challenge

1. See, for instance, the volume *Detraditionalization* (Hellas et al., 1996).
2. This has been observed by Kieran Flanagan in a new Preface to his study on theology and culture, Flanagan (1999).
3. *Telos*, 113, Fall 1998.
4. See the article by the translator, Robert Wallace, on the background to the debate (Wallace, 1981).
5. This sense of secularization – the rationalization of belief systems – can be compared to the two other dominant uses of the term: secularization as the institutional separation of Church and state, and secularization as the decline in religious beliefs.
6. The main difference is that for Weber the transformation of salvation is to be understood as part of the universal process of disenchantment. He tends to use the term 'secularization' in the sense of modernization, meaning the decline of religious belief. That is, secularization for Weber comes in the wake of religious rationalization, for once the disenchantment of religion is complete, the process of modernization begins.
7. This notion of secularization has more recently been taken up by Marcel Gauchet (1997), who sees the Judeo-Christian tradition as a self-negation of religion. His thesis is that the modern struggle for liberation was first articulated in religion and that, ultimately, there is no difference between monotheism and modernity. The fundamental 'paradox of religion' is that the more powerful God became, the more he withdrew from the temporal world, leaving humans to their own fate (Gauchet, 1997, p. 30). See also Kalyvas (1999) and Larmore (1996, pp. 42–3).
8. This latter position is frequently referred to as essentialism.
9. See, for instance, Eisenstadt (1973) and Gusfield (1966) for a similar perspective.
10. For a discussion of this, see Delanty (2000a).
11. See Taylor (1989) for a fuller account of his philosophical position.
12. See also Tiryakian's (1992) essay on enchantment in modernity.
13. See also his earlier work, Botwinick (1993).
14. For a critical review see Vatter (1999), Pickstock (1998) and see also on religion and deconstruction Berry and Wernick (1993) and Taylor (1984).
15. In this context mention might be made of the negative theology of Michael Theunissen, who offers a different view on negativity. See Thornhill (1998).

3 The Pathogenesis of Modernity: The Limits of Enlightenment

1. On the implications of the Holocaust for social theory, see Fine and Turner (2000). See also Cheyette and Marcus (1998) for views on different interpretations of the significance of modernity for Jews.
2. This will be discussed with reference to the idea of community in Chapter 7. On nostalgia and modernity and postmodernity, see Turner (1990).
3. It may be remarked that he is closer to Benjamin (1973b), whose philosophy of history was based on the redemption of memory.

4. Strauss will be discussed in detail in Chapter 4.
5. See the symposium on Bourdieu's work on Pascal in the *European Journal of Social Theory*, 2, 3, 1999.
6. On Voeglin see McNight (1978).
7. In her hierachy of orders, labour has a lesser worth than work, for it involves less self-conscious activity.
8. It is presumably for this reason that she never entirely rejected Heidegger after his own political inclinations became apparent. See Fine (2000).
9. See Eliot's *Notes Towards the Definition of Culture*, in particular the essay 'The Unity of European Culture' (Eliot, 1948).
10. See the chapter 'Hannah Arendt and the Political' in Lefort (1988).

4　The Impossibility of Modernity: Cultural Crystallization and the Problem of Contingency

1. Perry Anderson (1992, p. 326) points out that Gehlen derived the term from Pareto.
2. The best example of this thesis is Daniel Bell's *The End of Ideology* (1962).
3. For a discussion see Niethammer (1993) and Habermas (1987b, pp. 5–6).
4. See Anderson's (1992) history of this debate.
5. For a wide-ranging account of notions of the end of history, see Bull (1995).
6. This is suggested by Heller and Feher (1988, pp. 3–4).
7. See his correspondence on modernity with Karl Löwith in the 1940s (Strauss, 1983).
8. For a Nietzschean interpretation of Strauss, see Drury (1981). See also Pippin (1997, pp. 209–32) and the special issue of *The Review of Politics*, 53, 1, 1991, on Leo Strauss.
9. On Strauss's relationship to postmodernism, see Smith (1994).
10. See Larmore (1996, Chap. 3) for a discussion on Strauss's political philosophy.
11. On modernity and the idea of unattainability, see Friese and Wagner (1999a).
12. For a contemporary interpretation of Luhmann see the special issue of *New German Critique*, 61, 1994; in particular the essays of Müller (1994) and Arato (1994), as well as Luhmann's essay 'The Modernity of Science' (Luhmann, 1994a).
13. This theory is outlined in Luhmann (1995). See also Luhmann (1982) and (1990b).
14. See Luhmann's engagement with Lyotard's (1988) concept of the 'differend', Luhmann (1994b). See also Knodt (1994) and Rasch (1994).

5　Rescuing Modernity: The Recovery of the Social

1. Originally a lecture in 1980 on receiving the Adorno Prize.
2. See the essays in Habermas (1989b).
3. It may be remarked, however, that the German term, *Öffentlichkeit*, does not carry the same spatial connotations as the English or French. For a comprehensive overview of the literature on *Öffentlichkeit*, see Strum (1994).

4. See Piet Strydom's papers on triple contingency, Strydom (1999a, 1999d).

5. I have examined this and the question of the Occidental prejudice in Delanty (1997a).

6. See also a recent article on human rights, Habermas (1998b).

7. For a debate on this, see Bohman (1998).

8. See in particular, Chapter 11.

9. See Heller (1993) for an attempt to resolve some of the earlier problems in light of her more recent work on modernity.

10. This has also been pointed out by Grumley (1994) commenting on Heller's essay 'Modernity's Pendulum' (1992).

11. See Leledakis's reflections, Leledakis (1999).

12. For a fuller discussion on his social theory see Chapter 5 of my *Social Theory in a Changing World*, Delanty (1999a). See also Knöbl (1999).

13. I have commented on this in Delanty (2000b).

14. For another communications theoretic view on the contemporary situation, see Ferry (1994).

6 Postmodernism and the Possibility of Community

1. This chapter originally appeared in *Communitarianism and Citizenship*, edited by Emilios Christodoulidis (Avebury: Ashgate, 1998). I am grateful to the Editor for permission to reproduce this chapter, which I have revised for this book.

2. It must be pointed out that there are limits to the compatibility of Anderson's notion of 'imagined community' with postmodern perspectives, since his conception tends to be one of a relatively fixed and domesticated imaginary. This might be contrasted with Castoriadis's notion of the radical imaginary, where the stress is more on the transformative capacity of the imaginary.

3. The term has of course now been changed to EU, European Union. Nevertheless the appeal to political community is still present.

7 From Modernity to Postmodernity: Postdialectics and the Aestheticization of the Social

1. For a survey of some of the current trends, see de la Fuente (2000).

2. For useful histories and commentaries see Anderson (1998), Bertens (1995), Best and Kellner (1991), Lemert (1997), Rose (1991), Smart (1992).

3. On modernism and the avant-garde, see Bradbury and McFarlane (1991), Bürger (1984), Calinescu (1977).

4. See also Hassan (1987) on early postmodern developments.

5. On postmodern architecture see the famous works by Charles Jencks (1991) and Robert Venturi (1977). See also Kolb (1990) and Lillyman et al. (1994).

6. I have discussed this in Delanty (1999a, Chap. 4).

7. The term 'postmodernization' is used by Crook et al. (1992) to describe social change in contemporary society.

8. This has been commented by Dennis Wrong (1998, p. 90).

9. This was based on an essay originally published in the *New Left Review* in 1984.

10. Jameson's position has been expanded in works such as *The Seeds of Time* (1994).

11. For an overview of Baudrillard's work, see Baudrillard (1994a) and Kellner (1989).

12. For a good critical assesment of the politics of hyperreality, see King (1998).

13. A notable exception to this latter group is Eagleton (1996).

14. See also Silverman (1999) for an interpretation of postmodernism in terms of cultural fragmentation.

15. However, as Kurasawa (1999) has argued, this sense of an alternative to modernity was largely identified with non-western forces, such as Islam, which suggested to him the possibility of an alternative spiritual subjectivity.

16. For an overview of this debate, see Kelly (1994) and Ashenden and Owen (1999). See also Passerin d'Entreves and Benhabib (1996) and Flyvbjerg (1998).

17. On the Rorty–Foucault debate, see Norris (1993, Chap. 2).

18. See Rorty's critique of Lyotard, where he puts forward a position not too far removed from Habermas's (Rorty, 1992).

19. See Rorty (1985) on the Habermas–Lyotard debate.

20. On Lyotard's politics, see Fern Haber (1994), Lyotard (1993b) and Rojek and Turner (1998). On his aesthetic theory more broadly, see Lyotard (1993a).

21. This shift in the constitution of the self was anticipated by David Riesman in *The Lonely Crowd* (1950). Riesman argued that a shift was occurring from an 'inner-directed' character type to an 'outer-directed' type.

22. On postmodernity and responsibility, see Tester (1993). See also Delanty (1999c).

23. For a similar position see Yeatman (1994) or the work of Laclau and Mouffe.

24. For some further discussion on the self and modernity, see Seidler (1994).

25. A good example of this is Lash (1999).

26. We should be talking here in terms of contested modernities, see Lapidus (1987).

8 Further Reflections: Constructivism beyond Postmodernity

1. See also her later work, *La Folie du voir* (Buci-Glucksmann, 1986).

2. For further accounts of Benjamin and the culture of the eye, see Caygill (1998) and Gilloch (1996).

3. For a recent discussion of reflexivity, see May (1999, 2000).

4. See the Postscript to *The Rules of Art* (Bourdieu, 1996b). See also Bourdieu and Haacke (1995).

5. For a good overview of Bourdieu and one that places the idea of culture at the centre of his work, see Swartz (1997).

6. This view has also penetrated into the natural sciences. See Fuller (1997) and Wallerstein et al. (1996).

7. In *The Myth of Social Action* Colin Campbell (1996) has partly disagnosed this when the criticizes the social contextualism of social theory since the 1980s, but in my view he has mistaken social contextualism for culturalism.

8. On the concept of culture, see Münch and Smelser (1992).

9. These developments can be understood in terms of the knowledge society (Stehr, 1992). On culture and knowledge, see McCarthy (1996)

REFERENCES

Adorno, T. (1967). 'Cultural Criticism and Society'. In *Prisms*. Cambridge, MA: MIT Press.

Adorno, T. (1984). *Aesthetic Theory*. London: Routledge and Kegan Paul.

Adorno, T. (1990). *Negative Dialectics*. London: Routledge and Kegan Paul.

Agamben, G. (1993). *The Coming Community*. Minneapolis: University of Minnesota Press.

Ahmed, A. (1992). *Postmodernism and Islam*. London: Routledge.

Al-Azmah, A. (1992). *Islams and Modernities*. London: Verso.

Alexander, J. (1995). 'Modern, Anti, Post, and Neo: How Intellectuals Have Coded, Narrated, and Explained the "New World of Our Time" '. In *Fin de Siècle Social Theory*. London: Verso.

Alexander, J. (1998). *NeoFunctionalism and After*. Oxford: Blackwell.

Allison, D. (ed.) (1985). *The New Nietzsche*. Cambridge, MA: MIT Press.

Anderson, B. (1991). *Imagined Communities* (revised edn). London: Verso.

Anderson, P. (1992). 'The Ends of History'. In *A Zone of Engagement*. London: Verso.

Anderson, P. (1998). *The Origins of Postmodernity*. London: Verso.

Antonio, R. (1995). 'Nietzsche's Antisociology: Subjectified Culture and the End of History'. *American Journal of Sociology*, 101, 1, pp. 1–43.

Apel, K.-O. (1980). 'The a priori of the Communication Community and the Foundation of Ethics: The Problem of a Rational Foundation of Ethics in the Scientific Age'. In *TheTransformation of Philosophy*. London: Routledge and Kegan Paul.

Arato, A. (1994). 'Civil Society and Political Theory in the Work of Luhmann and Beyond'. *New German Critique*, 61, pp. 129–42.

Arendt, H. (1958). *The Human Condition*. Chicago: University of Chicago Press.

Arendt, H. (1961a). 'The Crisis in Culture'. In *Between Past and Future: Six Exercises in Political Thought*. London: Faber and Faber.

Arendt, H. (1961b). 'Tradition and the Modern Age'. In *Between Past and Future: Six Exercises in Political Thought*. London: Faber and Faber.

Arendt, H. (1964). *Eichmann in Jersualem: A Report on the Banality of Evil*. New York: Viking.

Arendt, H. (1965). *On Revolution*. New York: Viking Press.

Arendt, H. (1978). *The Life of the Mind* (2 vols). London: Secker and Warburg.

Arnason, J. (1989). 'The Imaginary Constitution of Modernity'. *Revue européene des sciences sociales*, 20, pp. 323–37.

Arnason, J. (1991). 'Modernity as a Project and as a Field of Tension'. In A. Honneth and H. Joas (eds), *Communicative Action*. Cambridge: Polity.

Arnason, J. (1995). *Social Theory and Japanese Experience: The Dual Experience*. London: Routledge and Kegan Paul International.

Ashenden, S. and Owen, D. (eds) (1999). *Foucault Contra Habermas*. London: Sage.

Ashheim, S. (1992). *The Nietzschean Legacy in Germany, 1890–1990*. Berkeley: University of California Press.

Augé, M. (1995). *Non-Places: Introduction to an Anthropology of Supermodernity*. London: Verso.

Avineri, S. and de-Shalit, A. (eds) (1992). *Communitarianism and Liberalism*. Oxford: Oxford University Press:

Barthes, R. (1975). *The Pleasure of the Text*. New York: Hill and Wang.

Bartos, O. (1996). 'Postmodernism, Postindustralism, and the Future'. *The Sociological Quarterly*, 37, 2, pp. 307–25.

Baudelaire, C. (1964). 'The Painter of Modern Life'. In *The Painter of Modern Life and Other Essays*. London: Phaidon Press.

Baudrillard, J. (1975). *The Mirror of Production*. St Louis, MO: Telos Press.

Baudrillard, J. (1981). *For a Critique of the Political Economy of the Sign*. St Louis, MO: Telos Press.

Baudrillard, J. (1983). *In the Shadows of the Silent Majorities*. New York: Semiotext(e).

Baudrillard, J. (1989). *America*. London: Verso.

Baudrillard, J. (1993). *Symbolic Exchange and Death*. London: Sage.

Baudrillard, J. (1994a). *Baudrillard: A Critical Reader*, edited by D. Kellner. Oxford: Blackwell.

Baudrillard, J. (1994b). *The Illusion of the End*. Cambridge: Polity.

Bauman, Z. (1987). *Legislators and Interpreters: On Modernity, Postmodernity and Intellectuals*. Cambridge: Polity.

Bauman, Z. (1989). *Modernity and the Holocaust*. Cambridge: Polity.

Bauman, Z. (1991). *Modernity and Ambivalence*. Cambridge: Polity.

Bauman, Z. (1992). *Intimations of Postmodernity*. Cambridge: Polity.

Bauman, Z. (1993). *Postmodern Ethics*. Oxford: Blackwell.

Bauman, Z. (1995). *Life in Fragments: Essays in Postmodern Morality*. Oxford: Blackwell.

Baumann, G. (1991). *Contested Cultures: Discourses of Identity in a Muti-Ethnic London*. Cambridge: Cambridge University Press.

Beck, U. (1992). *Risk Society*. London: Sage.

Beck, U., Giddens, A. and Lash, S. (1994). *Reflexive Modernization: Politics, Tradition and Aesthetics in the Modern Social Order*. Cambridge: Polity.

Becker, C. (1932). *The Heavenly City of the Eighteenth-Century Philosophers*. New Haven, CT: Yale University Press.

Bell, D. (1962). *The End of Ideology: The Exhaustion of Political Ideas in the Fifties*. New York: Free Press.

Bell, D. (1976). *The Cultural Contradictions of Capitalism*. London: Heinemann.

Bell, D. (1977). 'Return of the Sacred'. *British Journal of Sociology*, 27, 4, pp. 419–49.

Benatouil, T. (1999). 'A Tale of Two Sociologies: The Critical and Pragmatic Stance in Contemporary Sociology'. *European Journal of Social Theory*, 2, 3, pp. 379–96.

Benedict, R. (1935). *Patterns of Culture*. London: Routledge and Kegan Paul.

Benhabib, S. (1996). *The Reluctant Modernism of Hannah Arendt*. London: Sage.

Benjamin, W. (1970). 'Theses on the Philosophy of History'. In *Illuminations*. London: Jonathan Cape.

Benjamin, W. (1973a). *Charles Baudelaire: Lyric Poet in the Age of High Capitalism*. London: New Left Books.
Benjamin, W. (1973b). *Illuminations*. London: Fontana.
Benjamin, W. (1977). *The Origin of German Tragic Drama*. London: Sage.
Berman, M. (1982). *All That is Solid Melts into Air*. New York: Simon and Schuster.
Bernstein, R. (ed.) (1985). *Habermas and Modernity*. Cambridge: Polity.
Bernstein, R. (1992). *The New Constellation: The Ethical-Political Horizons of Modernity/Postmodernity*. Cambridge, MA: MIT Press.
Berry, P. and Wernick, A. (eds) (1993). *Shadow of Spirit: Postmodernism and Religion*. London: Routledge.
Bertens, H. (1995). *The Idea of the Postmodern: A History*. London: Routledge.
Best, S. and Kellner, D. (1991). *Postmodern Theory: Critical Interrogations*. London: Macmillan.
Blanchot, M. (1988). *The Unavowable Community*. Barrytown, NY: Station Hill Press.
Blond, P. (1998). 'The Primacy of Theology and the Question of Perception'. In P. Heelas (ed.), *Religion, Modernity and Postmodernity*. Oxford: Blackwell.
Bloom, A. (1987). *The Closing of the American Mind*. New York: Simon and Schuster.
Blumenberg, H. (1983). *The Legitimacy of the Modern Age*. Cambridge, MA: MIT Press.
Bohman, J. (1998). 'The Globalization of the Public Sphere'. *Philosophy and Social Criticism*, 24, 2–3, pp. 199–216.
Boltanski, L. and Thévenot, L. (1999). 'Critical and Pragmatic Sociology'. *European Journal of Social Theory*, 2, 3, pp. 359–77.
Borkenau, F. (1981). *End and Beginning: On the Generation of Cultures and the Origin of the West*. New York: Columbia University Press.
Botwinick, A. (1993). *Postmodernism and Democratic Theory*. Philadepphia: Temple University Press.
Botwinick, A. (1997). *Maimonides to Nietzsche: Skepticism, Belief, and the Modern*. Ithaca, NY: Cornell University Press.
Bourdieu, P. (1984). *Distinction: A Social Critique of the Judgement of Taste*. London: Routledge and Kegan Paul.
Bourdieu, P. (1990). *The Logic of Practice*. Cambridge: Polity.
Bourdieu, P. (1996a). *The State Nobility*. Cambridge: Polity.
Bourdieu, P. (1996b). *The Rules of Art: Genesis and Structure of the Literary Field*. Cambridge: Polity.
Bourdieu, P. (1997). *Practical Reason*. Cambridge: Polity.
Bourdieu, P. (1999). 'Scattered Remarks'. *European Journal of Social Theory*, 2, 3, pp. 334–40.
Bourdieu, P. (2000). *Pascalian Meditations*. Cambridge: Polity Press.
Bourdieu, P and Haacke, H. (1995). *Free Exchange*. Cambridge: Polity.
Bourdieu, P. and Wacquant, P. (1992). *An Invitation to Reflexive Sociology*. Chicago: University of Chicago Press.
Bourricaud, F. (1987). ' "Universal Reference" and the Process of Modernization'. In S.N. Eisenstadt (ed.), *Patterns of Modernity, vol. 1: The West*. London: Pinter.
Bradbury, M. and McFarlane, J. (eds) (1991). *Modernism: A Guide to European Literature, 1890–1930*. Harmondsworth: Penguin.
Bruce, S. (1998). 'Cathedrals to Cults: The Evolving Forms of the Religious Life'. In P. Heelas (ed.), *Religion, Modernity and Postmodernity*. Oxford: Blackwell.
Buci-Glucksmann, C. (1986). *La Folie du voir*. Paris: Éditions Galilee.

Buci-Glucksmann, C. (1994). *Baroque Reason: The Aesthetics of Modernity.* London: Sage.

Bull, M. (ed.) (1995). *Apocalypse Theory and the Ends of the World.* Oxford: Blackwell.

Bürger, P. (1984). *Theory of the Avant-Garde.* Minneapolis: University of Minnesota Press.

Cahoone, L. (1988). *The Dilemma of Modernity: Philosophy, Culture, and Anti-Culture.* New York: State University of New York Press.

Calhoun, C. (1983). 'The Radicalness of Tradition: Community Strength or Venerable Disguise and Borrowed Language'. *American Journal of Sociology,* 88, 5, pp. 886–914.

Calhoun, C. (ed.) (1993). *Habermas and the Public Sphere.* Cambridge, MA: MIT Press.

Calhoun, C. (1995). *Critical Social Theory.* Oxford: Blackwell.

Calinescu, M. (1977). *Faces of Modernity.* Bloomington: Indiana University Press.

Callinicos, A. (1989). *Against Postmodernism: A Marxist Critique.* Cambridge: Polity.

Campbell, C. (1996). *The Myth of Social Action.* Cambridge: Cambridge University Press.

Caputo, J. (1997). *The Prayers and Tears of Jacques Derrida: Religion Without Religion.* Bloomington: Indiana University Press.

Carver, T. (1998). *The Postmodern Marx.* Manchester: Manchester University Press.

Cascardi, A. (1992). *The Subject of Modernity.* Cambridge: Cambridge University Press.

Castells, M. (1996). *The Information Age,* Vol. 1: *The Rise of the Network Society.* Oxford: Blackwell.

Castells, M. (1997). *The Information Age,* Vol. 2: *The Power of Identity.* Oxford: Blackwell.

Castells, M. (1998). *The Information Age,* Vol. 3: *End of Millennium.* Oxford: Blackwell.

Castoriadis, C. (1987). *The Imaginary Institution of Society.* Cambridge: Polity.

Castoriadis, C. (1991). *Philosophy, Politics, Autonomy: Essays in Political Philosophy.* Oxford: Oxford University Press.

Castoriadis, C. (1993a). *World in Fragments: Writings on Politics, Society, Psychoanalysis, and the Imagination.* Cambridge: Polity.

Castoriadis, C. (1993b). 'The Retreat from Autonomy: Postmodernism as Generalized Confusion'. In *World in Fragments: Writings on Politics, Society, Psychoanalysis, and the Imagination.* Cambridge: Polity.

Caygill, H. (1998). *Walter Benjamin: The Colour of Experience.* London: Routledge.

Chadwick, O. (1993). *The Secularization of the European Mind in the Nineteenth Century.* Cambridge: Cambridge University Press.

Cheyette, B. and Marcus, L. (eds) (1998). *Modernity, Culture and 'the Jew'.* Cambridge: Polity.

Christodoulidis, E. (ed.) (1998). *Communitarianism and Citizenship.* Aldershot: Ashgate.

Clarke, J.J. (1997). *Oriental Enlightenment: The Encounter Between Asian and Western Thought.* London: Routledge.

Cohen, A. (1985). *The Symbolic Construction of Community.* London: Tavistock.

Cohen, J. and Arato, A. (1992). *Civil Society and Political Theory.* Cambridge, MA: MIT Press.

Connolly, W. (1988). *Political Theory and Modernity.* Oxford: Blackwell.

Connolly, W. (1995). *The Ethos of Pluralization*. Minneapolis, MN: University of Minnesota Press.

Connor, S. (1997). *Postmodern Culture: An Introduction to Theories of the Contemporary* (2nd edn). Oxford: Blackwell.

Corlett, W. (1993). *Community Without Unity: A Politics of Derridian Extravagance*. Durham, NC: Duke University Press:

Cotterrell, R. (1995). *Law's Community*. Oxford: Clarendon.

Critchley, S. (1999). 'The Other's Decision in Me. (What are the Politics of Friendship?)'. *European Journal of Social Theory*, 1, 2, pp. 259–79.

Crook, S. (1991). *Modernist Radicalness and its Aftermath*. London: Routledge.

Crook, S., Pakulski, J. and Waters, M. (1992). *Postmodernization: Change in Advanced Society*. London: Sage.

Cupitt, D. (1998). 'PostChristianity'. In P. Heelas (ed.), *Religion, Modernity and Postmodernity*. Oxford: Blackwell.

Dallmayr, F. (1996). *Beyond Orientalism: Essays on Cross-Cultural Encounter*. New York: State University of New York Press.

Debord, G. (1994). *The Society of the Spectacle*. New York: Zone Books.

de la Fuente, E. (2000). 'Sociology and Aesthetics: A Literature Survey'. *European Journal of Social Theory*, 3, 2.

Delanty, G. (1995a). *Inventing Europe: Idea, Identity, Reality*. London: Macmillan.

Delanty, G. (1995b). 'The Limits and Possibility of a European Identity: A Critique of Cultural Essentialism'. *Philosophy and Social Criticism*, 21, 4, pp. 15–36.

Delanty, G. (1996a). 'The Frontier and Identities of Exclusion in European History'. *History of European Ideas*, 22, 2, pp. 93–103.

Delanty, G. (1996b). 'The Resonance of Mitteleuropa: A Habsburg Myth or Anti-Politics?' *Theory, Culture and Society*, 14, 4, pp. 93–108

Delanty, G. (1997a). 'Habermas and Occidental Rationalism: The Politics of Identity, Social Learning and the Cultural Limits of Moral Universalism'. *Sociological Theory*, 15, 3, pp. 30–59.

Delanty, G. (1997b). 'Models of Citizenship: Defining European Identity and Citizenship'. *Citizenship Studies*, 1, 3, pp. 285–303.

Delanty, G. (1997c). *Social Science: Beyond Realism and Constructivism*. Buckingham: Open University Press.

Delanty, G. (1998a). 'The Idea of the University in the Global Era: From Knowledge as an End to the End of Knowledge?' *Social Epistemology*, 12, 1, pp. 3–25.

Delanty, G. (1998b). 'Rethinking the University: The Autonomy, Reflexivity and Contestation of Knowledge'. *Social Epistemology*, 12, 1, pp. 103–13.

Delanty, G. (1998c). 'Redefining Political Culture in Europe Today: From Ideology to the Politics of Identity'. In U. Hedetof (ed.), *Political Symbols, Symbolic Politics: Europe between Unity and Fragmentation*. Aldershot: Ashgate.

Delanty, G. (1999a). *Social Theory in a Changing World*. Cambridge: Polity.

Delanty, G. (1999b). 'Self, Other and World: Discourses of Nationalism and Cosmopolitanism'. *Cultural Values*, 3, 3, pp. 365–75.

Delanty, G. (1999c). 'Biotechnology in the Risk Society: The Possibility of a Global Ethic of Societal Responsibility'. In P. O'Mahony (ed.), *Nature, Risk and Responsibility: Discourses of Biotechnology*. London: Macmillan.

Delanty, G. (1999d). 'The Foundations of Social Theory: Origins and Trajectories'. In B.S. Turner (ed.), *The Blackwell Companion to Social Theory* (2nd revised edn). Oxford: Blackwell.

Delanty, G. (2000a). 'Nationalism'. In G. Ritzer and B. Smart (eds), *Handbook of Social Theory*. London: Sage.

Delanty, G. (2000b). 'The Resurgence of the City: The Spaces of European Integration'. In E. Isin (ed.), *Politics and the City*. London: Routledge.

Delanty, G. (2000c). *Citizenship in a Global Age*. Buckingham: Open University Press.

Deleuze, G. and Guattari, F. (1983). *Anti-Opedius*. Minneapolis: University of Minnesota Press.

Derrida, J. (1977). *Of Grammatology*. Baltimore: Johns Hopkins University Press.

Derrida, J. (1978). *Writing and Difference*. London: Routledge and Kegan Paul.

Derrida, J. (1992). *The Other Heading: Reflections on Today's Europe*. Bloomington: Indiana University Press.

Derrida, J. (1994). *Spectres of Marx: The State of the Debt, the Work of Mourning and the New International*. London: Routledge.

Derrida, J. (1997). *The Politics of Friendship*. London:Verso.

Derrida, J. and Vattimo, G. (eds) (1998). *Religion*. Cambridge: Polity.

Deutsch, K. (1957). *Political Community in the North Atlantic Area*. Princeton, NJ: Princeton University Press.

de Vries, H. and Weber, S. (eds) (1997). *Violence, Identity and Self-Determination*. Stanford, CA: Stanford University Press.

Drury, S. (1988). *The Political Ideas of Leo Strauss*. London: Macmillan.

Dupré, L. (1993). *Passage to Modernity: An Essay in the Hermeneutics of Nature and Culture*. New Haven: Yale University Press.

Durkheim, É. (1915). *The Elementary Forms of the Religious Life*. London: Allen and Unwin.

Durkheim, É. (1960). *The Division of Labour in Society*. Glencoe, IL: Free Press.

Eagleton, T. (1996). *The Illusions of Postmodernism*. Oxford: Blackwell.

Eder, K. (1985). *Geschichte als Lernprozess? Zur Pathogenese politischer Modernität in Deutschland*. Frankfurt: Suhrkamp.

Eder, K. (1992). 'Contradictions and Social Evolution: A Theory of the Social Evolution of Modernity'. In H. Haferkamp and N. Smelser (eds), *Social Change and Modernity*. Berkeley: University of California Press.

Eder, K. (1999). 'Societies Learn and Yet the World is Hard to Change'. *European Journal of Social Theory*, 2, 2, pp. 195–215.

Eisenstadt, S.N. (1973). *Tradition, Change, Modernity*. London: Wiley.

Eliot, T.S. (1948). *Notes Towards the Definition of Culture*. London: Faber and Faber.

Epstein, M. (1995). *After the Future: The Paradoxes of Postmodernism and Contemporary Russian Culture*. Amherst, MA: University of Massachusetts Press.

Etzioni, A. (1995). *The Spirit of Community*. London: Fontana.

Featherstone, M. (1991). *Consumer Culture and Postmodernism*. London: Sage.

Featherstone, M., Lash, S. and Robertson, R. (eds) (1995). *Global Modernities*. London: Routledge.

Feher, F. and Heller, A. (1994). *Biopolitics*. Aldershot: Avesbury.

Fern Haber, H. (1994). *Beyond Postmodern Politics: Lyotard, Rorty, Foucault*. London: Routledge.

Ferry, L. (1994). 'Ancient, Modern, and Contemporary'. In M. Lilla (ed.), *New French Thought: Political Philosophy*. Princeton, NJ: Princeton University Press.

Ferry, L. and Renaut, A. (1990). *Heidegger and Modernity*. Chicago: University of Chicago Press.

Fine, R. (2000). 'Crimes against Humanity: Hannah Arendt and the Nuremberg Debates'. *European Journal of Social Theory*, 3.

Fine, R. and Turner, C. (eds) (2000). *Social Theory after the Holocaust*. Liverpool: Liverpool University Press.

Fisher, M. and Abedi, M. (1990). *Debating Muslims: Cultural Dialogue in Postmodernism and Tradition*. Madison: University of Wisconsin Press.

Flanagan, K. (1999). *The Enchantment of Sociology: A Study of Theology and Culture*. London: Macmillan.

Flyvbjerg, B. (1998). 'Habermas and Foucault: Thinkers of Civil Society'. *British Journal of Sociology*, 49, 2, pp. 210–33.

Foucault, M. (1997). 'What is Enlightenment?' In *Michel Foucault: The Essential Works*, Vol. 1: *Ethics*. London: Allen Lane.

Frazer, E. and Lacey, N. (1993). *The Politics of Community: A Feminist Critique of the Liberal–Communitarian Debate*. Hemel Hempstead: Harvester Wheatsheaf.

Freud, S. (1946). *New Introductory Lectures on Psychoanalysis* (3rd edn). London: Hogarth Press.

Friese, H. (ed.) (2001). *The Moment: Time and Rupture in Modern Social Thought*. Liverpool: Liverpool University Press.

Friese, H. and Wagner, P. (1999a). 'Inescapability and Attainability in the Sociology of Modernity'. *European Journal of Social Theory*, 2, 1, pp. 27–44.

Friese, H. and Wagner, P. (1999b). 'Not all that is Solid Melts into Air: Modernity and Contingency'. In M. Featherstone and S. Lash (eds), *Spaces of Culture: City, Nation, World*. London: Sage.

Frisby, D. (1986). *Fragments of Modernity: Theories of Modernity in the Work of Simmel, Kracauer and Benjamin*. Cambridge, MA: MIT Press.

Frisby, D. and Featherstone, M. (eds) (1997). *Simmel on Culture*. London: Sage.

Fukuyama, F. (1992). *The End of History and the Last Man*. Harmondsworth: Penguin.

Fuller, S. (1997). *Science*. Buckingham: Open University Press.

Fuller, S. (1998). 'Divining the Future of Social Theory'. *European Journal of Social Theory*, 1, 1, pp. 107–26.

Gadamer, H.-G. (1979). *Truth and Method* (2nd edn). London: Sheed and Ward.

Gane, M. (ed.) (1993). *Baudrillard Live: Selected Interviews*. London: Routledge.

Gauchet, M. (1997). *The Disenchantment of the World*. Princeton, NJ: Princeton University Press.

Gehlen, A. (1963). 'Über kulturelle Kristallisation'. In *Studien zur Anthropologie und Soziologie*. Neuwied: Luchterhand.

Gehlen, A. (1980). *Man in the Age of Technology*. New York: Columbia University Press.

Gehlen, A. (1988). *Man: His Nature and Place in the World*. New York: Columbia University Press.

Gellner, E. (1992). *Postmodernism, Reason and Religion*. London: Routledge.

Gellner, E. (1998). *Language and Solitude: Wittgenstein, Malinowski and the Hapsburg Dilemma*. Cambridge: Cambridge University Press.

Giddens, A. (1984). *The Constitution of Society: Outline of a Theory of Structuration*. Cambridge: Polity.

Giddens, A. (1990). *The Consequences of Modernity*. Cambridge: Polity.

Giddens, A. (1991). *Modernity and Self-Identity*. Cambridge: Polity.

Giddens, A. (1994). 'Living in a Post-Traditional Society'. In U. Beck, A. Giddens and S. Lash, *Reflexive Modernization: Politics, Tradition and Aesthetics in the Modern Social Order*. Cambridge: Polity.

Gilloch, G. (1996). *Myth and Metropolis: Walter Benjamin and the City*. Cambridge: Polity.

Goldman, H. (1988). *Max Weber and Thomas Mann: Calling and the Shaping of the Self*. Berkeley: University of California Press.

Goldmann, L. (1964). *The Hidden God*. London: Routledge and Kegan Paul.

Goudsblom, J. (1980). *Nihilism and Culture*. Oxford: Blackwell.

Gouldner, A. (1970). *The Coming Crisis of Western Sociology*. New York: Equinox.

Graff, G. (1979). 'The Myth of the Postmodern Breakthrough', *Literature Against Itself: Literary Ideas in Modern Society*. Chicago: University of Chicago Press.

Gray, R. (1989). *The Imperative of Modernity: An Intellectual Biography of José Ortega y Gasset*. Berkeley: University of California Press.

Grumley, J. (1994). 'Watching the Pendulum Swing: Agnes Heller's Modernity'. *Thesis Eleven*, 37, pp. 127–140.

Guardini, R. (1998). *The End of the Modern World*. Wilmington, DE: ISI Books.

Gusfield, J. (1966). 'Tradition and Modernity: Misplaced Polarities in the Study of the Social Change'. *American Journal of Sociology*, 72, pp. 351–62.

Habermas, J. (1973). *Kultur and Kritik*. Frankfurt: Suhrkamp.

Habermas, J. (1976). *Legitimation Crisis*. London: Heinemann.

Habermas, J. (1979). *Communication and the Evolution of Society*. London: Heinemann.

Habermas, J. (1981). 'Modernity versus Postmodernity'. *New German Critique*, 22, pp. 3–14.

Habermas, J. (1984). *The Theory of Communicative Action*, Vol. 1: *Reason and the Rationalization of Society*. London: Heinemann.

Habermas, J. (1987a). *The Theory of Communicative Action*, Vol. 2: *Lifeworld and System: A Critique of Functionalist Reason*. Cambridge: Polity.

Habermas, J. (1987b). *The Philosophical Discourse of Modernity*. Cambridge, MA: MIT Press.

Habermas, J. (1989a). *The Structural Transformation of the Public Sphere*. Cambridge: Polity.

Habermas, J. (1989b). *The New Conservatism: Cultural Criticism and the Historians' Debate*. Cambridge, MA: MIT Press.

Habermas, J. (1989c). 'The New Obscurity'. In *The New Conservatism: Cultural Criticism and the Historians' Debate*. Cambridge, MA: MIT Press.

Habermas, J. (1989d). 'The Public Sphere: An Encyclopedia'. In S. Bronner and D. Kellner (eds), *Critical Theory and Society*. London: Routledge.

Habermas, J. (1989e). 'Modern and Postmodern Architecture'. In *The New Conservatism: Cultural Criticism and the Historians' Debate*. Cambridge: Polity.

Habermas, J. (1992). *Postmetaphysical Thinking*. Cambridge: Polity.

Habermas, J. (1993). 'Further Reflections on the Public Sphere'. In C. Calhoun (ed.), *Habermas and Modernity*. Cambridge, MA: MIT Press.

Habermas, J. (1994). 'Struggles for Recognition in the Democratic Constitutional State'. In A. Gutmann (ed.), *Multiculturalism: Examining the Politics of Recognition*. Princeton, NJ: Princeton University Press.

Habermas, J. (1996). *Between Facts and Norms: Contributions to a Discourse Theory of Law and Democracy*. Cambridge: Polity.

Habermas, J. (1998a). *The Inclusion of the Other: Studies in Political Theory*. Cambridge, MA: MIT Press.

Habermas, J. (1998b). 'Remarks on Legitimation through Human Rights'. *Philosophy and Social Criticism*, 24, 2/3, pp. 157–71.

Habermas, J. and Luhmann, N. (1971). *Theorie der Gesellschaft oder Sozialtechnologie*. Frankfurt: Suhrkamp.

Hall, D. (1991). 'Modern China and the Postmodern West'. In E. Deutsch (ed.),

Culture and Modernity: East–West Philosophic Perspectives. Honolulu: University of Hawaii Press.

Halton, E. (1995). *Bereft of Reason: On the Decline of Social Thought and Prospects for Its Recovery.* Chicago: University of Chicago Press.

Harré, R. (1998). *The Singular Self.* London: Sage.

Harvey, D. (1990). *The Condition of Postmodernity: An Inquiry into the Origins of Cultural Change.* Oxford: Blackwell.

Hassan, I. (1987). *The Postmodern Turn: Essays in Postmodern Theory and Culture.* Columbus: Ohio State University Press.

Heelas, P. (ed.) (1998). *Religion, Modernity and Postmodernity.* Oxford: Blackwell.

Heelas, P., Lash, S. and Morris, P. (eds) (1996). *Detraditionalization: Critical Reflections on Authority and Identity.* Oxford: Blackwell.

Hegel, G.W.F. (1952). *The Philosophy of Right.* Oxford: Oxford University Press.

Hegel, G.W.F. (1977). *Phenomenology of Mind.* London: Routledge and Kegan Paul.

Heidegger, M. (1957). *Holzwege.* Frankfurt: Klostermann.

Heidegger, M. (1959). *An Introduction to Metaphysics.* New Haven, CT: Yale University Press.

Heidegger, M. (1968). *What is Called Thinking?* New York: Harper and Row.

Heidegger, M. (1977). 'The Age of the World Picture'. In *The Question Concerning Technology and Other Essays.* New York: Harper and Row.

Heidegger, M. (1978). 'Letter on Humanism'. In *Martin Heidegger: Basic Writings.* London: Routledge and Kegan Paul.

Heilbron, J. (1995). *The Rise of Social Theory.* Cambridge: Polity.

Held, D. (1995). *Democracy and the Global Order: From the Modern State to Cosmopolitan Governance.* Cambridge: Polity.

Heller, A. (1982). *A Theory of History.* London: Routledge and Kegan Paul.

Heller, A. (1984). *Everyday Life.* London: Routledge and Kegan Paul.

Heller, A. (1990). *Can Modernity Survive?* Cambridge: Polity.

Heller, A. (1992). 'Modernity's Pendulum'. *Thesis Eleven,* 31, pp. 1–13.

Heller, A. (1993). *A Philosophy of History in Fragments.* Oxford: Blackwell.

Heller, A. (1999). *Theory of Modernity.* Oxford: Blackwell.

Heller, A. and Feher, F. (1988). *The Postmodern Political Condition.* New York: Columbia University Press.

Herf, J. (1986). *Reactionary Modernism: Technology, Culture, and Politics in Weimar and the Third Reich.* Cambridge: Cambridge University Press.

Hobsbawm, E. and Ranger, T. (eds) (1983). *The Invention of Tradition.* Cambridge: Cambridge University Press.

Honneth, A. (1993). *Critique of Power: Reflective Stages in a Critical Theory of Society.* Cambridge, MA: MIT Press.

Honneth, A. (1995). *The Fragmented World of the Social.* New York: State University of New York Press.

Honneth, A. (1996). *The Struggle for Recognition: The Moral Grammar of Social Conflicts.* Cambridge, MA: MIT Press.

Honneth, A. (1999). 'Reply to Kalyvas'. *European Journal of Social Theory,* 2, 2, pp. 249–52.

Hookway, C. (1990). *Skepticism.* London: Routledge.

Horkheimer, M. and Adorno, T. (1979). *Dialectic of Enlightenment.* London: Verso.

Hughes, H. (1958). *Consciousness and Society: The Reconstruction of European Social Thought, 1890–1930.* New York: Vintage.

Hughes, H. (1966). *The Obstructed Path: French Social Thought in the Years of Desperation, 1930–1960*. New York: Harper and Row.

Husserl, E. (1965). 'Philosophy and the Crisis of European Man'. In *Phenomenology and the Crisis of Philosophy*. New York: Harper.

Huyssen, A. (1984). 'Mapping the Postmodern'. *New German Critique*, 32, pp. 5–52.

Jacobsen, D. (1997). *Rights Across Borders: Immigrants and the Decline of Citizenship*. Baltimore: Johns Hopkins University Press.

Jameson, F. (1981). *The Political Unconsciousness: Narrative as a Socially Symbolic Art*. London: Methuen.

Jameson, F. (1984). 'Postmodernism, or, the Cultural Logic of Late Capitalism'. *New Left Review*, 146, pp. 53–92.

Jameson, F. (1990). *Late Marxism: Adorno, or, the Persistence of the Dialectic*. London: Verso.

Jameson, F. (1991). *Postmodernism, or, the Cultural Logic of Late Capitalism*. Durham, NC: Duke University Press.

Jameson, F. (1994). *The Seeds of Time*. New York: Columbia University Press.

Jameson, F. and Miyoshi, M. (eds) (1998). *The Cultures of Globalization*. Durham, NC: Duke University Press.

Jay, M. (1984). *Adorno*. Cambridge, MA: Harvard University Press.

Jay, M. (1992). 'Scopic Regimes of Modernity'. In S. Lash and J. Friedman (eds), *Modernity and Identity*. Oxford: Blackwell.

Jencks, C. (1991). *The Language of Post-Modern Architecture* (6th edn). London: Academy Editions.

Joas, H. (1996). *The Creativity of Action*. Cambridge: Polity.

Joas, H. (1998). 'The Autonomy of the Self: The Median Heritage and its Postmodern Challenge'. *European Journal of Sociology*, 1, 1, pp. 7–18.

Jonas, H. (1996). *The Gnostic Religion: The Message of the Alien God and the Beginnings of Christianity*. Boston: Beacon Press.

Jones, R.F. (1961). *Ancients and Moderns: A Study of the Rise of Scientific Movements in Seventeenth-Century England*. Berkeley: University of California Press.

Jones, S. (ed.) (1995). *CyberSociety: Computer-Mediated Communication and Community*. London: Sage.

Judt, T. (1992). *Past Imperfect: French Intellectuals, 1944–1956*. Cambridge: Cambridge University Press.

Kalyvas, A. (1999). 'Review Essay: Marcel Gauchet'. *European Journal of Social Theory*, 2, 4, pp. 99–108.

Kandinsky, V. (1977). *Concerning the Spiritual in Art*. New York: Dover.

Kant, I. (1929). *Critique of Pure Reason*. London: Macmillan.

Kant, I. (1970). 'Idea for a Universal History with a Cosmopolitan Purpose'. In *Kant: Political Writings*, edited by H. Reiss. Cambridge: Cambridge University Press.

Kant, I. (1996). 'An Answer to the Question: What is Enlightenment?' In J. Schmidt (ed.), *What is Enlightenment? Eighteenth-Century Answers and Twentieth-Century Questions*. Berkeley: University of California Press.

Kellner, D. (1989). *Jean Baudrillard: From Marxism to Postmodernism and Beyond*. Cambridge: Polity.

Kelly, M. (ed.). (1994). *Critique and Power: Recasting the Foucault/Habermas Debate*. Cambridge, MA: MIT Press.

Kierkegaard, S. (1980). *The Sickness unto Death*. Princeton, NJ: Princeton University Press.

King, A. (1998). 'A Critique of Baudrillard's Hyperreality: Towards a Sociology of Postmodernism'. *Philosophy and Social Criticism*, 24, 6, pp. 47–66.

Knöbl, W. (1999). 'Social Theory from a Sartrean Point of View: Alain Touraine's Theory of Modernity'. *European Journal of Social Theory*, 2, 4, pp. 403–27.

Knodt, E. (1994). 'Towards a Non-Foundationalist Epistemplogy: The Habermas/ Luhmann Controversy Revisted'. *New German Critique*, 61, pp. 77–100.

Kolb, D. (1990). *Postmodern Sophistications: Philosophy, Architecture, and Tradition.* Chicago: University of Chicago Press.

Koselleck, R. (1985). *Futures Past: On the Semantics of Historical Time.* Cambridge, MA: MIT Press.

Koselleck, R. (1988). *Critique and Crisis: Enlightenment and the Pathogenesis of Modern Society.* Oxford: Berg.

Kracauer, S. (1995). *The Mass Ornament and Other Essays: Weimar Essays.* Cambridge, MA: Harvard University Press.

Kurasawa, F. (1999). 'The Exotic Effect: Foucault and the Question of Cultural Other'. *European Journal of Social Theory*, 2, 2, pp. 147–65.

Laclau, E. and Mouffe, C. (1985). *Hegemony and Socialist Strategy: Towards a Radical Democratic Politics.* London: Verso.

Lapidus, I.M. (1987). 'Islam and Modernity'. In S.N. Eisenstadt (ed.), *Patterns of Modernity*, Vol. 2: *Beyond the West.* London: Pinter.

Larmore, C. (1996). *The Morals of Modernity.* Cambridge: Cambridge University Press.

Lasch, C. (1979). *The Culture of Narcissism.* New York: Norton.

Lasch, C. (1985). *The Minimal Self: Psychic Survival in Troubled Times.* London: Pan.

Lasch, C. (1991). *The True and Only Heaven: Progress and its Critics.* New York: Norton.

Lash, S. (1990). *Sociology of Postmodernism.* London: Routledge.

Lash, S. (1994). 'Reflexivity and its Doubles: Structures, Aesthetics, Community'. In U. Beck, A. Giddens and S. Lash, *Reflexive Modernization: Politics, Tradition and Aesthetics in the Modern Social Order.* Cambridge: Polity.

Lash, S. (1999). *Another Modernity, A Different Rationality.* Oxford: Blackwell.

Lash, S. and Urry. J. (1994). *Economies of Signs and Space.* London: Sage.

Latour, B. (1993). *We Have Never Been Modern.* Hemel Hempstead: Harvester Wheatsheaf.

Law, J. (1994). *Organizing Modernity.* Oxford: Blackwell.

Lawson, H. (1985). *Reflexivity: The Post-Modern Predicament.* London: Hutchinson.

Lefebvre, H. (1984a). *Everyday Life in the Modern World.* New Brunswick, NJ: Transaction Books.

Lefebvre, H. (1984b). 'The Bureaucratic Society of Controlled Consumption'. In *Everyday Life in the Modern World.* New Brunswick, NJ: Transaction Books.

Lefebvre, H. (1991). *The Production of Space.* Oxford: Blackwell.

Lefebvre, H. (1995). *Introduction to Modernity.* London: Verso.

Lefebvre, H. (1996). *Writings on Cities*, translated by E. Kofman and E. Lebas. Oxford: Blackwell.

Lefort, C. (1986). *The Political Forms of Modern Society.* Cambridge: Polity.

Lefort, C. (1988). *Democracy and Political Theory.* Cambridge: Polity.

Leledakis, K. (1999). 'An Appreciation of Cornelius Castoriadis'. *European Journal of Social Theory*, 2, 1, pp. 95–8.

Leledakis, K. (2000). 'Derrida, Deconstruction and Social Theory'. *European Journal of Social Theory*, 3, 2.

Lemert, C. (1997). *Postmodernism is Not What You Think it is.* Oxford: Blackwell.

le Rider, J. (1993). *Modernity and Crises of Identity: Culture and Society in Fin-de-Siècle Vienna*. New York: Continuum.
Lichtblau, K. (1999). 'Differentiations of Modernity'. *Theory, Culture and Society*, 16, 3, pp. 1–30.
Lichternman, P. (1996). *The Search for Political Community: American Activists Reinventing Commitment*. Cambridge: Cambridge University Press.
Liebersohn, H. (1988). *Fate and Utopia in German Sociology, 1870–1923*. Cambridge, MA: MIT Press.
Lilla, M. (1998). 'The Politics of Jacques Derrida'. *New York Review of Books*, June 25, pp. 36–41.
Lillyman, W., Moriarty, M. and Neuman, D. (eds) (1994). *Critical Architecture and Contemporary Culture*. Oxford: Oxford University Press.
Love, V. (1988). *Marx, Nietzsche and Modernity*. New York: Columbia University Press.
Löwith, K. (1949). *Meaning in History: The Theological Presuppositions of the Philosophy of History*. Chicago: University of Chicago Press.
Löwith, K. (1995). *Martin Heidegger and European Nihilism*. New York: Columbia University Press.
Luhmann, N. (1979). *Trust and Power*. London: John Wiley.
Luhmann, N. (1982). *The Differentiation of Society*. New York: Columbia University Press.
Luhmann, N. (1985). *A Sociological Theory of Law*. London: Routledge and Kegan Paul.
Luhmann, N. (1986). *Love as Passion: The Codification of Intimacy*. Cambridge, MA: Harvard University Press.
Luhmann, N. (1990a). 'The World Society as a Social System'. In *Essays in Self-Reference*. New York: Columbia University Press.
Luhmann, N. (1990b). *Essays in Self-Reference*. New York: Columbia University Press.
Luhmann, N. (1990c). *Political Theory and the Welfare State*. Berlin: de Gruyter.
Luhmann, N. (1993). *Risk: A Sociological Theory*. Berlin: de Gruyter.
Luhmann, N. (1994a). 'The Modernity of Science'. *New German Critique*, 61, pp. 9–23.
Luhmann, N. (1994b). 'Speaking and Silence'. *New German Critique*, 61, pp. 25–37.
Luhmann, N. (1995). *Social Systems*. Stanford, CA: Stanford University Press.
Luhmann, N. (1998). *Observations on Modernity*. Stanford, CA: Stanford University Press.
Lunn, E. (1982). *Marxism and Modernism: An Historical Study of Lukács, Brecht, Benjamin and Adorno*. Berkeley: University of California Press.
Lyotard, J.-F. (1984). *The Postmodern Condition*. Minneapolis: Minnesota University Press.
Lyotard, J.-F. (1988). *The Differend*. Minneapolis: Minnesota University Press.
Lyotard, J.-F. (1992). *The Postmodern Condition Explained*. Minneapolis: Minnesota University Press.
Lyotard, J.-F. (1993a). *Toward the Postmodern*. New York: Humanities Press.
Lyotard, J.-F. (1993b). *Political Writings*, edited by B. Readings and K.P. Geiman. London: UCL Press.
Lyotard, J.-F. (1994). 'A Postmodern Fable on Postmodernity, or: In the Megalopolis'. In W. Lillyman, M. Moriarty and D. Neuman (eds), *Critical Architecture and Contemporary Culture*. Oxford: Oxford University Press.

McCarthy, D. (1996). *Knowledge as Culture: The New Sociology of Knowledge*. London: Routledge.

McFarlane, J. (1991). 'The Mind of Modernism'. In M. Bradbury and J. McFarlane (eds), *Modernism: A Guide to European Literature, 1890–1930*. Harmondsworth: Penguin.

MacIntyre, A. (1953). *Marxism: An Interpretation*. London: SCM Press.

MacIntyre, A. (1967). *Secularisation and Moral Change*. Oxford: Oxford University Press.

MacIntyre, A. (1968). *Christianity and Marxism*. New York: Schocken Books.

MacIntyre, A. (1971). *Against the Self-Image of the Age: Essays on Ideology and Philosophy*. London: Duckworth.

MacIntyre, A. (1981). *After Virtue: A Study in Moral Theory*. London: Duckworth.

MacIntyre, A. (1988). *Whose Justice? Which Rationality?* London: Duckworth.

MacIntyre, A. (1990). *Three Rival Versions of Moral Enquiry*. London: Duckworth.

MacIntyre, A. and Ricoeur, P. (1969). *The Religious Significance of Atheism*. New York: Columbia University Press.

McMylor, P. (1994). *Alasdair MacIntyre: Critic of Modernity*. London: Routledge.

McNight, S. (ed.) (1978). *Eric Voeglin's Search for Order in History*. Baton Rouge and London: Lousiana State University Press.

Maffesoli, M. (1996a). *The Time of the Tribes: The Decline of Individualism in Mass Society*. Sage: London.

Maffesoli, S. (1996b). *The Contemplation of the World*. Minneapolis: Minnesota University Press.

Mannheim, K. (1952). 'Competition as a Cultural Phenomenon'. In *Essays in the Sociology of Knowledge*. London: Routledge and Kegan Paul.

Maravall, J.A. (1986). *Culture of the Baroque: Analysis of a Historical Structure*. Minneapolis: Minnesota University Press.

Marcuse, H. (1964). *One-Dimensional Man*. London: Routledge and Kegan Paul.

Marx, K. (1976). *Capital*, Vol. 1. Harmondsworth: Penguin.

May, T. (1999). 'Reflexivity in the Age of Reconstructive Social Science'. *International Journal of Methodology*, 1, 1, pp. 7–24.

May, T. (2000). 'A Future for Critique: Positioning, Belonging and Reflexivity'. *European Journal of Social Theory*, 3, 2.

Mellos, K. (1994). 'The Postmodern Challenge to Community'. *History of European Ideas*, 19, 1–3, pp. 131–6.

Melucci, A. (1996). *The Playing Self: Person and Meaning in the Planetary Society*. Cambridge: Cambridge University Press.

Meštrović, S. (1991). *The Coming Fin de Siècle: An Application of Durkheim's Sociology to Modernity and Postmodernism*. London: Routledge.

Meštrović, S. (1994). *The Balkanization of the West: The Confluence of Postmodernism and Postcommunism*. London: Routledge.

Meyrowitz, J. (1986). *No Sense of Place: The Impact of Electronic Media on Social Behaviour*. Oxford: Oxford University Press.

Michelfelder, D. and Palmer, R. (eds) (1989). *Dialogue and Deconstruction*. New York: State University of New York Press.

Milbank, J. (1990). *Theology and Social Theory: Beyond Secular Reason*. Oxford: Blackwell.

Miller, D. and Walzer, M. (eds) (1995). *Pluralism, Justice and Equality*. Oxford: Oxford University Press.

Mills, C. Wright (1970). *The Sociological Imagination*. Harmondsworth: Pelican.

Misztal, B. (1996). *Trust in Modern Society*. Cambridge: Polity.

Miyoshi, M. and Harootunian, H. (eds) (1989). *Postmodernism and Japan*. Durham, NC: Duke University Press.

Morris, P. (1996). 'Community Beyond Tradition'. In P. Hellas, S. Lash and P. Morris (eds), *Detraditionalization*. Oxford: Blackwell.

Morrison, K. (1998). 'Durkheim and Schopenhauer'. *Durkeimian Studies*, 4, pp. 15–23.

Mouffe, C. (1993). *The Return of the Political*. London: Verso.

Mouzelis, N. (1999). 'Modernity: A Non-European Conceptualization'. *British Journal of Sociology*, 50, 1, pp. 141–59.

Mulhall, S. and Swift, A. (1996). *Liberals and Communitarians* (2nd edn). Oxford: Blackwell.

Müller, H. (1994). 'Luhmann's Systems Theory as a Theory of Modernity'. *New German Critique*, 61, pp. 39–54.

Mumford, L. (1961). *The City in History*. Harmondsworth: Penguin.

Münch, R. and Smelser, N. (eds) (1992). *Theory of Culture*. Berkeley: University of California Press.

Nancy, J.-L. (1991). *The Inoperative Community*. Minneapolis: Minnesota University Press.

Nicholson, L. and Seidman, S. (eds) (1995). *Social Postmodernism: Beyond Identity Politics*. Cambridge: Cambridge University Press.

Niethammer, L. (1993). *Posthistoire: Has History Come to and End?* London: Verso.

Nisbet, R. (1953). *The Quest for Community*. Oxford: Oxford University Press.

Nisbet, R. (1967). *The Sociological Tradition*. London: Heinemann.

Norris, C. (1993). *The Truth about Postmodernism*. Oxford: Blackwell.

O'Neill, J. (1986). 'The Disciplinary Society: From Weber to Foucault'. *British Journal of Sociology*, 37, 1, pp. 42–60.

O'Neill, J. (1972). *Sociology as a Skin Trade: Essays Towards a Reflexive Sociology*. London: Heinemann.

O'Neill, J. (1995). *The Poverty of Postmodernism*. London: Routledge.

O'Neill, J. (1999). 'What Gives (with Derrida)?' *European Journal of Social Theory*, 2, 3, pp. 131–45.

Ortega y Gasset, José (1961). *The Modern Theme*. New York: Harper.

Outhwaite, W. (1999). 'The Myth of Modernist Method'. *European Journal of Social Theory*, 2, 1, pp. 5–25.

Owen, D. (1994). *Maturity and Modernity: Nietzsche, Weber, Foucault and the Ambivalence of Reason*. London: Routledge.

Pagels, E. (1979). *The Gnostic Gospels*. New York: Random House.

Pangle, T. (1991). 'On the Epistolary Dialogue between Leo Strauss and Eric Voeglin'. *Review of Politics*, 53, 1, pp. 100–25.

Parsons, T. (1935). 'Service'. In *Encylopedia of the Social Sciences*, Vol. 13. New York: Macmillan.

Parsons, T. (1966). *Societies: Evolutionary and Comparative Perspectives*. Englewood Cliffs, NJ: Prentice Hall.

Passerin D'Entreves, M. and Benhabib, S. (eds) (1996). *Habermas and the Unfinished Project of Modernity*. Cambridge: Polity.

Pickstock, C. (1998). 'Review Essay: Postmodern Theology'. *Telos*, 110 (Winter), pp. 167–79.

Pippin, R. (1997). *Idealism as Modernism: Hegelian Variations*. Cambridge: Cambridge University Press.

Pocock, J. (1987). 'Modernity and Anti-Modernity in the Anglophone Political

Tradition'. In S.N. Eisenstadt (ed.), *Patterns of Modernity*, Vol. 1: *The West*. London: Pinter.

Poole, R. (1994). *Modernity and Morality*. London: Routledge.

Rancière, J. (1995). *On the Shores of the Political*. London: Verso.

Rasch, W. (1994). 'In Search of the Lyotard Archipelago, or: How to Live with Paradox and Learn to Like it'. *New German Critique*, 61, pp. 55–75.

Readings, B. (1996). *The University in Ruins*. Cambridge, MA: Harvard University Press.

Ricoeur, P. (1974). *The Conflict of Interpretations*. Evanston, IL: Northwestern University Press.

Ricoeur, P. (1994). *Oneself as Another*. Chicago: Chicago University Press.

Riesman, D. (with Reuel Denney and Nathan Glazer) (1950). *The Lonely Crowd*. New Haven, CT: Yale University Press.

Robertson, R. and Turner, B.S. (eds) (1991). *Talcott Parsons: Theorist of Modernity*. London: Sage.

Rojek, C. and Turner, B. (eds) (1998). *The Politics of Jean-François Lyotard: Justice and Political Theory*. London: Routledge.

Rorty, R. (1979). *Philosophy and the Mirror of Nature*. Princeton, NJ: Princeton University Press.

Rorty, R. (1983). 'Postmodernist Bourgeois Liberalism'. *Journal of Philosophy*, 80, pp. 583–89.

Rorty, R. (1985). 'Habermas and Lyotard on Postmodernity'. In R. Bernstein (ed.), *Habermas and Modernity*. Cambridge: Polity.

Rorty, R. (1989). *Contingency, Irony, and Solidarity*. Cambridge: Cambridge University Press.

Rorty, R. (1992). 'Cosmopolitanism without Emancipation: A Response to Lyotard'. In S. Lash and J. Friedman (eds), *Modernity and Identity*. Oxford: Blackwell.

Rose, G. (1991). *The Post-Modern and the Post-Industrial*. Cambridge: Cambridge University Press.

Rose, G. (1992). *The Broken Middle*. Oxford: Blackwell.

Rose, G. (1993). *Judaism and Modernity*. Oxford: Blackwell.

Rosen, S. (1989). *The Ancients and the Moderns: Rethinking Modernity*. New Haven, CT: Yale University Press.

Rundell, J. (1987). *Origins of Modernity: The Origins of Modern Social Theory from Kant to Hegel and Marx*. Cambridge: Polity.

Sandel, M. (1982). *Liberalism and the Limits of Justice*. Cambridge: Cambridge University Press.

Schabert, T. (1986). 'Modernity and History'. In A. Moulakis (ed.), *The Promise of History*. New York: de Gruyter.

Scheler, M. (1972). *Ressentiment*. New York. Schocken.

Schiller, F. (1998). 'Extracts from *On the Aesthetic Education of Man*'. In J. Rundell and S. Mennell (eds), *Classical Readings in Culture and Civilization*. London: Routledge.

Schmidt, J. (ed.) (1996). *What is Enlightenment? Eighteenth-Century Answers and Twentieth-Century Questions*. Berkeley: University of California Press.

Schmitt, C. (1970). *Political Theology*. Cambridge, MA: MIT Press.

Schmitt, C. (1985). *The Crisis of Parliamentary Democracy*. Cambridge, MA: MIT Press.

Schopenhauer, A. (1970). *Essays and Aphorisms*. Harmondsworth: Penguin.

Seidler, V. (1994). *Recovering the Self: Morality and Social Theory*. London: Sage.

Seidman, S. (1998). *Contested Knowledge: Social Theory in the Postmodern Era* (2nd edn). Oxford: Blackwell.

Selznick, P. (1992). *The Moral Commonwealth: Social Theory and the Promise of Community*. Berkeley: University of California Press.

Sennett, R. (1978). *The Fall of Public Man*. New York: Vintage.

Silverman, M. (1999). *Facing Modernity: Contemporary French Thought on Culture and Society*. London: Routledge.

Simmel, G. (1971). 'The Metropolis and Mental Life'. In D.N. Levine (ed.), *Georg Simmel on Individuality and Social Forms*. Chicago: University of Chicago Press.

Simmel, G. (1978). *The Philosophy of Money*. London: Routledge and Kegan Paul.

Simmel, G. (1986). *Schopenhauer and Nietzsche*. Amherst: University of Massachusetts Press.

Smart, B. (1992). *Modern Conditions, Postmodern Controversies*. London: Routledge.

Smart, B. (1999). *Facing Modernity: Ambivalence, Reflexivity and Morality*. London: Sage.

Smart, N. (1998). 'Tradition, Retrospective Perception, Nationalism and Modernism'. In P. Heelas (ed.), *Religion, Modernity and Postmodernity*. Oxford: Blackwell.

Smelser, N. (1997). *Problematics of Sociology*. Berkeley: University of California Press.

Smith, G.B. (1994). 'The Post-Modern Strauss'. *History of European Ideas*, 19, 1–3, pp. 191–7.

Smith, G.B. (1996). *Nietzsche, Heidegger and the Transition to Postmodernity*. Chicago: University of Chicago Press.

Soja, E. (1996). *ThirdSpace: Journeys to Los Angeles and Other Real-and-Imagined Places*. Oxford: Blackwell.

Sorel, G. (1950). *Reflections on Violence*. New York: Collier.

Sousa Santos, B. de (1995). *Toward a New Common Sense: Law, Science and Politics in the Paradigmatic Transition*. London: Routledge.

Soysal, Y. (1994). *Limits of Citizenship: Migrants and Postnational Membership in Europe*. Chicago: University of Chicago Press.

Stauth, G. (1992). 'Nietzsche, Weber, and the Affirmative Sociology of Culture'. *Archives of European Sociology*, 33, pp. 219–47.

Stehr, N. (1992). *Knowledge Societies*. London: Sage.

Strauss, L. (1964). 'The Crisis of Our Time'. In H.J. Spaeth (ed.), *The Predicament of Modern Politics*. Detroit: University of Detroit Press.

Strauss, L. (1975). 'The Three Waves of Modernity'. In *Political Philosophy: Six Essays by Leo Strauss*. Indianapolis: Bobbs-Merrill.

Strauss, L. (1983). 'Correspondence Concerning Modernity: Karl Löwith and Leo Strauss'. *Independent Journal of Philosophy*, 4, pp. 105–19.

Strum, A. (1994). 'A Bibliography of the Concept of *Öffentlichkeit*'. *New German Critique*, 61, pp. 161–202.

Strydom, P. (1987). 'Collective Learning: Habermas's Concessions and Their Implications'. *Philosophy and Social Criticism*, 13, 3, pp. 265–81.

Strydom, P. (1992). 'The Ontogentic Fallacy'. *Theory, Culture and Society*. 9, pp. 65–93.

Strydom, P. (1993). 'Sociocultural Evolution or the Social Evolution of Practical Reason? Eder's Critique of Habermas'. *Praxis International*, 13, 3, pp. 304–22.

Strydom, P. (1999a). 'Triple Contingency: The Theoretical Problem of the Public in Communication Societies'. *Philosophy and Social Criticism*, 25, 2, pp. 1–25.

Strydom, P. (1999b). 'Hermeneutic Culturalism and Its Double: A Key Problem in the Reflexive Modernization Debate'. *European Journal of Social Theory*, 2, 1, pp. 45–69.

Strydom, P. (1999c). 'The Challenge of Responsibility for Sociology'. *Current Sociology*, 47, 3, pp. 1–21.

Strydom, P. (1999d). 'Review Essay: The Contemporary Habermas: Towards Triple Contingency?' *European Journal of Social Theory*, 2, 2, pp. 253–63.

Strydom, P. (1999e). 'The Civilization of the Gene: Biotechnological Risk Framed in the Responsibility Discourse'. In P. O'Mahony (ed.), *Nature, Risk and Responsibility: Discourses of Biotechnology*. London: Macmillan.

Strydom, P. (2000). *Discourse and Knowledge: The Making of Enlightenment Sociology*. Liverpool: Liverpool University Press.

Sugimoto, Y. and Arnason, J. (eds) (1995). *Japanese Encounters with Postmodernity*. London: Routledge and Kegan Paul International.

Swartz, D. (1997). *Culture and Power: The Sociology of Pierre Bourdieu*. Chicago: University of Chicago Press.

Szakolczai, A. (1998). 'Reflexive Historical Sociology'. *European Journal of Social Theory*, 1, 2, pp. 209–27.

Sztompka, P. (1998). 'Trust, Distrust and Two Paradoxes of Democracy'. *European Journal of Social Theory*, 1, 1, pp. 19–32.

Taylor, C. (1989). *Sources of the Self*. Cambridge, MA: Harvard University Press.

Taylor, C. (1991). *The Malaise of Modernity*. Toronto: Anansi.

Taylor, M.C. (1984). *Erring: A Postmodern A/theology*. Chicago: University of Chicago Press.

Taylor, P.J. (1999). *Modernities: A Geohistorical Interpretation*. Cambridge: Polity.

Tester, K. (1993). *The Life and Times of Post-Modernity*. London: Routledge.

Therborn, G. (1995). 'Routes to/through Modernity'. In M. Featherstone, S. Lash and R. Roberston (eds), *Global Modernities*. London: Sage.

Thornhill, C. (1998). 'Intersubjectivity and Openness to Change: Michael Theunissen's Negative Theology of Time'. *Radical Philosophy*, 88, March/April, pp. 6–18.

Tiryakian, E. (1992). 'Dialectics of Modernity: Reenchantment and Dedifferentiation as Counter-Processes'. In H. Haferkamp and N. Smelser (eds), *Social Change and Modernity*. Berkeley: University of California Press.

Tiryakian, E. (1996). 'Three Metacultures of Modernity: Christian, Gnostic, Chthonic'. *Theory, Culture and Society*, 13, 1, pp. 99–118.

Tönnies, F. (1963). *Community and Society*. New York: Harper and Row.

Toulmin, S. (1990). *Cosmopolis: The Hidden Agenda of Modernity*. Chicago: University of Chicago Press.

Touraine, A. (1995). *Critique of Modernity*. Oxford: Blackwell.

Touraine, A. (1997). *What is Democracy?* Boulder, CO: Westview.

Touraine, A. (1998a). 'Can We Live Together, Equal and Different?' *European Journal of Social Theory*, 1, 2, pp. 165–78.

Touraine, A. (1998b). 'Sociology without Society'. *Current Sociology*, 46, 2, pp. 119–43.

Toynbee, A. (1954). *A Study of History*, Vol. 8. London: Oxford University Press.

Trend, D. (1997). *Cultural Democracy*. New York: State University of New York Press.

Trotsky, L. (1931). *The Permanent Revolution*. London: Pathfinder Press.

Turner, B.S. (ed.) (1990). *Theories of Modernity and Postmodernity*. London: Sage.

Turner, B.S. (1991). *Religion and Social Theory*. London: Sage.

Turner, B.S. (1994). *Orientalism, Postmodernism and Globalism*. London: Routledge.

Unger, R. (1987). *Social Theory: Its Situation and its Task: A Critical Introduction to Politics, A Work in Constructive Theory*. Cambridge: Cambridge University Press.

Urry, J. (2000). *Sociology Beyond Society.* London: Routledge.
Varela, T., Thompson, E. and Rosch, E. (1991). *The Embodied Mind: Cognitive Science and Human Experience.* Cambridge, MA: MIT Press.
Vattimo, G. (1988). *The End of Modernity: Nihilism and Hermeneutics in Postmodern Culture.* Baltimore: Johns Hopkins University Press.
Vatter, M. (1999). 'Review: Derrida and Vattimo on Religion'. *European Journal of Social Theory,* 3, 4.
Vattimo, G. (1992). *The Transparent Society.* Cambridge: Polity.
Veblen, T. (1970). *The Theory of the Leisure Class.* London: Allen and Unwin.
Venturi, R. (1977). *Complexity and Contradiction in Architecture.* London: The Architectural Press.
Voeglin, E. (1952). *The New Science of Politics.* Chicago: University of Chicago Press.
Voeglin, E. (1975). *From Enlightenment to Revolution.* Durham, NC: Duke University Press.
Wagner, P. (1994). *A Sociology of Modernity: Liberty and Discipline.* London: Routledge.
Wagner, P. (1998). 'Certainty and Order, Liberty and Contingency'. In J. Heilbron, L. Magmusson and B. Wittrock (eds), *The Rise of the Social Sciences and the Formation of Modernity.* Dordrecht: Kluwer.
Wagner, P. (1999). 'After Justification: Repertoires of Evaluation and the Sociology of Modernity'. *European Journal of Social Theory,* 2, 3, pp. 341–57.
Wallace, R. (1981). 'Progress, Secularization and Modernity: The Löwith–Blumenberg Debate'. *New German Critique,* 22, pp. 63–79.
Wallerstein, I., Calestous, J., Fox Keller, E., Kocka, J., Lecourt, D., Mudimbe, V.Y., Mushakoji, K., Prigogine, I., Taylor, P.J., Trouillot, M.-R. and Lee, R. (1996). *Open the Social Sciences: Report of the Gulbenkian Commission on the Restructuring of the Social Sciences.* Stanford, CA: Stanford University Press.
Walzer, M. (1983). *Spheres of Justice.* New York: Basic Books.
Weber, M. (1948a). 'Science as a Vocation'. In H.H. Gerth and C. Wright Mills (eds), *From Max Weber.* London: Routledge and Kegan Paul.
Weber, M. (1948b). 'Politics as a Vocation'. In H.H. Gerth and C. Wright Mills (eds), *From Max Weber.* London: Routledge and Kegan Paul.
Weber, M. (1948c). 'Religious Rejections of the World and Their Directions'. In H.H. Gerth and C. Wright Mills (eds), *From Max Weber.* London: Routledge and Kegan Paul.
Weber, M. (1978). *The Protestant Ethic and the Spirit of Capitalism.* London: Allen and Unwin.
Weinstein, D. and Weinstein, M. (1993). 'Simmel and the Theory of Postmodern Society'. In B.S. Turner (ed.), *Theories of Modernity and Postmodernity.* London: Sage.
Wellmer, A. (1971). *Critical Theory of Society.* New York: Continuum Books.
Wellmer, A. (1991). *The Persistence of Modernity: Essays on Aesthetics, Ethics and Postmodernism.* Cambridge: Polity.
Welsch, W. (1997). *Undoing Aesthetics.* London: Sage.
Williams, R. (1976). 'Community'. In *Keywords.* London: Fontana.
Wilkinson, I. (1999). 'Where is the Novelty in Our Current "Age of Anxiety"?' *European Journal of Social Theory,* 2, 4, pp. 445–67.
Wilson, R. and Dissanayake, W. (eds) (1996). *Global/Local: Cultural Production and the Transnational Imaginary.* Durham, NC: Durham University Press.
Wittrock, B. (1998). 'Early Modernities: Varieties and Transitions'. *Daedalus,* 127, 3, pp. 19–40.

Wittrock, B. (forthcoming). 'Modernity: One, None or Many'. *Daedalus*.

Wolin, S. (1961). *Politics and Vision: Continuity and Innovation in Western Political Thought*. London: Allen and Unwin.

Wrong, D. (1998). *The Modern Condition: Essays at Century's End*. Stanford, CA: Stanford University Press.

Wuthnow, R. (1989). *Communities of Discourse: Ideology and Social Structure in the Reformation, the Enlightenment, and European Socialism*. Cambridge, MA: Harvard University Press.

Yack, B. (1998). *The Fetishism of Modernities: Epochal Self-Consciousness in Contemporary Social and Political Thought*. Notre Dame, IN: Notre Dame University Press.

Yeatman, A. (1994). *Postmodern Revisionings of the Political*. London: Routledge.

Zimmerman, M. (1990). *Heidegger's Confrontation with Modernity: Technology, Science and Art*. Bloomington: Indiana University Press.

Zuidervaart, L. (1994). *Adorno's Aesthetic Theory: The Redemption of Illusion*. Cambridge, MA: MIT Press.

INDEX